T0244615

LET'S START THE REVOLUTION

LET'S START THE REVOLUTION

Tools for Displacing the Corporate State and Building a Country that Works for the People

RALPH NADER

Skyhorse Publishing

Skyhorse Publishing books may be purchased in bulk at special discounts for sales promotion, corporate gifts, fund-raising, or educational purposes. Special editions can also be created to specifications. For details, contact the Special Sales Department, Skyhorse Publishing, 307 West 36th Street, 11th Floor, New York, NY 10018 or info@skyhorsepublishing.com.

Skyhorse® and Skyhorse Publishing® are registered trademarks of Skyhorse Publishing, Inc.®, a Delaware corporation.

Visit our website at www.skyhorsepublishing.com.

Please follow our publisher Tony Lyons on Instagram @tonylyonsisuncertain.

10 9 8 7 6 5 4 3 2 1

Library of Congress Cataloging-in-Publication Data is available on file.

Cover design by David Ter-Avanesyan

Print ISBN: 978-1-5107-8185-6
Ebook ISBN: 978-1-5107-8186-3

Printed in the United States of America

To all the voters who work to elaborate the "We the People" preamble to our Constitution that includes "establish Justice, insure domestic Tranquility, provide for the common defense, promote the general Welfare and secure the Blessing of Liberty to ourselves and our Posterity, do ordain and establish this Constitution for the United States of America."

Contents

Acknowledgments

I wish to acknowledge the intense labors of Mark Green, the vibrant presentations of some two dozen civic leaders who made possible our project WinningAmerica.net in 2022, ripe for 2024, the support of Gloria Jarecki, David I. Kelley, and Katrina vanden Heuvel, and the few members of Congress who understood the critical importance of our effort. I also am grateful for the assistance of my sister, Dr. Claire Nader, who provided helpful recollections and sagacious commentary on the manuscript, John Richard for his wise counsel, and Shinee Picon for her close attention to detail in our efforts to strengthen the civic community and our democracy. This is a work very much still in progress.

CHAPTER 1

"What's Past Is Prologue . . ."

To me, the election results in the 2020 presidential race were stunning. Sure, Joe Biden won both the popular vote by a wide margin of some seven million voters and the Electoral College by 306 to 232, but less than a switch of one hundred thousand votes out of the 160 million cast in four swing states would have allowed the vestigial Electoral College to select Donald Trump as president for a second term. How could the election be so close? After all, Trump's record was brazen and in plain sight. According to the *Washington Post*, he lied or made misleading statements more than 30,573 times through four years of delusional fantasies, egomaniacal ignorance (note the fatal response to the COVID-19 pandemic), profited from corruption and self-dealing, and always delivered for giant corporations and the super-wealthy by huge tax cuts. He also canceled health, safety, and economic regulation of business at the expanse of the lives, health, and safety of all Americans. He froze the minimum wage, cut social safety programs for children and mothers, and bloated the military budget at the expense of the public works programs that he bragged he would create for the people. Not the least offenses were his serious serial violations of federal law.

1

He repeatedly predicted a rigged election against him while encouraging voter suppression and other electoral shenanigans in the many states controlled by Republicans. It is hard to believe someone with his mental instability, family corporate greed, and his executive and judicial appointees believing corporations are to be favored over real people still has Republican voters' support. Mark Green and I wrote two books on Trump—*Fake President: Decoding Trump's Gaslighting, Corruption, and General Bullsh*t* (2019) and *Wrecking America: How Trump's Lawbreaking and Lies Betray All* (2020). These books are factual and useful to anyone wanting to understand and counter Trump's continuing assault on our democracy.

Back to my question—How could the 2020 election have been so close? How could the House and Senate outcomes have been so close even though the Democratic Party squeezed by as the victor in November 2020?

The answers start with the long slide over the years into the Democratic Party's decrepitude, its self-isolation from blue-collar America, its obsessive preoccupation with dialing[1] for the same strings-attached corporate campaign dollars sought by the GOP, and its endless capacity for rejecting introspection and wallowing in scapegoating. The Democrats abandoned their base and let the Republicans turn states solid Red. It's never the Democratic Party leaders' fault; it's never time to look into the mirror and reassess their blunders, arrogance, cronyism, stupidities, lassitude, and chronic lack of preparing new leaders for a new generation of elected candidates up to the demands of the times. Imagine if they acted as if people mattered, first and foremost.

The more money the Democratic Party raised, the more it measured its success vis-à-vis the Republicans in dollar terms, further draining any authenticity from its rhetoric regarding workers, consumers, and children. The Democrats failed to fight for environmental protection, health and safety laws, and Medicare for All. Military and foreign policy by the Democrats only differed from the Republicans from 2000 to 2020 because the GOP became even more hawkish and bloodthirsty after 9/11, keeping a step ahead of the Democrats rushing to ditto-head them, as with the undeclared[2] war and criminal, full-scale invasions of Afghanistan and Iraq.

Then there were the eight-hundred-pound gorillas in the rooms. The Democratic Party's candidates chose to have polit-ical/media consultants run their campaigns. These consultants and firms were corporate conflicted: having corporate clients undermining their alleged fiduciary relationship with con-gressional candidates. As Kathleen Curry—a veteran political adviser in Connecticut—told me: "When their candidates lose, they invariably blame the candidates, not themselves." Win or lose, the largest such consulting firms keep getting rehired, and the media keeps ignoring their central role in losing elections.

In a conversation with Elizabeth Moynihan years ago, she told me she just fired the consultants in charge of the reelec-tion campaign of her husband, Senator Patrick Moynihan, and took full control of it herself. "Ralph," she added, "These consultants are destroying the Democratic Party." That was in 1998, and they've never finished their lucrative job doing just this ever since. While the media chronicles the regular reports of candidates' fundraising, it rarely looks into the ways these consultants control their candidates' campaigns, the messaging, and who is permitted to enter the force fields they create around candidates. Had reporters made a minimum effort to do so, they would have discovered a key to why the Democrats keep losing so many elections they should be winning easily, or winning others so closely that the Blue Dog Democrats are able to hand-cuff their party's better agendas. Consultants are control freaks. They isolate their clients from progressive citizen organizations, thereby blocking crucial, campaign-winning agendas, strategies, and language from reaching and motivating voters.

The Democratic Party apparatus has become isolated. It knows how to reach out for money, but it is too inbred to know or want to know how to reach out to people for votes and coun-sel. That's when it is not entirely slumbering in GOP-safe states and seats.

The stagnation by self-paralysis of the Democratic Party was described by John Kenneth Galbraith in *Harper's Magazine* back in 1970 when he saw the encroachments of corporate power as stripping the party of its very raison d'être coming out of the Roosevelt/Truman years of electoral supremacy. Years later, Robert Reich, a staunch Democrat and former Secretary of Labor under Clinton, penned an op-ed (2001) in the *Washington Post* that began with the words "The Democratic Party is stone dead. Dead as a doornail."

However, with the GOP becoming more extreme, more corporate, and more militaristic under George W. Bush and Dick Cheney, the Democratic Party went into a tailspin after

Obama's victory in 2008 and taking major control of both the Senate and the House. Whether born of complacency or a young president, who in the words of veteran House member Maxine Waters, didn't seem "to want to run with his congressional candidates," the elections of 2010 spelled disaster for the party and for anything left of Obama's modest legislative agenda. Caught napping, the party lost big in the 2010 redistricting contests to gerrymandering supremacy, especially in swing states such as Pennsylvania, Wisconsin, Michigan, and Ohio.

By 2017, the Democratic Party had lost control of both Houses of Congress, over one thousand state legislative seats, with the Republicans controlling the state legislatures in thirty-two states to fourteen held by the Democrats. The GOP had twice the number of governors. It was worse than the numbers revealed. Democrats lost in Pennsylvania and Wisconsin, where they received the most votes but were overwhelmed by minority-rule gerrymandering. They were defeated by fevered GOP politicians who were openly opposed to the long-overdue rights of workers, consumers, women, and children and ignored essential environmental issues and the deteriorating or nonexistent public services desired by huge majorities in the polls. They were defeated by state lawmakers bent on obstructing voters of certain demographics from being counted or even being able to vote. State Republicans opened the doors to more corporate welfare and less enforcement against corporate crimes or criminal negligence. In Georgia and Florida, they made residential consumers pay for electricity from nuclear plants long before they were providing any electricity—paying for so-called construction works in progress. As for polluting the air and waterways of both conservative and liberal families, it was "open sesame" time for the Republican Party.

None of these collapses led the Democratic Party to engage in postmortems, political introspection, and learning from their defeats. Instead, they energetically scapegoated third parties and independent candidates or whined about GOP shenanigans they should have foreseen and forestalled. Moreover, they celebrated when they lost by narrower margins than some polls predicted. These patterns of responses are the seeds of decay.

Rejecting the truism that *policy* must precede *messaging* to be authentic, the Democrats effectively conveyed the widespread impression of not standing for anything, of hollow rhetoric few believed, of an inability to change the failing guard and enlist fresh human energies, replacing incompetence and sinecurism. In 2014, former Senator Gary Hart told me that people in Denver didn't know what the Democratic Party stood for—a refrain that was repeated in blue states without shaking the party's establishment from measuring its prowess by how much campaign cash they were raising.

Indeed, they have become very good at raising enormous amounts of money, often exceeding the Republicans by ample margins. However, the more they took in, the more they wasted on repetitive, irritating television and social media ads concocted by their corporate consultants eager for their 15 percent commission at the expense of a far more effective ground game for voter turnout. Working with people from the community for voter turnout drives—person to person—is commission-free.

There was one continual achievement by these political/ media firms, other than juggling their lucrative corporate business with their candidate clients. They assiduously avoided the glare of investigative coverage by the media reporters covering campaigns. That enhanced their avoidance of any responsibility for their losses.

For example, while observers recall the $120 million blown on Jaime Harrison's hapless campaign against Republican senator and regular loudmouth Lindsey Graham and the $80 million spent on Amy McGrath's campaign against Senator Mitch McConnell based on her being a fighter pilot in Iraq, it is doubtful whether they can recall the consultants who spent such vast sums, nor the politicians—such as Senator Chuck Schumer of New York—who chose these candidates and assigned these firms. Both candidates lost by comfortable margins. Their party didn't bother analyzing the campaigns for future applications. Instead, Harrison was promoted to become the head of the Democratic National Committee (DNC) as a consolation prize for his disastrously uninspiring campaign. His selection as the majordomo for advancing Democrats campaigning all over the country was another example of cronyism.

The victory by Biden over Trump in 2020 and the razor-thin wins by Democrats to control the House and the Senate continued to avoid any resets in spite of foreboding erosion among traditional party bases in the Black and Hispanic communities. These warnings were prominently related in a rare, thirty-three-page report titled "Autopsy: The Democratic Party in Crisis" (November 2017) by veteran Democratic partisans Norman

Solomon, Karen Bernal, Pia Gallegos, and Sam McCann. Their energetic analysis and recommendations were motivated by the mid-2017 rollout of the Democratic Party's new slogan "A Better Deal," chosen from a cluster of proposed slogans by an expensive firm allegedly skilled in memorable phrasemaking. Instead "A Better Deal" was so full of tedious blather as to constitute an alternative to the sleeping pill merchants. It lolled in political slumberland, rescued from further circulation by the 2018 congressional midterm victory over the Trumpsters following two years of Trumpism-driven pushback. Again, the Democratic Party leadership persisted in their mode of being "too cautious, too corporate and too removed from the emerging passions of the current era . . . that major structural changes are not needed, in the party or in the country," the Autopsy report observed.

The report's authors knew very well the necessities, anxieties and dreams that embodied the daily struggles of millions of families. As students of history and electoral successes, they recognized agendas and messages that could persuade people that the Democratic Party was on their side, while the GOP sided with the wealthy, symbolized by prioritizing Wall Street greed and rapacity over Main Street values. Their closing advice to their party in late 2017 serves as a present-day clarion call:

> For the Democratic Party, the goal of outreach cannot be only to get votes. The enduring point of community outreach is to build an ongoing relationship that aims for the party to become part of the fabric of everyday life. It means acknowledging validity and power of people-driven movements as well as recognizing and supporting authentic progressive community leaders. It

means focusing on how the party can best serve communities, not the other way around. Most of all, it means persisting with such engagement on an ongoing basis, not just at election time. When insincerity and a poor record of community engagement are detected, the outcome is a depressed turnout on Election Day. Democratic Party pros have routinely discounted the political importance and electoral impacts of genuine enthusiasm at the grassroots. But passionate supporters and vital movements are crucial to lifting the fortunes of the party and the country.[3]

As we shall see later in this narrative, the Democratic Party goes out of its way to avoid connecting with reformist citizen/neighborhood groups, or with labor and cooperative organizations, other than to ask for donations featuring the specter of looming Republican atrocities. With a few exceptions, candidates do not campaign *with* these people; they posture before them with scripted, endlessly repetitive "politicalese." Voters are very good at turning off their phoniness. What is worse, behind the candidates' practiced smiles and handshakes are deaf ears to listening to their friendly critics with significant experience in communicating to people about the common good because they practice what they preach.

That closed-mind syndrome, fortified by the barriers of political consultants who remind candidates where they get their money, is pervasively cult-like. The low-energy Democratic Party is half of an exclusive political two-party duopoly, shielded by its own enacted protections from competition. It is a political monoculture, impervious to the winds of change and evolution. This is bad for the Democratic Party and for the citizenry.

I was not a silent observer of the Democratic Party's inability to take advantage of what Trump delivered to them regularly during his four years of some 30, 573 public lies and fake promises, compiled by the dutiful Glenn Kessler of the *Washington Post*.[4] No politician in American history handed an opposing party more brazen and open abuses, outrages, bigotry, and violations of the Constitution and federal laws. In late 2019, before Speaker Nancy Pelosi's drive to impeach Trump because he pressured Ukrainian president Volodymyr Zelenskyy to damage a political rival in exchange for the Trump administration releasing $391 million of United States taxpayer funds that Congress had appropriated on a bipartisan basis to provide military assistance to Ukraine, constitutional law expert Bruce Fein and I submitted to Pelosi eleven other evidence-backed impeachable offenses by Trump, committed not once but over and over again. These include constant "obstruction of justice," which his former national security aid, John Bolton, described "as a way of life in the White House."

I relayed these counts, written in ready-to-go legal language, in a lengthy telephone conversation with Speaker Pelosi, whom I've known since she entered Congress. She listened respectfully and replied that she wanted "airtight cases" as she believed the impeachment over the Ukraine offense to be. I explained how other impeachable offenses were airtight and in plain sight—such as ignoring over 120 congressional subpoenas and other offenses with far greater "kitchen-table" impact on the citizenry than the more remote Ukraine count. Further, I urged, more counts would force GOP Senate majority leaders to call a variety of witnesses who would cast the president and the GOP in a very bad light. For example, Trump systemically stripping away enforcement and enforcers from protecting the health, safety, and economic well-being of all the people would be hard to defend. Her voice told me she felt she had her hands full, and she could not take on such a mass of indictments, which she could get through the House, but which would consume her time and attention to the detriment of other pressing matters. My impression is that she was satisfied with a House impeachment and did not want to use the political capital and evidence amassed by several ongoing investigations by four of her House committees for a conviction in the Senate—even if she could get it—to expel a sitting president before an election year. Even trying to get to a Senate conviction that would lead Trumpsters into the riotous streets, as Trump had previously warned would happen, was too disruptive a scenario in her mind, not to mention the vitriol that would come down on her and the Democratic Party from Trump's hateful hordes. She is a politician after all, and had had more than her share of hate directed relentlessly at her persona. She didn't hold back, however, during our conversion—at one time she exclaimed: "He's [Trump] a liar, a thief, and a crook. He should be in prison."

Earlier, Bruce Fein and I had visited the offices of Jamie Raskin, Jim McGovern (then chair of the House Rules Committee), and Jerry Nadler, chair of the House Judiciary Committee, among others. They all sympathized with our case for expanding the number of impeachment counts. A quietly exasperated Jerry Nadler told us in his office that additional impeachment counts were drafted and directly sent to Speaker Pelosi, but to no avail. Mark Green and I had just published a comprehensive book on Trump's business and political career, *Fake President*, which helped authenticate our impeachment proposals. But impeachment did not exhaust our strategies to arrest Trump's lawlessness. We also urged the House and Senate to employ their inherent contempt power to summarily sanction Trump's defiance of congressional subpoenas with fines or detention without the protracted delay of seeking a federal court order demanding compliance. All this took a lot of effort on Capitol Hill, and all we got back in return was the shoulder shrug expression "It's up to Nancy." A couple of lawmakers substituted the word "Commander" for Nancy. It was well known that Speaker Pelosi preferred the more suave Representative Adam Schiff of California over Judiciary Committee Chairman Nadler (D-NY) as the House Managers for the Senate impeachment trial of President Donald J. Trump. Many viewed Schiff as being more compliant with Pelosi's limited scope for impeachment. Schiff also had more experience as a prosecutor than Representative Nadler.

We didn't stop with Congress. I made dozens of calls to congressional reporters, legal reporters, editors, and columnists of the major newspapers and the so-called independent media. The message we received back, in various phrasings or non-responses, was that unless our expansion of the impeachment counts received traction among members of Congress, what we were proposing, never mind the documentation, was not newsworthy.

I was left with my weekly columns, which commenced in January 1971. My columns about Trump started with what seemed to me to be persuasive negative information—Trump's open, brutish admission of assaulting women and the two dozen credible accusations by women charging him in convincing detail with assault and battery. All this was well-known to members of Congress, yet there were no investigations and no public hearings regarding probable felonies, crimes, and impeachable offenses. Representative John Conyers and Senator Al Franken were pressured to resign from Congress amid a media uproar over accusations far, far less egregious and infrequent than those of the serial violent misogynist sitting in the White House. Had the bully and sexual predator become too terrible to challenge, too much of an unrepentant criminal sexual marauder gravely abusing his power and public trust, to justify impeachment and removal from office? Such offenses are rooted in state statutory criminal laws. In addition, he paid hush money to a porn star late in the election year of 2016, which is itself a violation of federal campaign laws and comes with criminal penalties. A few congressional legislators publicly condemned Trump and rec-ommended investigations to hold him accountable. Then there was an interminable silence going into the presidential election year. There was no time to lose. I composed a lengthy letter "to the women in Congress" (at the suggestion of some male legislators) and personally delivered it to some 105 offices, over-whelmingly those of women, in the House of Representatives (the Senate was Republican controlled). Hour after hour I went in and out of House offices, identifying myself and leaving the letter with the receptionist or on occasion meeting with women staffers. I saw their frustrated, reddened faces and moistened eyes when inaction regarding this outrageous, repulsive behavior was urgently raised with them directly. Overall, the response in the offices where staff chose to discuss this sexual violence broke down into, "It's all up to Nancy," whose staff also received the letter, or "It won't do anything because he's Teflon," or "We don't need all the hassle and hate mail."

In the succeeding days, I waited for any responses from the over one hundred legislators. There came five polite acknowledgments but with no comment. My follow-up telephone calls to Nancy Pelosi, Jackie Speier, Maxine Waters, and other senior members resulted in messages taken and not returned. Similar disinterest followed my conversations with reporters who had covered Trump's transgressions earlier. Even women's group leaders had given up on anything affecting this recidivist, hardened, browbeating lout. This brutish record, it turned out, was not even used by the Democrats in the November presidential campaign. To recognize the moral decay over a short time, remember that a married Senator Gary Hart had to drop his presidential race against Walter Mondale in 1984 because he was photographed with a young woman on a motorboat in Florida.

My next effort was to have the Democrats firmly pick up what polls around the world have shown to be the number one revulsion about government—corruption. Trump displayed that trait without reservations, both as a dictatorial American führer and a flagrant violator of any laws, regulations, or constitutional restraints that should impede what he encapsulated in his July 2019 declaration: "I have an Article II, where I have the right to do whatever I want as President." Well, he wasn't kidding. Right up to January 6, 2021, and beyond. Having read his assertion of impunity, I was astonished that the Democrats didn't pick it up and run with it to challenge this unprecedented asserting by the self-anointed dictator. Month after month, it was ignored. The media followed suit. Had the expectation level for Trump's descent into lawlessness become so low, so banal, that it was not taken seriously even though it was being practiced openly? It is as if our collective national numbness can only muster the response of, "There he goes again," and leave it at that. Or could it be that any of the many countervailing forces choose not to engage in a dogfight with Trump and his retaliatory frothings and slander by name which, remarkably, was amplified verbatim by the major media? Imagine the *New York Times* rarely gave Trump's targets the right to reply in the pages of the paper.

Trump's corruption is not just the traditional kind of enriching himself from his high office, of steering government contracts to his cronies, or of purging the civil service of law enforcement regulators going after his campaign contributors and business buddies. It is also the institutional corruption of appointing regulators whose desired task is to shut down their agencies, such as the federal cops on the Wall Street beat over at the Consumer Financial Protection Bureau. Or similarly paralyzing the Environmental Protection Agency (EPA),[5] Occupational Safety and Health Administration (OSHA),[6] the Federal Trade Commission (FTC),[7] National Highway Traffic Safety Administration (NHTSA),[8] and the Centers for Disease Control (CDC),[9] even weakening nursing home protections[10] and cutting inspections of food and drug imports.[11] Trump pushed to slash budgets established to reduce preventable deaths, injuries, and illnesses. He appointed cronies to stifle the CDC[12] while demanding budget cuts for the CDC[13] and trivializing the emergence of the deadly COVID-19 pandemic, costing many American lives.[14]

In late February 2020, I wrote: "Whether it is the air you breathe, the water you drink, the vehicles you ride in, or the toxins in your workplace, Trump's corporatist wrecking crew is running federal agencies into the ground. While corporate outlaws fill Trump's coffers and hotels with riches, he gives them and his family huge tax escapes and starves infrastructure. The word 'corruption' cannot fully embrace how this foulmouthed, self-indicting megalomaniac is tearing apart our country, our democratic practices and our moral norms. Protections for children, the elderly, veterans and workers are all on Trump's chopping block."

The GOP is far more adroit in charging corruption against the Democrats for campaign purposes with far less material. From Thomas Dewey's painting the Truman administration as corrupt in 1948, based on a couple of cases, to the current major highlighting of Hunter Biden's use of the Biden name to reap profits, the GOP thinks the issue resonates with many voters. Despite numerous Trump appointees having to resign due to blatant malfeasance, the Democratic Party has chosen not to focus on such corruptions of public government. When it comes to this widely understood revulsion, the party rarely misses an opportunity to miss an opportunity. My conversations with numerous Democratic legislators on Capitol Hill were met with nodding acquiescence followed by tossing the ball to the clueless Democratic National Committee (DNC). Yet nothing keeps these lawmakers from making corruption a front-and-center issue in their own campaigns and press releases. Could it be the fear that Trump and his Trumpsters will retaliate by falsely charging them with fraud and crookery? The media regularly and supinely picked up and repeated Trump and company's erroneous claims. The answer is that probably it's on their mind as an inhibiting factor. Denying themselves such a modest profile of political moxie is inexcusable. Let someone else take the heat.

The Democrats do not have a strategy to counter Trump's media usage. He worked to dominate the twenty-four-hour news cycle with outlandish charges, lies, lurid predictions, and gigantic boasts. As president, he openly said his tweets and other assertions had to be covered because they gave radio/TV/social media higher ratings and more profits. No politician in American history came close to such 24/7 media saturation. He kept them amply supplied over three shifts.

On the other side, the Democrats haughtily declined to feed the media machine with rebuttals. Why lower themselves to his gutter, no one believes his crazed pronouncements, they thought. They failed to understand that veracity does not matter to people looking for emotional connections, to identify themselves with his prejudices, his recognition of their feelings of being abandoned by West Coast and East Coast elites. As one fifty-two-year-old factory worker moving from Ohio to Georgia told a reporter: "The media says Trump is crazy. But he's saying things that I'm thinking. Does that mean I'm crazy?"

Such aloofness by the Democrats allowed Trump to dominate the media daily, sometimes by the hour. Just as liberals allowed talk radio to be dominated by Trump-touting right-wing talk shows day after day. There are few, if any, parallels in American history where one party had such a dominant, aggressive, partisan soliloquy of *words* concocting phony issues to cover its own absence of positions or *records* in the public interest.

Although intensifying, this imbalance in speaking to the public has been going on for a long time. In 2004, referring to this mismatch, author and former prominent Republican political analyst Kevin Phillips asserted that the "Republicans go for the jugular while the Democrats go for the capillaries." This default was more than a failure of communication in the contest for the hearts and minds of voters. It has become a failure of conviction, a turning of the back on the values of the New Deal agenda for working families. An updated Democratic progressive agenda could provide the basis for a formidable contest with the GOP in basic bread-and-butter perceptions and realities. Consider the bland Democratic Party Platform, so flaccid that the GOP decided in 2020 not even to have a platform. Senator Mitch McConnell would tell inquiring reporters that he'd tell them about their agenda after the election. This political sneer could never have crossed McConnell's lips were he confronted with vibrant, credible commitments to the people—a covenant for all the people—by the Democrats.

CHAPTER 2
Floundering Democratics

In the early weeks of 2022, Mark Green and I spoke many times about the many political vacuums that the Democrats were not filling, seemingly oblivious even to their existence. Mark was a lifelong Democrat, having run for office in New York several times, being elected New York City's "Public Advocate," and having narrowly lost to the extravagant spending of Michael Bloomberg for the office of mayor. More pertinently, he had authored or coauthored twenty-six books and edited the two bulging volumes on Democratic Party policies for the Bill Clinton and Barack Obama presidential campaigns. He observed that the Democrats were failing in not highlighting the terrible Republican votes in Congress, thereby defaulting on a cardinal principle behind winning politics—contrast and comparison. Surveys showed that such an approach gets out more of the vote than simply sending self-touting letters, postcards, or emails and making robocalls. Although I had persuaded Representative John Larson (D-CT), head of the House Democratic Caucus, in 2014 to post the worst votes by the GOP in the House (including voting to protect corporations that outsource American jobs overseas in violation of the National Labor Relations Act and weakening protections for battered immigrant women who are legally here),[1] his highly usable list was not promoted by the Democratic National Committee (DNC) or the Democratic Congressional Campaign Committee (DCCC) to the candidates in the field. This was just as inexplicable as was the paucity of Democratic lawn signs compared to those of the GOP in the swing states. In 2018, Jamie Raskin, tired of waiting for the Democratic Party, put out his own compilation titled "Outrageous Things the GOP House Majority Did in My First Term."

Again, the Democratic Party and other candidates didn't pick them up. If you're asking, "Why not?," the answer is that they felt no need to explain, or referred you to their consultants if they even bothered to respond. Any eager-beaver grassroots Democratic vote-getter needed such a list with clear descriptions of the bills the GOP opposed or proposed. The go-getter was left with what they could find with Google. If anything, the Democrats' fundraising appeals were defensive in content (e.g., defend Social Security) and limited in number of issues. Based on their haughty belief that voters could not process more than a very few themes in the campaign, every two years, themes were poll-tested and singled out for endless repetition, to the exclusion of many other matters on the minds of hard-pressed individuals and families. Thus, in 2018, Nancy Pelosi decided that broadening the number of Americans with health insurance would do the trick. Well, it certainly helped, but why not diversify the menu for the majority of people who are insured or the millions without a livable minimum wage, say of $15 or more per hour. In 2022, following the Supreme Court *Dobbs* decision reversing *Roe v. Wade*, the Democrats ran very heavily on the woman's right to choose. Polls decidedly favored that position. But it crowded out other appeals for changes and reforms in people's minds. The independent voters and the many stay-at-home Democrats need to have more answers to their implicit questions as to why they should vote at all, why the election should matter to them personally.

Coming from years in the citizen movement, running a variety of citizen groups, Mark and I were keenly aware of another vacuum—a big yawning one. The Democratic Party behaved as if organized citizen communities didn't exist and that it was not worth engaging with their ways and means of persuading the citizenry to act in their own self-interest.

Starting in January 2022, I began calling Democratic Party officials to see why they were ignoring what these groups have to offer over the entire range of substantive campaigning as if people matter first. To put it mildly, it was very hard to get through the voicemails, the screeners, and the preoccupation with raising money daily, hourly, always. From the party apparatchiks to the candidates, that was the obsession—outdialing the GOP for often the same dollars from the same special interests. About ten years ago, Representative Marcy Kaptur (D-OH) told me that during the election years, she would go to the House Democratic Caucus meetings, and from start to finish, all the talk was about raising money, meeting quotas, and being urged to spend more time going for the almighty dollars. She was distressed that the agendas, issues, and reforms and the needs of the people were simply not on the table. Given the accelerating surge in the sheer amount raised since then by both major parties, the laser-beam focus on getting ever more campaign cash is greater than ever, leaving the essential purposes of politics in a democracy languishing in the darkness. Pandering and staying mum on matters such as raising minimum wage, universal single-payer health insurance, curbing military contracting waste and bad military policies, the corporate crime wave, and certainly campaign finance reform, were a few of the agenda items not conducive to getting large donors and support of large secretive political action committees (PACs). It was as if Bernie Sanders's historic breakthrough in 2016, raising huge campaign monies averaging twenty-seven dollars for each donor over the internet, was merely an addition to the customary ways of maxing out by individuals and PACs.

As the days passed, I saw once again the emergence of candidates trivializing their exalted potential who were unwilling to even wonder why they weren't championing the grave issues of concentrated power impoverishing our country. It didn't matter if candidates had safe seats or were running in competitive races. Their messages were flat and timid. Matters of peace or war, corporate commercial control, and the diminution of the role of the citizenry were not topics addressed before their audiences and conventions.

Ever since Representative Tony Coelho (D-CA) showed the Democratic Party in 1979 how easy it was to raise major money from commercial interests and their PACs, the consequences were rife and real. Coelho was chair of the House Democrats' election campaign committee. In that position, he started the sharp downward slide of the Democratic Party, in the waning years of the Carter administration, toward corporatist capture. We lost major legislation, including a proposed effective consumer protection agency, in those two years—1979 and 1980. The signs, increased with the arrival of Reagan, a cruel man with a smile, who avoided responding to citizen groups. Democrats in the Congress showed less interest in public hearings and less interest in backing legislation protecting and advancing the interests of the traditional Democratic Party constituencies—workers, consumers, and low-income families and their health, safety, and economic well-being. Low morale settled in the minds of the most progressive lawmakers.

One was the fairly progressive Senator Paul Sarbanes (D-MD), whom I knew at Princeton before he became a Rhodes Scholar. As chair of the Senate Banking Committee, he should have been an active champion of long-delayed consumer protection hearings and legislation. At a meeting in his Senate office, I questioned his inaction in personal terms as his being "an underachiever." He simply shrugged and said any bills wouldn't go anywhere because Reagan would veto them. Going to the mat to build popular support and be stronger to prevail another day was not on his horizon. I had more than a few of these interactions with our supposed allies on Capitol Hill. They debilitated themselves and were rewarded with campaign cash—a surefire formula for complacency and isolation from the gestating civic community.

CHAPTER 3

Early Warnings

It is not my personality to become jaded, a trait which is bad for the requisite civic stamina over the long haul. In 1992 I talked with Steve Grossman, chairman of the Massachusetts Democratic Party from 1991 to 1992. As chair of the Massachusetts party, he had cleared the way for my getting on the Massachusetts presidential ballot in 1992 as a Democratic primary candidate. He was known as a progressive Massachusetts Democrat. From 1997 to 1999, he was the chairman of the Democratic National Committee (DNC). When he took this job, we discussed a wide range of necessary changes in our country's political economy, and I handed him and his aide documentation, writings, and specific legislative wording behind each issue. Included were practical ways to empower the citizenry in their various roles as consumers, workers, environmentalists, patients, owners of the public commons, small savers, ratepayers, and more. The reception was encouraging as we showed that going with these missions seriously in the Democratic Party Platform was just, popular, and frugal. These issue and platform plank recommendations would answer the question, "Whose side are you on?" and show the Democrats were "siding with the people" regardless of their political labels.

To add a light touch, I gave Mr. Grossman a couple of copies of a cartoon paperback titled *Why Dogs Are Better Than Republicans* (1996) by the very witty Jennifer Berman. We departed with the assurance that after the staff had the time to digest and reflect on the materials, they would get back to us with their responses. A few days passed. The telephone rang from the DNC and a staffer asked if they could get more copies of *Why Dogs Are Better Than Republicans*. We obliged and sent them a dozen copies. We never heard from them again. They went incommunicado on the policy materials.

A few years later in December 2003, I received a call from Senator John Kerry (D-MA) who requested having dinner. We met in a private enclave at the Jefferson Hotel near the White House. I arrived first with an armful of similar reports, because I knew he was planning to run for the Presidency. Years earlier, as an ambitious Vietnam vet, he sought me out for a long afternoon chat in our offices, where I sensed his political energy. He came to our dinner and sat down with the abrupt declaration "I'm going to take on the bastard." I recall thinking the word "the bastard" is an understatement in describing a world-class war criminal, like George W. Bush. (Well, Kerry had voted for the resolution supporting the Bush/ Cheney criminal invasion of Iraq.)

As the discussion continued, we were like two ships passing in the night. He seemed to be asking for my advice. I readily proposed what his candidacy should stand for and press forward in an open run *with* the people. What he really wanted was to persuade me not to run in 2004 because he said we were both on

the same wavelength on so many issues. I politely indicated perhaps not, and that were I to run outside the Democratic Party,
it would be to make it easier for someone like him to adopt
progressive policies. We parted in a friendly manner, with his
assurance that he would look through the materials I handed to
him. That was pretty much it with Senator Kerry. Later I saw a
television clip of his almost bellowing to a New Jersey business
audience, "I am Not a Redistributionist." In the midst of the
2004 presidential campaign, my campaign volunteers marched
down to his campaign headquarters in Washington, D.C., with
one major reform on each of twelve silver platters. Neither he
nor, unfortunately, the media, was amused. Another effort unre-
quited by Thomas Jefferson's Party.

There were other attempts to inform the Democrats that
flopped. This was a party so marinated in corporate campaign
cash, so compromised by viewing the military budget as a jobs
program, so wedded to Wall Street, so willing to take for granted
labor and minority support, that possibly the only way to wake
them up was for them to lose big-time to the Republicans. The
GOP obliged the Democrats again and again, by winning, but
this didn't awaken the Democrats.

During one of those roundtables on the Sunday morning
network news show (around 2019) where the press turns to
punditry, I heard the *New York Times* investigative reporter,
Michael Schmidt, explain that the Democrats couldn't seem to
get their arms around Trump. Essentially the same observation
came from Robert Weissman, president of Public Citizen, speaking about the national civic groups' inability to get to Trump.

Mark and I thought we could throw some light on this seeming conundrum. The more outrageous Trump became with his howling lies and "twistifications" (Jefferson's word) of realities, the more inoculated he was from conventional criticism. We wrote a book titled *Fake President* in 2019 that was unlike the covey of books about Trump. It was to be read and to be used to grasp Trump's fakeries and corrupt practices so as to reach the Trumpsters themselves in terms of their own self-interest, awakening a sense that he did more than not deliver for their livelihoods. He betrayed his campaign promises made for blue-collar workers, and at their expense, while he enriched the super-rich. The next year we updated and refined its laser beams in *Wrecking America: How Trump's Lawbreaking and Lies Betray All*. We thought, given our backgrounds of advocacy and candidacies, that the political reporters and the Democratic Party apparatus would take some notice. Our publisher, Skyhorse, sent out scores of these books to the requisite lists. Almost no one was interested. Especially silent were the Democratic operatives and the Democratic incumbents on Capitol Hill. They knew all about Trump and still couldn't believe his supporters would continue to wake up each day believing his nutty tweets. What these people were lacking was that level of humility that could have provided them with the necessary curiosity, imagination, and tactical judgment—independent of their control-freakish consultants who, of course, also knew it all. If you had any doubts, all you had to do was ask them.

I decided to write an op-ed on why Trump voters were still sticking with him through thick and thin, through his daily distracting wordplay and media exposés, a small number of which would have doomed a conventional politician in the polls if not before a grand jury. It was written with a little tongue in cheek—too much so for the *Washington Post* and the *New York Times*. But the *Boston Globe*'s op-ed editor Marjorie Pritchard published it.[1] My points showed how Trump had connected with his supporters' egos, their emotional identities, their sense of grievance over their abandonment. Once they locked their sense of identity with his rhetoric of victimhood and their loss of status and power, taken away by an increasingly multiethnic populace, it was very difficult to unlock their adhesion to his personality of defiance, promise, and restoration. Recall his "I alone can fix this." For Trump followers to separate themselves from his flawed vison would require them to go outside Donald's frames of reference. They would need to accept that the problems of our political economy cannot be solved with pompous slogans and dog whistles that pit people against each other.

Ever since Hillary Clinton blew hundreds of millions of dollars on saturation television ads in 2016 repeating the refrain that "Donald Trump isn't fit to be president," the Democrats still can't find the handle. Many still cling to the fervent belief that some forthcoming disclosure, some over-the-cliff faux pas, some over-the-top racist tumble, some revealed bribe, some lawsuit by the IRS, or a Department of Justice prosecution will bring him down. Trump, it turns out, has a better read of why his supporters stick with him. He turns any detracting news into the latest elaboration of his victimhood, and tells his flock that he is defending not only himself but them, from similar persecution and degradation. "They're not coming for me," he would say at his rallies. "They're coming for you. I'm just standing in their way."

In 2023, when his indictments began, he asserted he needed "one more indictment" to seal his victory in 2024. Clearly such a unique figure in America's political history deserved some unique oppositional thinking. In a discussion about Trump's survivability and his tendency to become even stronger with time with Speaker Nancy Pelosi, she noted that polls showed the only crack in his base of backers was that many didn't think he delivered on his promises. (They were amenable, though, to his scapegoating.) She had no other explanations, adding that she could hardly bear to be in the same room with the Trumpsters and their nasty closed minds.

During his term in office, Trump confounded the Democrats by holding on and expanding his base a little, despite the tumult that exploded from his delays and denials regarding the COVID-19 pandemic and his ridicule of the medical scientists as he suggested people might try drinking bleach to stop contagion.

Facing these steady support polls and not finding a way to reduce Trump's numbers for election-tipping margins in swing states, any normal political party would turn their attention to the other part of the voter equation. One that Rev. Jesse Jackson and Bishop James Barber have urged to be recognized. I'm referring to turning out a decisive percentage of the approximate 125 million nonvoters predicted as staying home in November. I always thought that would be the easier alternative, given their abundance and that many of them should be considered low-income Democratic voters. However, it is not easy to get nonvoters registered and to the polls using the usual methods—telephone banks, postcards, registration drives, door-knocking, all-audience television ads. Poorer voters have felt betrayed by both parties. When they ask themselves why they should vote, the answer isn't strong. Promises by Democratic candidates fall on deaf ears, since even that of keeping up the minimum wage with inflation or productivity has not been delivered. Other bread-and-butter issues are also seldom discussed in Democratic campaigns.

What more would it take, in addition to communicating more specifically and authentically? In January 2018, I composed a memo suggesting a more intensive and earlier interaction with voters. The objective was to bring out ten million nonvoters in swing states for the 2018 midterm congressional elections, in preparation for the 2020 presidential campaign. Using the best demographic data, neighborhoods and projects would be selected, influencers located, perceived unmet necessities would be documented through extensive research and conveyed through periodic lunches, suppers, or coffee with the potential voters. While voters who are unable to get to the polls would be shown how to vote via the absentee ballot, in-person voting would build élan developing free transportation, going to the polls in buses, vans, or sedans, followed by culinary gatherings to coalesce some solidarity for future improvements in their lives. These human touches seemed to be personal, eyeball-to-eyeball interactions that would produce a successful turnout.

With local influencers and leaders of extended families and social clubs, the turnout would have a festive quality highly anticipated in the weeks before the election. Such a drive would start its gatherings three or four months before voting day, with preparations by organizers starting in the spring. Given the stakes—both tangible and intangible—the proposed budget of $500 million could be considered a bargain. Just think of the monetary value of corporate tax reform, improved public services, cutting government contract waste, lower drug prices, higher minimum wages, and consumer protection refunds and reliefs—for starters.

The exponential spiral of what is spent on congressional campaigns makes the estimated budget far more realizable than would have been the case a dozen years earlier. In the 2020 Democratic presidential primaries, Michael Bloomberg spent a billion dollars just for his candidacy and only won American Samoa.

I sent this proposal to several very rich liberal persons and to the usual Democratic Party institutions. Some of the former demurred as already being way over their regular donations to the party and too ambitious for their allotted time for politics, busy as they already were. Others I did not hear from. As for the Democratic Party, either the recipients referred me to some other office, or they did not acknowledge getting my memo. I'm sure were any of them to read its preelection and postelection ambitions, they might have peeked from the silos and exclaimed something like—"what the heck is this off-the-wall fantasy about?"

I then tried to interest some political writers who I thought, mistakenly, might be interested in pondering something other than the daily tedium of covering "politics as usual." One of them, the national political writer for the *Washington Post*, Dan Balz, I actually got on the telephone. It was a short, polite exchange, with me informing him I was going to send the memo for him to consider writing about in one of his many columns. Duly sent. Duly heard nothing in response. Others were similarly unresponsive. Had I been able to get some incumbents to cosign, perhaps it would have been considered newsworthy enough for some column inches. But then incumbents would have seen backing such a budget as possibly drawing away from their quotas, or upsetting to their relationships, or far too labor-intensive and untested.

Reducing the post-voting celebratory paid-for supper or lunch would have cut the budget significantly and made it more "realistic." Or the GOTV number count could have been reduced. These and other adjustments could have been discussed, but no one was interested in doing so.

Big elections require big ideas with sweeping ranges for sweeping results. Narrowing down on each candidate and each district is of course essential but, as recent election years have shown, it is not likely that the Democratic Party wakes up and tries to launch a GOTV movement without interference from their political/media consultants. No one collects 15 percent commissions for organizing these personal gatherings, exchanges, and transportation to the polling stations. Refreshing as the proposed idea was to some, it needed some major donors—national

and local and excitable grassroots—to launch. Media noncover-
age of these political/media consultants continue year after year,
even though they are riddled with corporate conflicts of interests which editors and reporters usually like to harpoon in other
contexts. Granted, they like to stay in the shadows and have
their candidates' campaign offices put out the press releases.
Organizationally, there are a small number of big firms which in
turn contract out to literally hundreds of consultants or experts
in various fields. But the "Big Boys" control the terrain, tempo,
and substance to make their clients comfortable, protect them
from being ostracized by avoiding the all-important "concentrated power" issues, and reassure them that their playbook will
provoke few surprises and smooth a path to victory. There are
so many safe Democratic seats in the House and the Senate (as
there are for the GOP) that this advice extends to the few challengers where such complacency does not work, given how hard
it is to unseat incumbents. One cannot beat the GOP incumbent
by adhering to a tactic of "protective imitation."

Listening to an array of congressional and gubernatorial
debates on C-SPAN Radio, I found it took me some time to
know whether the Democratic or the Republican candidate was
speaking. The spell of doubt was usually broken by the moderator identifying them for his/her next question.

Interestingly, the GOP candidates or incumbents are not as
fearful of what comes at them from the Democratic side when
they express their crazed assertions and vituperatives as are the
Democrats. That is a key reason why their "Teacher" Trump
hurls his invectives daily in personal terms without receiving his

own medicine in return. As a result, he learned early on to accuse the Democrats of what he is doing—as in bribing, lying, cheating, stealing, rigging elections, destroying democracy, wrecking the economy, and so forth.

He also holds the stage with his pejorative nicknames for others, which the "liberal" press such as the *New York Times* and *Washington Post* repeat verbatim, including his CAPITAL LETTERS. How strange is it that the Democrats have not developed all kinds of nicknames for Trump through their many emissaries? The options are endless: "Dangerous Donald," "Trump the Chump," "Faker Trumper," "Serial Criminal Trump," "Trumpy Dumbty," "Der Führer Trump," "Delusionary Donald," "Crooked Donald," and "Lying Donald"—some taken from his own nicknames of Ted Cruz, Marco Rubio, and Hillary Clinton. Before dozens of his campaign rallies, the crowd would roar, "Lock her up," referring to Hillary. Interestingly the chant was suspended for a while after President Trump went to watch a Nationals baseball game and heard the crowd chant, "Lock him up." It is long known that bullies need their own medicine. Democrats say they do not want to stoop to his level, which would be indisputable if the media did not become Trump's faithful bullhorn to tens of millions of people. Democrats need to play hardball. There has to be a tit-for-tat reaction until he realizes he has to pay a price for his unanswered railings. The Nazi propaganda machine reveled in demonstrating that the Big Lie, repeated again and again, gains believers. Trump's Big Lies further embed his daily soliloquies ever deeper among voters who react emotionally to candidates and do not do much homework about whom they might vote for and against. The difference between Trump's nicknames and those by his responding opponents is one of significant veracity.

Having finished our first book on Trump (*Fake President*) in 2019, I used its practical contents in an attempt to convey how to both persuade some of his hesitant supporters and motivate others who don't usually vote to feel the chaos, anxiety, dread, and fear that will come to them should the Trump Dump grab the White House for another four years. You know, politically active people have to do their part, pick up their oars, so to speak, regardless of the probabilities of them reaching significant numbers of nonvoters or uninformed people at all levels. Ever since I came to Washington in 1963—hitchhiking from Connecticut to save money and, on the way, meeting interesting people ready to talk during the monotonous drives—I learned that getting a no for an answer has been a routine experience for citizens or consumer advocates. That is the plain language of how the status quo voices respond. Locating myself in a phone booth by a gas station, I would make endless calls to the offices of members of Congress to see if they were interested in a visit to talk about how cars could be designed far more safely than the current models pumping horsepower and style. The receptionist would pick up the senator's or representative's phone and immediately ask, "Who are you with?" I would look around and say it's just me, a young lawyer who knows how important federal safety standards would be to save many lives and reduce injuries and air pollution. Some would say, okay, come on down, and a staffer would hear me out. But most times, the answer was a curt, "No." A cold call from a nobody to regulate the most powerful industry in the country, with mighty General Motors (GM) at the helm? Forget it.

However, in the intervening half century plus, I harbored the prospect that my name (*U.S. News & World Report* had me in 1974 as the fourth most influential person in the United States) might evoke some lingering memories on Capitol Hill when some people called me a majordomo of the place in terms of getting public hearings and getting Congress to pass legislation. Unfortunately, a new generation of staff has a minimal recollection of the recent history of where they work.

Many senior staff left, especially during the Bush years, tired of waiting to be able to get anything done. At the same time, the K Street lobbyists, not satisfied with their overwhelming number scurrying in and out of congressional offices daily, developed a toxic revolving-door system, with the active support of some GOP legislative leaders. Corporate lobbying firms placed their people as staff to members of Congress, in full anticipation that these plants would carry their know-how and know-who back to their corporate offices at much higher salaries.

Observing this decline in public-spirited congressional staff was Michael Pertschuk, former chief of staff to the powerful Senator Warren Magnuson. There, with great persuasiveness and stamina in the 1960s and 1970s, he guided through Congress many significant bills to protect the people's health and safety. He wanted to have the current congressional staff learn about those days when staff worked to convince their lawmakers to enact legislation as if people mattered first. Pertschuk started the drive in Congress to harness the tobacco industry and its 450,000 fatal victims yearly in the United States. His quiet influence and adroit connections with civic groups and the media led people to describe him as the 101st senator.

In 2017, he completed his book tellingly titled *When the Senate Worked for Us* and journeyed in his mid-eighties to Capitol Hill from Santa Fe, New Mexico, to meet with members and staff. Alas, no one was interested except Representative David Price (D-NC) who knew Pertschuk when Price was a graduate student at Yale writing a book on the House and Senate Commerce Committee. The newspapers exclusively covering Congress were not interested either. The editor of *The Hill* bluntly told me that the book "was just about history!"

There are still some people around who think history has importance for today's world, however, it's being downplayed in too many high school curricula. History tells us there were times when members of Congress and staff were more accessible. That was before the growth of corporate lobbying and the internet, email, voicemail, and the touted age of information. The blackout of citizens wanting to engage with their members of Congress is now near complete. Unless you are a campaign contributor, a social buddy, or an ordinary citizen wanting help to get through the bureaucracy to resolve an impasse or delay at, say, the Veterans Administration, the Social Security Administration, the Small Business Administration, or the IRS, reaching your elected officials is almost impossible. The lawmakers call helping constituents with personal problems "casework," which they see as helping them look good back home. They can devote up to half of their staff to handle such requests. Remember, they're supposed to be legislators and overseers of the vast executive branch departments and agencies. History also instructs us that until the 1990s, Congress was in session five days a week, not counting recesses. Now they work three days a week, interspersed with fast walking to nearby campaign offices where they make their endless fundraising calls.

I cannot overstate the chronic lack of civic community access on serious issues to both congressional offices and their committee staff. The stark difference between access in the 1960s and 1970s now also extends to the executive agencies—conservative and liberal/progressive organizations—that don't raise money for campaigns directly or indirectly are largely shut out of the public policymaking process. Yes, members will respond to causes they already are espousing but these are so exclusive of the great challenges confronting our country and the world as almost to be deemed peripherally self-serving.

The 2020 presidential election year scared progressives, especially after the Democratic Party's orchestrated coup against Bernie Sanders in favor of Joe Biden during and right after the South Carolina primary. The Trumpsters were actively working to suppress the Democratic vote. A Trump collaborator he chose to become Postmaster General hindered the prompt delivery of mail, including absentee ballots. Biden was not seen by many Democrats as a winner, despite Trump regularly injuring himself with his displays of detestable language, fakery, lying, rampant lawlessness, self-enrichment, and open suspension of enforcing health and safety regulations, including those on imported food and drugs.

A frequent candidate for the presidency, Biden was always rumored to be one whenever the White House was Republican occupied. He was widely seen as a loser by both parties after having to drop out because of a charge of plagiarism in 1988. Known for his numerous gaffes, he was actually wished for by the GOP. I recall an amusing encounter with Republican Senator Christopher Bond (R-MO) in the greenroom at the CNN studios where we were both waiting to go on the air. I casually mentioned that Joe Biden might be running in 2004. Suddenly, the immaculately suited Ivy League senator dropped to his knees on the dusty carpet, placed his hands in prayerful mode, and cried out, "Oh please Dear God, may this be so."

In the terrifying COVID-19 pandemic year of 2020, a strong case could be made that without Trump's fumbling, sometimes-grotesque mishandling of this pandemic—denying, delaying, mocking, lying, underfunding, playing medical adviser, emitting false notices and signals, and evincing little compassion for massive fatalities and illnesses from his monetized mind—all massively covered by the media, Biden would have lost the Electoral College Vote.

There was much media regarding the large number of Americans whose lives could have been spared were federal action taken in January through March 2020 to reduce the virus's range of infection multiplying its contagion. Documentary filmmaker Eugene Jarecki developed a "Trump Death Clock," taking the best scientific evidence of this multiplier effect to estimate the accumulating preventable loss of American life had Trump acted promptly on the urgings of NIH and CDC scientists. The Trump Death Clock was located in Times Square in New York City and then later moved to other urban sites.

After Biden secured the Democratic nomination, worries grew about his prospects in November. Worrying overtime were Bill Hillsman, Jaron Bourke, and Drew Westen. Hillsman was a specialist in political messages to blue-collar workers and independent voters. He showed his skill in creating the political communications for the election of underdog candidate for governor, Jesse Ventura, and Senator Paul Wellstone. Bourke worked as a Democratic staff director on Capitol Hill for many years. Drew Westen was one of the most perceptive scholars of the Democratic Party in academe, teaching at Emory University in Atlanta. They knew well the failures of the Democratic Party to reach key New Deal constituencies corralled by the likes of the *Rush Limbaugh Show*. They knew the party was inbred, overly cautious, and willing to waver on issues of concern to key Democratic Party constituencies. Campaign contributions from industry and commerce have paved the way for the party's abandoning of many key positions and voters. As Hillsman said, "If the party doesn't know what it stands for, how is it going to persuade enough of the electorate that it really means to be on their side?" One would think this trio of longtime Democrats would get some resources and the callbacks to advise the Democratic candidates how to win big, so that the party could have a working mandate with a comfortable majority. Not so. Despite repeated efforts to break through the "force field" I've earlier described, they too were shut out.

Mark Green had similar experiences. He tried strenuously to contact party leaders in Washington, including the DNC. Thinking that he could meet with the head of the DNC, Tom Perez, he went down to Washington. They made him cool his heels in the waiting room with no meeting occurring. This is how the party headquarters treated a person who put together two major tomes on Democratic politics for Bill Clinton and Barack Obama's presidential runs, as previously noted. Whether out of insularity, arrogance, or cluelessness, excluding Mark and his knowledge about campaigning and messaging was just the way they treated all civic leaders. After all, they had professional consultants, mass-media and social-media experts to whom they paid millions in fees. Why would they tap people outside the electoral arena to win votes? Civic leaders didn't have the campaign cash to be recognized.

CHAPTER 4
Winning or Losing America

By March 2020, it was becoming increasingly clear that once again the Democratic Party machinery in Washington, D.C., was preparing a knockout prejudicial tactic against Bernie Sanders—coming off similar maneuvers on behalf of Hillary Clinton over Bernie in the 2016 presidential race. Their trump card was African American representative James E. Clyburn, an eighty-year-old veteran of South Carolina politics and one of the few elected politicians whose words could command votes in primaries. If Joe Biden, whose candidacy was sagging, could win the South Carolina primary and other presidential candidates would then drop out, the momentum would make Delaware Joe into the front-runner. The tactic worked with precision. Senator Amy Klobuchar (D-MN) and then-mayor of South Bend, Indiana, Pete Buttigieg suddenly dropped out, although they were on the ballot on Super Tuesday on March 3, 2020. They were contacted by the Democratic Party, the DNC, by various people like Terry McAuliffe and the Clintons, all of them basically saying: "Do it in order to save the party from Bernie Sanders and socialism. Do it for our Joe Biden, our boy, Obama's vice president, you know." Millions of Americans, especially young voters supporting Bernie Sanders, were left in the dust. Instead of a progressive nominee, they were left with voting either for Biden or Trump. As most voters want to cast their ballot for a winner, few of these Sanders backers were going to vote Green. The alternative to Dangerous Donald was to be Joe Biden, known to be a reliable custodian of the corporate state. After all, Delaware for generations has been the preferred state for giant corporations, such as Citigroup and GM, to obtain their charters. It was the state that led the "race to the bottom" for chartering corporations and interpreting them to favor the control of top executives over their shareholders and other stakeholders. It was and is the corporate bosses' most permissible paradise. In my presidential campaigns, to drive this point home, I would say that GM could buy Delaware in a weekend if DuPont was willing to sell it. That was the political breeding ground for Joe Biden, and early on he learned to say yes to his corporate paymasters.

Growing up in Delaware, Biden saw how variously true it was that DuPont "owned" Delaware. A colossus of a global chemical company, with powerful interlocking directorates, DuPont owned the two major newspapers in the state and influenced its state legislature to cut its property taxes using some of the "savings" to fund many of the charities, including antipoverty and pro–civil rights ones that might have given the company some trouble. Its corporate lawyers were the guardians of Delaware's permissive corporate code, which was a significant revenue source due to the thousands of corporate charters filed there. Delaware's congressional delegations were seen in Washington as deputies of DuPont's far-flung interests in legislation on Capitol Hill. There were very, very few mavericks in the state legislature.

DuPont's power in Delaware was conveyed to me long ago in classes at Harvard Law School. Our course on corporate law was filled with cases from Delaware's Chancery Court. Given the state's tiny size, I was puzzled enough to ask my professor why our casebook was so loaded with Delaware cases, as compared with, say, New York, Illinois, or California. He dryly replied that the case law was just more developed and detailed in Delaware.

Years later, intrigued, I invited two graduate students to write a report on DuPont in Delaware, which was turned into the singular book *The Company State* (1973). As was our practice with "Nader's Raiders" reports, we put the first edition out in mimeographed form to expedite its public release. Want to know how alert this company was to criticism? They called asking whether they could send a limousine to pick up the report early in the morning. Sure enough, a long Ford limo pulled up in front of our modest offices with five well-dressed men. The driver paid for five copies and gave one to each passenger. Each man promptly took a section and started reading on the way back to Wilmington. By the afternoon, the company had released its response to the many reporters covering the release of the report.

Clearly, rooted in this DuPont political landscape, Biden was not expected to come out for federal chartering of giant companies, as did presidents Teddy Roosevelt and William Howard Taft over a century ago and most recently Senator Elizabeth

Warren. But he was no conventional corporate Democrat. He was a toady of the big banks in Delaware, which extended to big banks throughout the United States. He was the waterboy—aggressively so—for the credit card industry and their rapacious interest rates and penalties, along with the cruel carving out of protections in the bankruptcy laws used by bankrupt student loan debtors. In other areas, Biden supported all the congressionally undeclared "Wars of Empire"[1] (he says proudly that he has taught separation of powers), all the corporate-managed trade agreements so inimical to American labor, consumers, and the environment—the ones that emptied so many communities of jobs in his beloved native Pennsylvania. And, of course, there was his bungling as chairman of the Senate Judiciary Committee—of the Clarence Thomas Supreme Court nomination. It wasn't just his ineptness regarding Anita Hill's courageous testimony. He did not persuade eleven of his fellow Democratic senators not to cross the aisle and make Thomas a winner by a vote of 52 to 48.

His main competitor for the Democratic nomination—Bernie Sanders—could pull vastly greater crowds, but that didn't stop the corporate Democratic operatives led by the Clintons from maneuvering Biden over the top at the Convention in July 2020. With that uninspiring public event, down went the progressive agenda of deconcentrating the power of the few plutocrats over the many to elevate the lives and livelihoods of all Americans. This was a quicker replay of the 2016 contest between Bernie Sanders and Hillary Clinton so full of dirty tricks, starting with the Nevada primary. Always accommodating to the Democratic

Party to maintain his voice and seniority within it, Bernie formally enrolled as an Independent. Someday he may write the full inside story of the sabotage of his two promising presidential campaigns.

So, after July, it was Biden vs. Trump. Neither were worthy of the citizenry, not to mention posterity. But Trump kept making it easier to choose the lesser of two evils. I do not endorse candidates—too sweeping, too indentured, and I might add, too pompous. I do support or oppose the positions taken by candidates, which is a freer way to authentically communicate with the public.

Trump almost made it too easy to condemn him—having made himself into a fumbling, flailing, and ferocious outlaw on a daily basis. To repeat, he gave Democrats the smoking gun of his sneering contempt for the Constitution and rule of law on July 19, 2019, in boasting, "Then I have an Article 2, where I have the right to do anything I want as president," and proceeded to prove it in volumes. It was hard to keep down the page count on Trump in Mark Green's and my book, *Fake President*, that came shortly thereafter. Yet stunningly, the Democratic campaigns hardly referred to his declaration of being above the law, that neither Nixon nor Bush dared to make, however much their decisions were lawless and unconstitutional. Over and over again, I would openly write and speak to candidates running for office urging them to remind the people of this assertion of dictatorship and how it had and would harm them—and leave them voiceless. To this day, I have never received any explanation about why they dropped this campaign gift. After all, didn't

Biden make our Trump-imperiled democracy an issue? Making this issue concrete with Dangerous Donald's own exclamation would have driven this abstraction to a more memorable level. Never underestimate how many arrows in their quiver that the Democrats fail to utilize. That is their MO, to the mind-boggling dismay of their many informed supporters. They have so much more political ammunition against the cruel and vicious GOP that would get them a greater voter turnout, including policies and programs that poll well in liberal and conservative circles. What can be expected when their political consultants keep telling them that the disgruntled have nowhere to go and that fundraising goals cannot be jeopardized?

This caution, bordering on political masochism, is revealed in the fundraising letters written in mechanical prose by their consultants. I have yet to detect any of these letters being written from the heart and the mind of the candidates. And no, it is not hard for anyone alert to the uses of language to detect.

Two such sandpapered letters came to me in July 2020 from House Speaker Nancy Pelosi—a record-breaking fundraiser for the Democrats. These letters are expensive to prepare by supposed experts in this medium. Her writers came up with this doozy on the envelope: "I Won't Back Down. Are You With Me?" I mused about the thousands of dollars paid to create a defensive and vague message and was doubtful it would tempt voters to tear open these envelopes and lunge for the return envelope to send the dough.

Bear in mind, this was at a time of Trumpian criminal enterprises, pandemic denial, a destructive rampant lawlessness, and a hyper-corrupt, lying Trump regime stiff-arming the people every day on behalf of the giant wrongdoing corporate tax-escapees. And Nancy tells us she's not backing down. Wow—what political moxie it takes to defend in her letters expensive Obamacare, making insurance companies ever richer, leaving some thirty million persons still uninsured and many more than that number of people underinsured, instead of bucking up to support full Medicare for All (that both Obama and Hillary Clinton in earlier times stated was the best option but not practical, given the powers that be).

Playing defense was embedded in the survey accompanying Nancy's fundraising letter.[2] We were asked to rank the following:

1. Defending choice [without adding maternal, neonatal, and childcare]
2. Stopping voter suppression [without expanding known ways to surge voter turnout]
3. Protecting Social Security [with benefits frozen for forty years instead of expanding the lone barrier to severe elderly poverty and repealing the huge Trump tax cut of 2017 for the rich and big corporations. Note that both were pressed for by Bernie Sanders's campaign which the Democratic Party rejected.]
4. "Fighting Climate Change and opposing Trump's weakening of environmental laws" [instead of displacing fossil fuels with renewables, as written in the Green New Deal advanced by Democratic Party progressives and younger voters]

There was no mention of the corporate crime wave bleeding liberal and conservative families alike through rip-offs, overcharges, billing fraud, toxic pollution, and many preventable harmful conditions in hospitals, nursing homes, farms, factories, and mines.

Nancy did have a line saying that she wanted "to hear from" me because she felt our "opinions are important." I again sent her four letters signed by me and constitutional law specialists which had been sent earlier, filled with important opinions that hadn't even been acknowledged, much less responded to by her office. Sending them again was met with similar incommunicado behavior, as expected when one responds with form letters.

Over at the White House, Trump continued to flout criminal laws relating to political campaigns without incurring the focused wrath of his Democratic opponents. As soon as the Treasury checks started going out to tens of millions of Americans cramped by the COVID-19 pandemic, Trump ordered civil servants to have his signature added to each check in the lower left-hand corner. This was a violation of the criminal statute known as the Hatch Act. Bruce Fein and I objected in a letter to the Justice Department, sent to the media and put on the internet. No reaction from the Democrats. In 2020, Trump had a major campaign rally on the White House lawn—something that had never been done in US history and a clear violation of the Hatch Act. Again, we objected in a letter made public to the Justice Department. Again, no response. Again, the Democrats remained silent.

In July 2020, Trump, in an interview with Fox's Chris Wallace—suggested presciently that he may not accept the results of the November election should he lose, saying, "I have to see."

On October 9, 2020, radio opinion host Rush Limbaugh, to whom Trump had given the Presidential Medal of Freedom Award at the White House on February 4, 2020, conducted a two-hour "radio rally" for Donald Trump to openly advance his 2020 presidential political campaign. Green Party presidential candidate Howie Hawkins demanded equal time on Limbaugh's show (which was transmitted over the public airwaves) citing section 315(a) of the Communication Act of 1934. Limbaugh ignored him. No reporter covered the story of this event that had an audience in the millions.

Speaker Nancy Pelosi gave Trump another pass and did not prompt a public hearing on any of these blatant violations of civil and criminal laws. Trump must have been chortling between his cheeseburgers and became further emboldened after the election, as we all know. Did you think we could get any response to all this from any Democratic official anywhere in Washington? We thought so, until, after many attempts, we did not.

As an example of the comparative level of aggressiveness between the two parties and campaigns, consider the broader unlawful collaboration between right-wing talk show hosts Sean Hannity and Rush Limbaugh and the Trump candidacy. These two members of the press flagrantly violated the federal election law prohibiting donating anything of value exceeding $2,800 to a presidential candidate. Widely covered by the media, Hannity and Limbaugh worked with Trump to turn their valuable radio and television programming time into a soapbox for his 2020 reelection efforts. The daring duo openly bragged about it, with Hannity going on stage at a Trump campaign rally. The in-kind programming contributions Hannity and Limbaugh made to Trump's campaign vastly exceeded $2,800 in value, simply based on the costs of sixty seconds of advertising on the respective shows. Trump violated the Federal Election Campaign Act in neglecting to report these in-kind contributions from Hannity and Limbaugh to the Federal Election Commission (FEC). Gridlocked with three Democrats and three Republicans, FEC action was unlikely. However, that should not have deterred the Democratic Party's lawyers from filing a formal complaint to add to the record of Trump the outlaw. It didn't help that no reporter or columnist of note took this trio to task for these election law violations.

To the Democrats in 2020, continually, daily violations of these and other laws didn't make it as a campaign issue, a rallying cry, or even a slogan lasering in on this chronic lawbreaker who had sworn to uphold the Constitution and the laws of the land. High-level Democrats seemed to always be afraid of Trump accusing them of the crimes that he himself had committed. That is his MO, to be sure, but why can't they surmount this verbal intimidation by a staggering prevaricator? They are weak-kneed!

It's that trait—weakness—that emboldens Trump. We all know this trait from elementary schoolyard bullying.

Privately, Trump intuits his openings against a party that runs scared. He may not read or think or know much about governing, but his street smarts tell him that the Democratic

Party leaders don't know who they are, or worse, who they *were*. FDR clobbered the Republicans on issues such as Social Security, minimum wage, and unemployment compensation. He pushed for unions, taxing the rich, and went after business crooks. He taunted the GOP. They called him a traitor to his class, and he said he welcomed their hatred. Trump knows these issues are very popular today, but the Democrats aren't pulling for their base. They've even allowed Trump to take the word "populist" from them. Add that to the Democrats letting the GOP take away the Bible, the flag, and the votes of many blue-collar workers—the core of FDR's New Deal base.

It wasn't only the Democratic Party that showed itself to be so AWOL. How about the party's alleged circle of organized supporters? Take the labor unions and their AFL-CIO Federation located on 16th Street in Washington, a couple of hundred yards from the White House. It's an imposing building with loads of staff. Close by is the headquarters of the U.S. Chamber of Commerce, right off Lafayette Square in front of the White House. I kept waiting for some energy from the AFL-CIO and its member unions comprising some thirteen million workers. Trump was the perfect "Ugly Politician" with a terrible anti-worker, lawless business background in New York and New Jersey. The labor federation's website took him to task, and they sent out emails. Unfortunately, there was very little action on the ground. There were few news conferences, picketing, or any other displays of urgency over the state of American labor. In 2023, only 10 percent of workers were members of unions. This percentage is about as low as one hundred years ago, thanks in part to anti-union laws. The main achievement of organized labor in recent election years was to raise money for the Democratic Party, without public conditions or public pledges of labor law reforms, minimum wage upgrade, card check to facilitate starting unions, strengthening a terribly underfunded, weak OSHA, and pulling back on the runway from American labor foreign trade agreements. Of course, they were for these advances. But they never negotiated for them because they and the Democrats know that labor unions had conceded they had nowhere else to go. They compounded their futility by early endorsement of corporate Democratic candidates. Talk about taking union leaders for granted. The Democrats have done it for years without a thought, and their neglect of the rank and file has come back to haunt them in many election losses.

In midsummer 2020, I called Damon Silvers, long considered an intellectual star at the AFL-CIO's 16th Street headquarters. During the conversation about how reluctant the Democrats were to use powerful and voter-motivating arguments and proposals, Damon said, "Ralph, they don't want to win." "What?" I exclaimed. He repeated the statement, giving me to understand that the Democrats who had safe seats didn't want the responsibility of governing. It was his way, I surmised, of saying that the Democrats just were not nearly as hungry for victory as were the ideological Republicans with their Tea Party, their Freedom Caucus inside Congress, and their evangelical constituencies in the red states. By inference, that hunger to win did not describe Big Labor, which never wanted to get ahead of the Democratic Party and pull it faster than it wanted to go.

In 2011, sitting in the large booklined office of Richard Trumka, the former coal miner who rose to head the AFL-CIO, I asked why they weren't really pressing Barack Obama to meet his pledge, during his 2008 presidential campaign, to press for a federal $9.50 minimum wage by 2011 (up from $7.25, which is where it remains today). Trumka stood up, pointed at the White House through his office window, and said: "I'm waiting for him [meaning Obama] to make the move, before I spend my time on this thing." His union members made more than that sum per hour, so he didn't have a leadership stake there and, I suppose, didn't want to step up front without Obama, who was stalling on this modest increase instead of leading the way.

All through 2020, I assembled information for my weekly columns, radio show/podcast, and tweets covering a wide variety of topics showing that good politics for electoral victory meant good benefits for all the people. Many of these materials are available on my website: nader.org.[3] The demographically focused Democrats seemed unable to recognize the appeal of long-overdue advances for the well-being of both liberal and conservative voters where they live and are similarly affected. The Democratic Party's woeful strategists believed in targeting categories of voters in ways that appeared inauthentic, expedient, without any follow-through on the ground. The vacuous sound of their advertisements, mailings, and handouts was partly due to their inability to deliver the next step to the neighborhoods for turnout. The local Democratic committees were very weak, with low membership participation, tiny budgets, and low energy for expanding registration levels and attracting the younger generation. They had no coherent public agenda, nor were they given to showing they cared for the people. Their consultants' slogan, ludicrously out of touch, was "Build Back Better." Build what? Better than who—Trump? This was a semantic loser if there ever was one. I would ask active Democrats if they could remember any of the television ads the party was producing that made television stations rich with hundreds of millions of dollars in ad buys. All they could do was nervously giggle. This was the party that our duopoly was offering up to save the Republic from Der Führer Trump, Tyrant Trump, Treacherous Trump—the muckraked subject of countless books, exposés, and compelling cartoons left unused by his opponents.

I tried to make case after case for the Democrats to move into a more effective mode to landslide the totally vulnerable GOP. Republicans were working overtime to actively keep certain people from voting, keep the votes from being fully counted, and even discriminately purging voter rolls. Trump and the Republicans gutted several lifesaving federal laws and regulations such as those dealing with safety assessments for potentially toxic chemicals, limits on carbon emissions from coal- and gas-fired power plants, and OSHA programs designed to reduce risks of workers developing lung disease.[4] In addition, they cut taxes on the superrich and profitable megacompanies to historically low barebones levels.[5] How many fastballs down the middle did the Democrats need? The Democrats should have taken the Republicans to task for blocking programs for children, women, and workers, neglecting public works that were historically routine and expected, and undermining clean air and water laws.

I called the brainy chair of the Ohio Democratic Party, David Pepper, for some enlightenment about the party's lack of energy. He said he had to raise money just to get more lawn signs in this key swing state because the National Party was not recognizing the GOP's far greater number of such signs. Signs signify party activity to passersby; they generate partisan talk. Silence is deadly for any party's prospects.

There was another disparity. The Democratic Party would bring in outsiders to get the vote out while the GOP was using home-grown and known people in the streets, neighborhoods, and communities. No contest in terms of which approach gets out more votes.

I wasn't so much interested in supporting the elections of marginally better candidates—both incumbents and challengers—in the Congress. To me, they had to be vocal carriers of mandates. My hope was to generate sharper foci among the voting public on fundamental bread-and-butter issues, on distinct shifts of power, on encouraging a few citizens to become much more active and leverage that energy among their circle of relatives, friends, and coworkers. There was little point in electing politicians without a perceived series of mandates from the people back home. Otherwise, elected officials go to Washington on a political "high" and let the corridor-walking commercial lobbyists fill the policy vacuum with callous corporate purpose.

After a while, watching and listening provides close observers of elections a sense of comparative levels of drive, momentum, and enthusiasm. One senses which of the two major party candidates and party committees are on the defense or are on the offense. The

GOP has made the most out of the least in these tugs-of-war. Not being able to run much on any record for the people, they run on bromides—lower taxes for corporations and the superrich, deregulation, bigger military budgets—which year after year fail to provoke pulverizing rebuttals by the Democrats in language the average family and taxpayers can grab on to. In column after column, I would rebut the cover-ups for less protections for health and safety and economic well-being, less taxes for the already undertaxed superrich, and the waste, fraud, and redundancy of the military budget at the expense of domestic public works. Other groups did the same with vibrant language and examples drawn from their special expertise. The tone-deaf Democrats remained on the defensive, in part because they too supported a runaway unauditable military budget and were taking great sums of campaign money from the nominally regulated companies.

The GOP also ran on fictitious issues, accusing Democrats of saturating public schools with "critical race theory," of being for "defunding the police," and any other number of fake charges.

Every day it was more likely that the Democrats were on the defensive, not the more culpable Republicans. Once a party becomes chronically defensive and does not have an attack attitude and message, it is hard to get out of that hole. Especially since the Democrats fall into the "elitist" trap of responding to the Grand Old Party with mockery and derision, something the Republican base and many undecided voters take personally and resent.

In trying to reach both the voters and candidates, I wrote columns with titles such as "Suggestions for Successful Elections in

2020 at All the Levels," "Trump: Letting Big Corporations Get Away with Whatever They Want," and "Why Do Americans Give Away So Much Control to Corporations?" I even wrote a column debunking the grotesque appropriation of the word "populist" to describe plutocratic Donald. These and other writings presented a cornucopia of actions taxpayers (the owners of the commons) could take to reclaim control of assets such as the public lands, public waterways, and the public airwaves. Imagine the benefits of investors in mutual fund and pension fund assets controlling their trillions of dollars of investments that are now under corporate control.

In September 2020, I offered ways for "the Democratic Party to rev the engines to topple Tyrant Trump. This followed an August 2020 column urging the Democrats to "Demolish Trump's Delusional Law-Breaking Dystopia." One would have thought that his blatant breaking of the laws and his collateral corruptions would be a top-ranked charge by the Democrats. Trump was in their face—delivering his acceptance of the party's nomination right on the White House premises, turning, as noted, this exalted residence into a federal crime scene by his violating a criminal statute called the Hatch Act.

In late September I wrote, "To Democratic Voters—Up Your Demands; To Trump Voters—See How He Didn't Deliver for You." Nearing voting day, I assembled thirty-one of my "Election Time Tweets for Getting Out The Vote."

The election saw the Republicans losing the Senate and the Democrats losing ground and coming perilously close to losing the House of Representatives—so close that Speaker Pelosi had to concede considerable power to a handful of Blue Dog Democrats who more than made up the margin of difference between the two parties.

It was a headshaking, frustrating time. I tried to reach the widest possible audience—*macro* to the public-at-large through columns, tweets, and weekly radio show and podcasts, and *micro* by countless telephone calls to politicians, political committees, reporters, columnists, editors, radio/TV producers, and reporters. The mediums were the internet, the Postal Service, and hand-delivered print materials. Realistically, did many read, open, or react? The internet was a "snare and a delusion"— lawyers' phrasing. So too were more traditional methods of reaching the audience. The COVID-19 pandemic obviously made connecting difficult. Remote work cleared out the inhabitants of newsrooms, and widespread fear and dread were more than distractions. The sheer news output on the tragic scenes in hospitals, the gross lack of preparedness, the crazed circuses at the White House press conferences, the adjustments that schools, stores, and hospitals were frantically making, crowded out efforts to civically nourish the contents of electioneering that year.

Other kindred citizen groups had long ago become accustomed to being frozen out of the electoral arenas and their public dialogues and debates. Continuing the daily grind in their specialized civic pursuits, these national organizations were largely observers. Once in a while they would write letters to the editor or submit an op-ed for a newspaper, mostly incurring rejection. They had very few calls to return from a media whose busy daily postings and official-source journalism dulled their curiosity and sense of newsworthiness. Media like NPR and PBS interviewed reporters for expertise on issues raised by the candidates, when they used to call genuine experts such as Bob McIntyre, former head of the Citizens for Tax Justice, for informative exchanges.

Excising citizen groups from electoral arenas was a minor devolution. Almost every step forward in the struggles for justice has started with a tiny number of citizens expanding in number to affect the political realms that eventually adopt reforms. The early twenty-first century couldn't have been more different than the bustling early twentieth century, when the progressive movement was at its height, and many conservatives of those days would be considered serious liberals today, especially on subjects related to concentrated corporate power and corporate crimes. A century later, the Prozac culture has taken hold.

Friends would think I was optimistically dazed, furiously tilting at nonexistent windmills, hoping somewhere out there in the internet gulag someone was taking notice. They amusingly suggested I try my hand at a politically instructive video game to reach a sliver of the giant gaming crowd. They saw my efforts as being adrift in a giant ocean of people who were preoccupied and predisposed. One wannabe satirist compared me to a person standing in the middle of a giant stadium crying out the question to a packed crowd: "What's the difference, my friends, between ignorance and apathy?" and receiving a bellowing response: "We don't know and we don't care."

I wasn't always faced with such deep inattention, though I tried to suppress remembering those vivifying times. *U.S. News & World Report* in 1974 named me as the Fourth Most

Influential American after the president, the Chief Justice, and the head of the AFL-CIO. In 2006 the *Atlantic* rated me as one of the 100 most influential Americans in our country's history. I never had such illusions, but media perceptions can affect reality. Experiencing the celestial black hole of 2020 was quite enough to be discouraging. My sustaining framework was how I started out in the early 1960s, hitchhiking to Washington from Connecticut to lobby Congress into regulating the auto industry. Talk about an exercise in wishful thinking. I recall being picked up by a truck driver in Delaware who asked where I was going. I quietly replied that I was going to Washington to get General Motors regulated for safer cars. He gave me a look that made me think he was about to head for the shoulder and drop me off for some passing dreamboat.

At that moment, he was right, of course. I didn't have one vote in Congress for such a Herculean objective. Lots of hard work over the following months ended with a unanimous vote in the Senate and House for the passage in 1966 of legislation that brought the sheriff to that reckless "Detroit Iron" of style and horsepower.

In the succeeding fifteen years, an astonishingly small cohort of activists brought enough compelling information about abuses to the media's attention to force Congress to enact laws governing the meat and poultry industries, regulating products like flammable fabric, chemicals, pesticides, and gas pipelines, and creating new federal regulatory agencies that were signed into law by President Nixon. People today know them by their acronyms: OSHA, EPA, NHTSA, and CPSC, covering workplace health/safety, the environment, auto safety, and assorted household products. We also fought successfully against corporate opposition to see President Richard Nixon, of all presidents, sign into law the fundamental air pollution and product safety legislation.

Later in 1974, I worked closely with Congressman John Moss (D-CA) and Senator Ted Kennedy (D-MA) to pass the historic Freedom of Information Act Amendments. That same year, the Safe Drinking Water Act was passed. Nixon's vetoes for the Water Pollution Bill and the Freedom of Information Act were overridden by Congress.

The ways we developed to defeat polluting industries again and again, and again, before they built up their counterattack, was simple. We would create task forces of law students, or recent law graduates, to put out powerful documented reports pressing for legislation and litigation. The media was enamored by this burst of youthful idealism (calling these young people "Nader's Raiders") and provided continual coverage of our follow-ups in Capitol Hill hearings. To mobilize the grassroots, we helped establish organizations such as Clean Water Action (CWA) headed by David Zwick, who was instrumental in drafting the 1972 Clean Water Act while a Harvard Law School student. CWA developed one of the largest door-to-door canvassing operations in the country. Buoyed by newspaper, radio, and television coverage, members of Congress saw the popularity and voter attractions of these quality-of-life improvements. It was a virtuous cycle of citizen advocacy, publicity, and then the Congress responding.

I knew it couldn't last. I was getting reports from many sources that corporate lawyers, like Lloyd Cutler, were meeting privately with editors at the *Washington Post* and *New York Times* to convey thinly veiled threats regarding why their clients might not want to place advertising in publications undermining the "free enterprise system." Family-owned, these papers were going or thinking of going public with shareholders. The *Times*'s new managing director, Abe Rosenthal, was more than receptive to corporate visits and started exerting a restraining hand on his subordinates not to be seen as antibusiness. He issued a rule that any citizen groups such as ours, which criticized a company, had to receive a response from the company or the story would be pulled. GM learned that simply not responding reduced *New York Times* coverage. The television networks took their cues from the leading newspapers—the *New York Times,* the *Washington Post,* and the *Wall Street Journal.*

As coverage began to shrink, we tried to make up for some of that slide by going on television talk shows such as those hosted by Phil Donahue, Mike Douglas, and Merv Griffin, whose audiences reached many millions of viewers. At this time, another base—Congress—was starting to falter, undermining President Jimmy Carter's modestly progressive agenda and the first-rate regulators he nominated. Commercial political action committees (PACs) were emerging in ever greater numbers. The arrival of Ronald Reagan in 1981 meant a never-before-seen wholesale takeover of Washington, D.C., by the corporations.

Reaganites actually gave companies open invitations to submit "wish lists" for deregulation, tax breaks, subsidies, and other privileges and immunities.

Democrats controlling Congress started raising money the way Republicans did, from the business community. Organized labor was getting weaker—losing jobs to automation and the export of jobs overseas. This added to their own internal stagnation.

The Reagan landslide victory over Carter in 1980 took with it the defeat of many of our key veteran allies such as Senators Warren Magnuson, Gaylord Nelson, and Frank Church.

When the history is written of this progressive citizen movement—also manifesting itself at the local and state levels—1980 will mark the year when the galvanized forces of corporatism—straddling business, government, and the media—drove this effort for a functioning democracy of "justice for all" into its unabated decline. It was not something that valiant civic advocates wanted to describe publicly lest they seem to be admitting their own diminishing influence. The ever-maturing corporate state was tailored to the corporate, political, and media world's ambitions of profit, status, and control. Sensing this looming demise, I passed to others the leadership of Public Citizen—the largest of the groups I founded—in order to be freer to incubate more citizen organizations and promote more civic power to make containing corporate power a national agenda. Unfortunately, funders and the existing groups remained on the ramparts fighting some specific abuses and harms at the retail level and not investing the necessary resources to make corporate power, control, and crime a national front-burner focus for fundamental structural accountability.

CHAPTER 5
Ideas and Action for Change

My presidential campaigns in 1996, 2000, 2004, and 2008 with the Green Party and as an Independent were an extension of my efforts to make the corporate domination of our political economy, our culture, and its interaction with the rest of the world a cornerstone of the public dialogue and debate at that more visible level. As before, I had great difficulty convincing my former colleagues running their groups of the necessity for fertilizing the electoral arenas so fully occupied by a two-party duopoly marginalizing the civil society from any participation. Public opinion understood this tightening of corporate compulsion. A national poll by *BusinessWeek* reported that over 70 percent of the respondents believed that "corporations have too much control over their lives." This was before the collapse of Wall Street in 2008 resulting in the loss of eight million jobs, huge taxpayer bailouts, and a steep recession, among other corporate-led calamities from the opioid industry's rising annual death toll to the intransigence of the omnicidal fossil fuel industry led by ExxonMobil. More recently, in 2024, a national poll had 82 percent of the respondents favoring higher taxes on the wealthy.

The onset of computerized billing and the internet has greatly enlarged billing frauds, bogus telephone marketing, and other rip-offs of consumers, leaving tens of millions of shoppers baffled, powerless, and put upon by the day.

Still, I trudged on, writing books and articles, granting interviews, and interviewing reformers on my radio/podcast show. I helped start new pro-justice organizations, including ones coming from my Princeton class of 1955 and Harvard Law School class of 1958. They were designed to be replicable models for diffusion like the student public interest research groups (PIRGs) we sparked in over twenty states during the 1970s.

The US Supreme Court dealt this diffusion ambition a severe blow when by a vote of 5 to 3 it invalidated in 1986 a California utility regulator's decision to allow a consumer group to solicit support through a paid-for insert in the billing envelopes of the legal monopoly Pacific Gas & Electric Company. The Court, assailed by Justice William Rehnquist's dissent, astonishingly ruled that such an insert violated the company's First Amendment right to remain silent and not have to respond. To this day, the decision marks the most radical interpretation of corporations—called artificial persons—having equal rights with real human beings. The Court ended a major drive to have inserts in the billings of electric, gas, water utilities, banks, insurance companies, large landlords, and even residential users of the Postal Service. Thousands of staffed consumer protection groups having a seat at the table were preempted. Millions of consumers who would have joined such groups were left without collective, skilled champions for their cause. Before the decision, we pressed for lawmakers to enact a few of these citizens utility boards or CUBs in Wisconsin, Illinois, New York, Oregon, San Francisco, and San Diego with government-required inserts soliciting such membership in the companies' billing envelopes. In just one negotiation, without filing a lawsuit, the Illinois group, called Illinois CUB, and its allies secured a $1.3 billion refund in 1993 to northern Illinois residents by the overcharging Commonwealth Edison Company.

This is not the space to go into any detail about the weakening of countervailing institutions to the increasing corporate supremacy over our society and the world. I have pointed them out in my weekly columns and books and in public conferences organized by the Center for Study of Responsive Law and other citizen groups. Suffice it to say that the Center's most elaborate conference initiative called "Breaking Through Power," held at the DAR Constitution Hall in 2016, brought together for eight days 161 civic leaders, thinkers, and civic doers—many of whom had made real change against great odds. Their succinct presentations went unreported by the media despite being well-advanced prior to and during the events. These eight days brought together a range of civic heroes never before convened in American history. Yet they were not considered worthy of on-site coverage by the press, print, radio, or television, including Public Radio and Public Broadcasting. See for yourself at our Breaking Through Power website.[1] It gets worse: the entire event was streamed free with fewer viewers than we expected. People did not learn about it in advance. Though Washington's WTOP daily promotes free business brands in its twice-an-hour business report, it declined our request to be interviewed about the forthcoming mega convocation. At WAMU, local NPR station host Kojo Nnamdi did an interview about the conference on May 31, 2016. Unfortunately, this was after the first four days of the conference had ended. The larger frame here is that the freezing out of civic actions by the mass media also took down the attentive audience for countless "kitchen-table" subjects. Years ago, the American people had made me into a national civic celebrity because the national media brought my work to their attention.

There are many factors in the mainstream media's avoidance of the civil society's activities beyond the desire for corporate advertising dollars and major papers and news chains going public with shareholders. Corporate lobbies became more aggressive in protesting stories they did not like. A new generation of journalists were required to post tidbits throughout the day and having to also shoulder burdens with smaller staffs to produce the copy. The public relying on "news" through the internet (Facebook, Twitter, etc.) forced the print editors to take up too much space with photographs, artwork, graphic displays, and features laced with more photos, sometimes displacing the newsworthy copy. The *New York Times* has combined these changes, and more, to adopting a magazine format with long, often excellent features on subjects such as the shrinking Amazon rainforest or the precipitous decline in groundwater in the United States. However, the price paid is the minimal attention to what civic groups are doing to improve our society. There is almost no regular reporting on efforts underway by citizens to get legislation, to win cases in court, or, heaven forbid, to introduce new ideas and strategies to strengthen our weakened democracy.

Had the *Times* and other major press followed this model in the 1960s and 1970s, there would have been no consistent reporting on the breakthrough reforms of our consumer, environmental, and worker safety laws, along with other major changes. Without such coverage, the lawmakers would not have been under pressure to adopt these proposals, much less hold public hearings to arouse public support.

Underneath these transformations and these pandering adjustments to shortened attention spans is a shocking ignorance by the media of the historic sine qua non role played by civic activity in almost all the blessings we have inherited from our forebears. Perhaps with the exception of the G.I. Bill of Rights at the end of World War II, just about every advance in justice started with one, two, three, or four citizens getting the ball rolling into incrementally large arrays of support, until they found themselves embraced by the political-legal systems of implementation.

If you asked editors and reporters why there are so few public hearings in Congress regarding the myriad of corporate abuses, some might point to the myriad of targeted corporate PACs. Perhaps the more perceptive ones may mention the shortened three-day week when Congress is in session. Even more astute journalists may take note of Congress stripping itself of the capacity to conduct such investigations due to reduced office and committee staff and advisory arms. The continuing defunding of the Office of Technology Assessment (OTA), commenced by Republican Speaker Newt Gingrich in 1995, is illustrative. But very few would look into the mirror and ascribe a significant part of the problem to inadequate or no reporting of many of the few such hearings that are conducted.

A case in point were the long-awaited hearings into the insurance industry by Chairman Peter Rodino (D-NJ) of the House Judiciary Committee in 1973. The insurance companies, who had long and weakly been regulated by the states, were given a pass by the feds over time. It took arduous groundwork to get Chairman Rodino to agree to such an unprecedented investigatory hearing. After day one, there was almost no reporting of the expert testimony. After day two, the same near blackout. On day three, Chairman Rodino turned to his chief staffer and asked, "What are we doing this for?" The hearing "petered" out soon thereafter. Subjects such as confronting the corporate crime wave, upgrading the antiquated federal corporate criminal code, or reviving the long-ago proposed federal chartering of large corporations are no longer the focus of thorough congressional hearings. Gone are meaningful congressional probes of the corporate hijacking of military budget/policy, or the corporate attack on people's freedom of contract and access to the courts with trial by jury.

I have dwelled in these pages on the background and context that emerged during conversations Mark Green and I had over our role in the 2022 congressional elections. Believe me, we were not seized by any delusions of grandeur, merely by a civic sense that we must do what we can and hope a multiplier effect would follow for greater quantitative impact on a more responsive

Congress. We started in late 2021, exchanging memos and telephone calls. Our reconnaissance persuaded us that we were not entering a crowded field. Long ago, the progressive civic community was shut out by Democratic Party operatives and their consultants. We were neither asked if we wanted to proactively volunteer our recommendations, nor did we find an open door or a returned phone call. Having run for elective office numerous times and having no further such aspirations, we believed our combined experience with long years running both citizen groups and knowing something about the dynamics of election campaigns could be an asset for receptive candidates running for seats in the Senate or the House of Representatives.

Mark, an open, loyal Democrat and twice elected as New York City Public Advocate, had many connections to incumbents from New York State. I cared about the agendas and mandates adopted in the most credible way by candidates, even Republicans, Greens, or Libertarians, who chose to pick up some or most of what we were systemically planning to offer. Consequently, we expected that Mark would get his calls returned, especially by their policy advisers, inasmuch, as noted, he had pulled together two large volumes full of policy for the Democratic Party in 1992 (Changing America: Blueprints for the New Administration: The Citizens Transition Project) and 2009 (Change for America: A Progressive Blueprint for the 44th President).

What were we thinking? We wanted to assemble an authentic, credible, fact-based agenda for concurring politicians for use in their daily campaigning. It would have a broad range and depth and be highly likely to appeal to voters self-described as conservative and liberal. Our slogan: "We all bleed the same color." We knew from the mass of insipid, repetitive, vacuous political advertising that if *policy* does not precede *message*, the message will go into the ether of amnesia or wedge the voters into divide-and-rule traps. Message without policy invites fake, phony manipulations of emotions that degrade voter expectations instead of elevating voter knowledge and electoral intelligence. Holding down deserving expectations so as to make the audience vulnerable to "twistifications" is an ultimate objective of political charlatans.

CHAPTER 6
Building on the Foundation

Having come fresh from extensive research on the Trump regime and the hard-right Republican Party he captured, we were prepared to shape the material from our books, *Fake President* and *Wrecking America*, into messages placing the Trumpsters on the defensive and to crisply, articulately, and proactively document the needs of all the American people. This approach fits findings that candidates who contrast their messages with their opponents' messages is more effective with voters than simple attack sallies, countless empty promises to or vague recitations of candidate accomplishments.

We wanted to focus on another technique used by politicians who have no record to try to convince ordinary people they care about people like them. GOP candidates like to talk about values—family values, patriotic values, religious values, hard work values, playing by the rules to succeed values, and so forth. The GOP has used these abstractions to flummox Democrats for years and put them on the defensive. As I shall illustrate, with regards to Senate majority leader Mitch McConnell's campaign, the way to boomerang such evasions is to throw the actual voting record or public position of the candidate directly against these abstract values to demonstrate their chronic manipulating falsehoods.

The Democratic Party's functionaries have not promoted a sense of mission on behalf of a beleaguered populace, identifying with their perceived needs and family aspirations and openly standing for them. This stems from an obsession with raising commercial money on an ever-more-insistent daily basis and the absence of any intellectual and principled dispositions. These failures are contagious. At an early 2022 major retreat for Democratic candidates in Virginia, people witnessed waves of defeatism and pessimism about the fall elections. The mainstream press would later report gloomy predictions by Democrats of their own defeat on more than one occasion in the succeeding months. That sense of doom, in contrast to GOP fervor, spread to the Democratic Party's workers and to more than a few voters who saw flat tires instead of charged-up engines. This is not a recipe for getting out more votes, either from the faithful nor from some of the 125 million eligible voters expected to stay home and not vote.

There were so many vacuums to be filled with appealing, graphic material by the Democratic Party if it replaced some of its bureaucrats with known but frustrated newcomers too long ignored.

Stagnation also occupied Congress. Newt Gingrich's rule changes concentrated power in the hands of the Speaker at the expense of Committee and Subcommittee Chairs. The leadership of the Democratic Party, principally Nancy Pelosi, followed suit and did not encourage the essential initiatives that can only come from freeing her House Democrats to develop their own policies, reforms, and investigations. Everything had to be cleared through "the commander," as some called her.

Violating the principle that none of us are as smart alone as all of us together, Pelosi developed an inside reputation of not listening to her members or advocacy organizations about matters of substance. This was in contrast to her unerring alertness to prospects of more large donors both in Washington and in the districts, to which she journeyed indefatigably to secure the allegiance of her indebted members.

Here is one consequential example of how this inverted ranking of priorities turned out. As noted earlier, Gingrich in 1995 defunded the crucial Office of Technology Assessment (OTA) inside Congress, effectively shutting down this modest $20 million budget for a staff of technical and scientific advisers to Congress. In 2008, after years of congress failing to fund OTA, the Democrats won a sizable majority in the House and Senate and won the White House with the Obama victory over McCain. I saw the Democratic control of both houses of Congress and the White House as the best opportunity yet to get the OTA funded. Representative Rush Holt (D-NJ), a former Princeton University scientist, was willing to take the lead. We organized petitions of former OTA officials, staff, and leading scientists, including several Nobel Laureates, to request the immediate funding and reopening of the OTA by the House and the Senate. Many members of Congress were unaware of how many tens of billions of dollars OTA could save the country by evaluating technology and producing scholarly reports on costly weapons systems, health threats in hospitals and workplaces, and product defects. OTA had a proven track record of assessing energy, agricultural, and environmental technologies. OTA research helped Congress prevent the ill effects of bad technology and encouraged Congress to adopt beneficial polices. A complete archive of OTA reports was created by the Federation of American Scientists.[1]

OTA reports would receive media coverage, and its testimony before committees would have enriched the legislative process and informed the people at large.

Obviously, corporations that wrongfully profit from congressional and public ignorance opposed the OTA. Look what Silicon Valley's internet giants have gotten away with year after year of flailing stupefaction on Capitol Hill. With OTA, that would not have occurred.

The major effort in 2009 didn't budge Nancy Pelosi, who privately saw it as a PAC-money-losing proposition. Her only made-public belief was that she didn't want to give the congressional Republicans an excuse to accuse her of starting another bureaucracy on Capitol Hill. Not surprisingly, the ever-cautious Barack Obama did not lift a finger to dissuade her and urge her to allow the appropriate House Committee to hold open hearings making the case. We had supplied Pelosi's office with a list of impressive witnesses. She declined a request to meet with a distinguished group of outside engineers, scientists, or with Democratic legislators arranged by Representative Holt. All this happened at a time of a House Democratic majority of 255 to 179 and a Senate with 59 and later 60 senators siding with the party. With such an inflexible stance, Pelosi, "the commander," proceeded to lose the House to a terrible version of the GOP in 2010, 2012, 2014, and 2016 before regaining control in 2018, 2020 and losing again in 2022. It's not as if the Democrats didn't need fresh vistas and self-renewals across the board.

Opportunities for revival and reinvigorating the body politic so as to arouse the citizenry for the common good were everywhere. Mark and I saw unused civic talent—honest, experienced, skilled people long engaged with people as people, not with political labels. We decided to find ways to marshal and focus their knowledge as volunteers for any candidates who want to represent the people in a thoughtful manner. Put the two together and, voilà, elections could be won decisively with open mandates, for both the immediate needs of individuals and families—these do make the news—and the larger potent perils: the looming omnicides of climate disruptions, multiple pandemics, nuclear, biological, and chemical warfare, corporate state suppression of democracy, and the ravaging consequences of mass poverty which are largely ignored in the heat of regular campaigning.

Even less portentous and on-the-ground abuses are not on the table. Corporate crime, corporate bailouts and subsidies, and campaign finance manipulations are all rejected by a large majority of the voters. Concentrated media control, political corruption, and single-payer health insurance are off the table. Except for Bernie Sanders, full Medicare for All and worker pay were at best throwaway lines by the candidates, leading people to see them as just that. Veteran House member John Larson's strong case for increasing Social Security benefits (frozen for over forty years) and gaining revenues from upper-income wealthies didn't make it on the table.

If one were to sum up the panicked state of the party, it would be to describe it, as I wrote in a column, as resembling a deer frozen in the headlights. In late February 2022, we began outlining the project that Mark named "Winning America." He had seen a documentary by Adam McKay on the GOP that called it the "party of death, destruction, and deceit." To bring these concepts home to people, we needed to portray the GOP as a party of anxiety, dread, and fear, reflecting a consistent denial of economic security, affordable healthcare, and protection from corporate predators at the workplace, and undermining family solidarity by crass mass marketing of bad stuff directly to children.

Reaching the ambitious Congresswoman Katie Porter (D-CA), I conveyed a list of such campaign-winning strategies. Twice she mentioned the need to shake up the leadership of her party. I did not know at the time that she was readying a run for the US Senate in 2024.

Mark was ready to strategize about the best way to present the list to Nancy Pelosi and other deciders. Would it be in the form of a handbook, would it use the word "fascism" to describe the Trumpsters, would it instead be a simpler list of "10 Ways the Dems can Win in 2022" with backup material? We finally decided on a far more labor-intensive approach and brought together over two dozen civic leaders, covering a wide range of needed changes resonating with regular people. The launching medium we chose, during the pandemic, was a Zoom conference for the candidates with succinct presentations about how to attract and convince voters to impact and elect the best available politicians. The conference would have to have prominent endorsers and one or two prominent introducers for this session scheduled for July 23, 2022. All this, of course, was easier conceived than finding the funding and getting it done. We had four months. Years ago, before the internet, voicemail, and information overload, that would have been plenty of time. With fewer communication technologies in the 1960s and 1970s, we were better able to communicate—two-way. People were more likely to return calls. Far more expensive conferences and logistics in real time were accomplished in less time. In 1979, right after the March 28th Three Mile Island nuclear near-catastrophe in Pennsylvania, we organized a massive rally on May 6, 1979, of about one hundred thousand people in less than four weeks.

Back to the Winning America project, once we gathered multiple lists of the people needed to succeed in a six-and-a-half-hour civic education for winning elections, the biggest obstacles were finding phone numbers and getting called back. Not only did we need many yeses from participants, but we needed to speak with each one of them to make sure that they were alert to the principal mission of the conference and willing to hone their arguments in practical terms. Since they were all volunteering, we were concerned that they, being busy, might just wing it with their standard speech. Not that we didn't try to raise funds to provide them with a modest honorarium. Scores of calls to liberal people of means registered zero. Katrina vanden Heuvel, Gloria Jarecki, and David K. Kelley came through with

$25,000, $20,000, and $10,000 respectively, with smaller contributions making up a tiny budget totaling $56,000. Never in a hundred years would I have predicted such a squeezing operational budget. The important and timely stakes and the quality of the event—provided free to the candidates and backed up by a willingness of the presenters to be called afterward by candidate staff for more pro bono consultations—wasn't enough to attract funders.

We thought we could get additional funds at least for a couple of additional staff. Hoping for some mass-media coverage didn't pan out. We didn't even get independent media coverage. Except for one columnist, Dana Milbank of the *Washington Post*, late in the fall campaign, this never-before-attempted project to civically persuade candidates into more formidable campaigns on an array of serious neglects was blacked out.

The media was a signal part of the environment that induced candidates to engage in their race to the bottom. To generalize, with few exceptions, the media was in its own rut. It reported regularly on how much candidates raised in dollars, but not how much they raised in time/hours of volunteers. It loved to report gaffes and poll results that asked the same limited questions or gave the comparative standing of the opposing candidates and parties. It published personal profiles of the candidates' backgrounds in not particularly useful ways for more informed voter choice. For instance, they usually ignored self-censored issues. The reporting repeated again and again the stump speech of the candidates but not what was again and again omitted. Reporters in the field covering the candidates were bored stiff.

Editors back at the office traded bored observations with their boring columnists.

As for third parties—why, since "they can't win," should the media cover their important agendas that were clearly off the table for any discussion by the taboo-afflicted two major parties? It is fortunate for sports fans that sports editors don't have an eradicating approach in not covering continually losing local teams. Notwithstanding the historic contributions of small parties—which never won a national election—such as coming forward first on the abolition of slavery, women's right to vote, farmer and industrial labor protections, many advances in democratic rights and the social safety net, the mass media rejected the contemporary offering of more voices and choices on the ballot.

The political bigotry against third parties (their candidates are called "spoilers") does not give them a chance to grow from year to year, especially being kept out of the debates and subject to a winner-take-all voting system. The proportional representation in some European democracies allowed Green and other start-up parties to gain a foothold and have a share of their parliament. Lucky for us that nature allows seeds to sprout and even to grow to replace existing monocultures.

As if this discriminatory political culture is not enough, states have enacted the highest barriers in the Western world by far to ballot access by small-party candidates. Provisions in these laws are constantly challenged in court with mixed results, notwithstanding the equal constitutional rights of such candidates to run for office and compete for votes.

For citizen groups such as ours, the absence of third-party competition took away some of the arguments that could be made to the Democrats to wake up or else. Instead, what reigns as a status quo glue is the belief that dissenters within the party have nowhere else to go. So, shut up and get in line. You don't want to waste your vote, do you?

None of these speed bumps daunted us. March and April were months of furious calling to start filling the six and a half hours, find endorsers, and sharpen the arguments to get people to say yes. One speed bump was gigantic. We did not have the phone numbers and emails of the campaign offices. Calling the congressional offices for discussing electoral politics of any kind was legally prohibited. The trained staff would have none of it. "You'll have to call the campaign," was the refrain without giving us contact numbers.

Groups who had numbers and emails, such as the Trial Lawyers PAC, would not share them. Nor would progressive members of Congress admit that they had the campaign contact information. The campaign arms of the House (Democratic Congressional Campaign Committee—DCCC), the Senate (Democratic Senatorial Campaign Committee—DSCC), and the Democratic National Committee (DNC) were similarly not divulging this information. Certainly, Speaker Pelosi had the list. But we couldn't ever get through to her.

We muddled along, getting a campaign contact here and there, but nothing like the efficiencies of having the entire list of congressional campaigns to alert and keep them current about the July 23rd Zoom presentations and with personal telephone conversations to enthuse them. In the process of making many calls and checking their campaign literature, we soon realized that the Democrats didn't even know how to boast about a century's worth of their past achievements and what they have enacted for the people under Biden. The GOP has become the Party of "No No No"—a gift to the Democrats that keeps on giving but not something the Democrats used to their advantage.

The Democratic Party was without compelling slogans, no energizing exhortations such as "Go vote yourself a raise, it's long overdue and you've earned it" for the twenty-million-plus workers making under $15 an hour. Or "Dump-the-Pay-or-Die Healthcare Gougers." "Win Medicare for All—More Efficient, Less Hassle, and More Lifesaving."

We kept looking for the one or two strategic geniuses, a few irrebuttable wordsmiths to take down the GOP and motivate more people to vote. No one came forward to suggest that they existed, as many did to point out very good fundraisers. It was as if they were waiting for their consultants. There was almost no spontaneous local creative energy.

One of our earliest calls was to Stan Greenberg, married to veteran Representative Rosa DeLauro (D-CT), who was a leading Democratic pollster and author of books on polls, voters, political parties, and elections. I described what we had in mind and went quickly over the range of issues. Would he join our effort, I asked? "No," he replied, saying that there were too many issues, and the one he thought was the most central was corporate power and the related economic agenda. I responded with the concurrence of its centrality, thinking my decades-long emphasis on corporate domination needed no elaboration. But the candidates were going to be expected to take other positions for which they need to be better prepared systemically. Greenberg may have had other reasons, because he showed little interest in what we continued to develop in the coming months.

Democratic pollster Celinda Lake was quickly enthusiastic on my call, made some suggestions, and said she would try to open some doors. Very few of the people who told us they would open some doors ever succeeded, giving them the benefit of the doubt that they tried.

Among the hardest doors to open were those to the media itself. Just about all reporters, editors, and columnists are on voicemail—you'd be lucky to reach one of them and make the arguments for covering what we were undertaking. They would politely listen, agree to receive more details, and then go incommunicado. These were often the political reporters and the assigning political editors—the latter presumably, we thought, looking for something new in a time of pack journalism.

The great *Washington Post* reporter Morton Mintz believed that reporters covering campaigns or participating in candidate debate forums should inject issues and reforms not part of the conventional campaign positions of the candidates and their limited pollsters. In 2004, he came up with many questions about matters usually unasked to put to candidates at debates, press conferences, or just one-on-one on the campaign trail. Many dealt with what would the candidates do about corporate crime, according corporations equal rights with real people, monopolistic practices in the drug, oil, and media businesses, corporate welfare and tax escapes, reforming campaign finance corruption, and universal health insurance. Mintz's peers looked on him as a maverick touting unrealistic public dialogues and making reporters into advocates. To which Mintz had a brief answer: if the subject matter is *important* for the public to know about, you go with it . . . period.

Beyond the Washington media world, I started to call the political editors at regional papers in Miami, Atlanta, Houston, Boston, St. Louis, Detroit, Iowa, Los Angeles, San Francisco, and Seattle. Perhaps they would like to hear about our project in the context of regional issues relating to a low minimum wage, governors not taking the federal money to include more poor families under Medicaid, and the controversies over public lands. Some took my calls and we had serious discussions, but they did not see why they should write about our project linking the civic community to the election campaign with a Zoom conference.

Since we were plowing new ground, we started in early 2022 to travel three parallel lanes. One was to organize the Zoom event on July 23rd, 2022, which would formally launch a flow of practical policies and advisories for willing candidates. A second lane was to have a prominent cluster of endorsers motivating the participants further into seeing the project as possessing visibility and recognition inside the political arena. A third lane would be to convince the media that what we were unfolding deserved to become part of the regular reporters' beat covering the 2022 election campaign, not just a one-time feature or column.

In the 1960s and 1970s, such a tripartite mission would not have been considered a difficult mountain climb. In 2022 with most everyone transfixed by screen time and inundated with messages, blather, and nastiness, getting people's attention to call back was like climbing a sheer cliff with a slippery rope.

Writing this disorderly narrative of what Mark and I, without any staff, had to do every day to move these lanes forward was not easy. Every day came with a flurry of Hail Marys. We were like salespeople making cold calls and knowing that a 5 percent response rate would be considered a great success. To make clearer a sense of urgency, we would write articles, send tweets, and speak to anyone willing to listen to us outline why a disaster in November was not an unlikely event. Mark wrote letters to E. J. Dionne, columnist for the *Washington Post*, to David Remnick, editor of the *New Yorker*, to Jaime Harrison, head of the DNC. My similar entreaties to David Marchese, the skilled interviewer for the *New York Times Magazine*, to Amy Goodman of *Democracy Now!*, to John Nichols, the political reporter for *The Nation* and the Madison, Wisconsin, newspaper, to columnists Eugene Robinson (*Washington Post*) and Charles Blow (*New York Times*) came up empty.

We would be careful to send out to all these reporters and editors the program for the July 23, 2022, Zoom event. As I shall point out, the presenters and the subjects they held forth on were not dull clichés. This was not an exercise in civicism. These participants were used to rough-and-tumble controversies, seeing close up the ugly underbelly of their avaricious, callous, or power-hungry antagonists. It didn't matter. Curiosity was not the media's strong suit. Even more remarkable was that neither National Public Radio (NPR), nor the Public Broadcasting Service (PBS), nor the progressive independent media showed any interest. None of them could frame what we were doing as to whether their readers or audiences would be interested in bringing their necessities and aspirations into the public debate of electoral campaigns. For years, the smaller progressive magazines have been trapped in their own silos and scarcely have covered their counterparts on the ramparts, save for civil rights street actions.

One of our star presenters was to be Hazel Henderson, the self-taught political economist born in the UK and lived in Florida. Hazel was a one-person truth and media machine, deconstructing conventional economists for being too abstract, empirically starved, and too tied to corporations. She did this with clarity of language and dry humor. I interviewed her for almost an hour on my radio show and podcast on May 7, 2022. She had told me she had stage four pancreatic cancer at age eighty-nine and didn't have long to live. If able, she agreed to be on the July 23rd tutorial. Unfortunately, she passed away on May 22, 2022. Earlier, I tried to have her interviewed by Amy Goodman and the *New York Times Magazine* interviewer David Marchese. I couldn't get through to make the case personally, though I left detailed messages. Hazel was a prolific writer, documentarian, speaker, convener, recruiter, and overall "futurist" (her self-description) with her own worldwide media network of activists. Single-handedly she could have shown the Democrats how to prevail, had they chosen to listen.

Over the course of the several months leading up to the 2022 elections, we spoke to a variety of activists, scholars, elected officials, candidates for office, reporters, and potential funders. It would be tedious, as it was to us most emphatically, to take the reader through all the day-by-day calls, emails, and letters to those who populated the three lanes we were developing. A scatter of examples might be enough, however, to provide the flavor of our listings.

I spoke to former California governor Jerry Brown about making opening remarks on July 23rd. Having known him for years, I can say that Jerry remains youthful in his discussions. His civic preoccupation was nuclear arms control and climate catastrophes. I went through our program. He was receptive, and after receiving our standard explanatory memo, he accepted our invitation.

I called Joan Claybrook, former auto safety regulator for Jimmy Carter and perennial lobbyist for auto safety, to reach speaker Nancy Pelosi for her endorsement—the most important endorsement to start momentum for turnout success and possibly media attention. Pelosi was the biggest fundraiser for the Democrats, and many of the Democrats in the House were dependent on her in many ways—a reliance she assiduously cultivated to deepen her own grip on the party.

I reached out to Annie Leonard, head of Greenpeace, to be on the panel, and she immediately accepted.

Mark received an endorsement blurb from Representative Carolyn Maloney (D-NY). At the same time, he told me that Representative Katie Porter (D-CA), for whom Mark has held fundraisers, turned down his request to endorse. She simply said she did not do such things.

I telephoned Representative Tim Ryan (D-OH), who was running for the US Senate against J. D. Vance, a favorite of *New York Times* coverage. I was referred to David Chase, his campaign manager, who called me back and heard my reasons for saying that Congressman Ryan would benefit greatly from listening to the civic leaders on July 23rd with staff and be free to request more details about the strategies, tactics, messaging, rebuttals, slogans, and ways to get out more votes. I also offered the slogan against his opponent "Why Take a Chance with Vance?" He thanked me and I never heard from him again, despite several calls including ones by helpful, politically active Ohioans.

Representative Jamie Raskin finally called back from Amherst, Massachusetts. He said he would happily endorse the July 23rd event and help urge members of the Progressive Caucus to attend. I called the next day to elaborate on the details and he welcomed being part of the program. His participation gave us a big lift since he had become a political celebrity for his work on the January 6th House Investigating Committee. Jamie is a lifelong learner and communicator. He liked Mark's suggestion to describe the Trumpsters as "dangerous extremists."

The brilliant social artist Mr. Fish agreed to do posters for our initiative. William Hartung agreed to go on the panel to speak about the military budget—his longtime expertise.

Mark spoke to pollster Celinda Lake, which resulted in her recommendation to highlight the "Freedom for Women" theme so often violated by Trumpian policies.

I called Representative Dwight Evans (D-PA), a former community organizer, who, during an earlier pre-pandemic meeting with half a dozen legislators, declared the big problem with the party was the messaging challenge. I was referred to Jason Green who heard me out and was promptly sent the memo. Our hope was that Congressman Evans would open doors to the Congressional Black Caucus. It didn't happen.

I reached Tom O'Brien, a former colleague, who was about to retire from the United Steelworkers Union in Pittsburgh. I asked for his help in urging labor leaders to call for repeal of the notorious anti-union law enacted back in 1947 known as the Taft-Hartley Act. The Democratic Party had never made this handcuff on union organizing and action a priority issue for repeal since the Republicans in Congress passed it over President Harry Truman's veto in 1947. He also liked the idea of the midnight campaign to reach the millions of workers who keep our society going during the midnight shift, but almost never are greeted by candidates for office.

Around this time, Bert Foer, an old friend and antitrust specialist, told about the six-and-a-half-hour time frame, replied that politicians wouldn't sit still for that long. Well, I replied, they sit long hours with consultants and during preparation for their ads. I added this is only a one-time display of patience on their raison d'être for wanting to be elected—presumably.

I spoke to Maureen Moriarty in my Congressman John Larson's (D-CT) office about him signing on as an endorser. I told her Mark would send her materials forthwith. On June 13, 2022, Representative Larson called me to say he was on board as an endorser and more. He agreed to send a letter to his colleagues to cosign and urge the progressive caucus to attend. He promised to urge Tim Ryan to get back to us and stressed that campaigning to increase Social Security benefits, after a freeze for forty years, would get more votes out.

Then totally unprovoked, he went after the Senate Democrats who allowed the threat of a GOP filibuster to stymie their action on over four hundred bills passed by the House and sent to die in the Senate. "Make them filibuster before the TV cameras against minimum wage increase and Social Security benefits—so long overdue for tens of millions of Americans," he declared. He excoriated the Senate Democrats for not holding enough hearings and not putting out conference reports. Pleasantly taken aback, I suggested he put this in an open letter and guaranteed that he would get mass-media coverage. Later I learned that House Speaker Pelosi frowned on such candor being made public. Obviously, she was okay with letting the Senate be a burial ground for House legislation. Anticipating this, she did not allow a vote in the House on the Social Security bill. Larson added the consultants and pollsters "minimize the ground game."

In the meantime, the media continued to report the gloom and doom, and anonymous predictions for November by Democratic politicians. One report recounted Biden hiring lawyers to fend off the coming GOP attacks and impeachment moves "when" they took control of Congress. This defeatism continued. Senator Rick Scott, (R-FL)who headed the National Republican Senatorial Committee, released his report *A 12 Point Plan To Rescue America: What Americans Must Do To*

Save This Country[2] which provided sweet fodder for use by the Democrats. Among other extremes—coming from the Senator from Florida, a state with millions of elderly voters—he declared that Social Security and Medicare should be sunsetted every five years, among other health, safety, and economic protections for the people. Majority leader Chuck Schumer picked up on this for a while and Senator Mitch McConnell, leader of the Senate GOP, immediately disowned it. By the fall typically few candidates were making this a poster child for the GOP's hidden agendas. I would have reprinted it as a cheap paperback to hand out with a graphic cover.

One suggestion we made to members and staff, coming after the July 23rd extravaganza, was to hold congressional hearings on major abuses of the people, starting with children, women, and workers ignored or harmed by the utterly monetized GOP ideologies. Paralleling campaigning back in the districts with ongoing congressional hearings in the fall was inconvenient, not something that was done. Consequently, it was never considered.

Following up on Congressman Larson's calls and promises, I contacted his chief of staff, Scott Stephanou. He said that seeing the Democrats as retaining the Senate in November was "seen as naive up here," adding that the defeatist attitude was widespread. A sure way to defeat themselves and not go for a broad reset of why the people should pull the Democratic lever, I added. Then I ran by him the whole "To Do" list from Representative Larson's call. It included contacting the DNC to be responsive to our calls and sending encouragement to attend on July 23rd to House members and to Hakeem Jeffries, Chair of the House Democratic Caucus, and so forth.

June 25, 2023, Mark got a high-level assistant to Hakeem Jeffries to call the DNC for the email addresses of all Democratic candidates running in the House and Senate. Mark is nothing but low-key persistent. Alarmingly, the DNC said no. Well, how about eighty names? Go ask the members' chiefs of staff one by one, was their retort. Sure. Try and get them on the phone and listen to their referring us to the campaign office without adding contact numbers and emails.

I had a conversation with Rob Weissman, head of Public Citizen, a large citizen group (citizen.org) that I founded in 1971. He thought because it proposed to take away what people already have, that the Scott report was especially damaging to the Republicans and should be a big issue repeated again and again by the Dems. This was about the time Biden attacked the "ultra-MAGAs," a moniker that delighted the Trumpsters who started selling T-shirts and caps with "Ultra-MAGA" as the latest moniker. Boomeranged!

A colleague suggested that Pelosi's close friend Representative Jackie Speier (D-CA) might be able to get us the MC's emails. A prominent lawyer friend promised to get the request to her. We never heard anything.

Mark was ready to "blast out" the invitation to members and their staffs to attend the proceedings on July 23rd, but was holding off on the hope that Pelosi would endorse our effort and shake loose the Democratic campaign email addresses. On June 25th, I spoke with Pelosi's campaign director Sydney Vermilyea, who took our request for her endorsement, noting our release was about to go out.

June 29, 2022—Mark spoke with Mary Plasencia, Pelosi's political aide, for some twenty minutes. She was pleasant but non-committal. Confirmations were sent to the speakers and two other key people at the DNC and the House campaign chair, Representative Sean Patrick Maloney (D-NY), who didn't return any of my or Mark's calls. Mark could have helped him in his own campaign, which he lost.

Week after week, more people were making calls on our behalf. They were elected officials, retired ones, civic advocates, and some retired journalists with their own circles and constituents. That they mostly came up empty was further evidence that the commercializing of elections in our country was increasingly distancing them from democracy, which doesn't pay to play. That is the Democracy of citizens and civic organizations that have access and policies recognized by a supposedly democratic media.

Jerry Brown, when I asked whether he would call his fellow Californian, Speaker Nancy Pelosi, to endorse and otherwise help the July 23rd launch, told me, "She doesn't return my calls anymore." Of course she doesn't. Jerry Brown is retired and doesn't count politically in her money-raising calculations. My stupid question.

In June I started to call a long list of members more likely to be receptive to attending and spreading the word to their colleagues. I reached Representative Diana DeGette, a thirteenth-termer from Colorado, and she got the point immediately—"I'm all in with you," she said, and promised she'd talk it up among her colleagues. She was deep into the pro-choice referendum in Kansas that was drawing national attention. (It won.) I liked this enthusiasm of the former state public defender.

It took a little longer to get to Representative Marcy Kaptur, a twentieth-termer and former White House aide from Toledo. She is free with her opinions, describing Ohio under the GOP as "a criminal state," wishing to get big special interest campaign money out of politics, telling me that her campaign manager just told her she had to raise $3 million for her safe seat against an opponent who had been present at the January 6th activities. I wanted her to get us to Tim Ryan, which she agreed to try to do. She mentioned his opposition to NAFTA and the extortionate price of insulin. I told her I would send a copy of the Kentucky Values that could be adapted quickly to Ohio values. She bewailed the Democratic leadership in Congress not talking about Social Security benefits.

Next to connect with was Representative Suzanne Bonamici, a sixth-termer from Oregon who was very gracious about the work we've done. As a college student, she was on the board of the student-run Oregon Student Public Research Group (OSPIRG), one of the first of nearly two dozen state PIRGs we helped launch in the 1970s. These groups filled the vacuum in university curricula for training in civic knowledge and skills. Their full-time staff focused on consumer, environmental, and other issues, with some PIRGs getting colleges to give course credit for some PIRG projects. She shared my urgency in getting out the vote better and offered to talk up the July 23rd event with her staff and her political circle.

I couldn't get through to Representative Andy Levin, a super-progressive who lost his primary after heavy opposition from AIPAC. Instead, I was referred to his campaign person, Megan Borowski, who liked the slogan "Freedom to Vote."

I spoke to Raja Krishnamoorthi, a third termer from Illinois and Harvard Law graduate, who knew our record of championing just causes. He confirmed his attendance and said he would get others to do so as well. We spoke about the collective thousand years of experiences by the presenters.

There were other members of Congress, such as Representative John Garamendi (D-CA), who had worked with us when he was the consumer-oriented California Insurance Commissioner. Sometimes the staff is unaware of these shared experiences and, seeing that we were not donors or from his district, just wouldn't place the telephone messages on his desk. I made several calls but never got through to him. We often tried calling the district offices, to no effect.

I did get through to a neighbor in Connecticut, Representative Jahana Hayes, deep into a very close race, yet she planned to attend, saying, "It works for me. . . . I'll plan to be on." After running through the various common themes of that day, she said she would have her staff connect with us for the link to the July 3rd event.

From Madison, Wisconsin, we spoke to Mark Pocan, considered the most progressive of all members by some observers. So, I upped my request for him to assume a big effort to attract members to the WinningAmerica.net event on July 23rd. He related that he too criticized the political consultants, promised to help with the progressive caucus and even go to the state electoral level. He allowed that Sean Maloney of the DCCC was "not the best," and lauded John Larson striving to get more sponsors for his Social Security bill that he thought would help the candidates in Iowa, Michigan, and Nebraska. During our short conversation, I sensed Representative Pocan's "minders" or staff tugging at him to get off the phone. Later when I tried to reach him in the fall, his staff briskly said that he was too busy to speak with us at any time. I told them that we had information to help Mandela Barnes against Senator Ron Johnson (R-WI), who won with just a 1 percent margin. Earlier, we couldn't get through to the Barnes campaign or any recommended major adviser. So Senator Johnson, probably the most loathed Republican in the Senate by his peers, got another six years of obstructive zaniness.

As a citizen organizer of stature in Chicago, Representative Jan Schakowsky (D-IL), actually wanted to return our call and discuss strategy. She agreed it was the Democrats' election to lose. I went through some of our conversations with other Democrats we called. With gasoline prices soaring, she stressed that the Democratic Party should jump on the legislation she cosponsored to impose an excess-profits tax on the oil companies, as the UK had enacted earlier.

There was one nonvoting member of Congress, representing what statehood backers call the colony of the District of Columbia. It's the only capital of any country in the world that doesn't give its people equal voting rights with the rest of their nation. Eleanor Holmes Norton, technically called a delegate, was a sixteen-term veteran advocate for statehood and other aspirations for D.C. equality. She said that none of the material about the Winning America project ever reached her. No matter, she said, that with her chief of staff Raven Reeder, she would "let everybody know about it."

On July 15th I spoke to Adam Smith, a thirteen-termer and chair of the House Armed Services Committee, a large committee well-armed by the Pentagon to do its bidding. He was very cordial, lauded our work, and agreed to spread the word to "our colleagues." While he didn't have time for a full six hours, he said he would attend part of the July 23rd event and have the staff cover the rest. I took this rare occasion to raise the issue of the unauditable Pentagon budget. All Secretaries of Defense have admitted the Pentagon was in violation of a statute, effective 1992, requiring all federal agencies and departments to supply Congress annually with an audited budget. Smith spoke of how old the DOD computers were and that "nobody in the Army knew who was working where" but he noted that some progress is being made toward an audit. Which, by the way, will cost taxpayers hundreds of millions of dollars a year.[3]

On July 15th I called Representative Peter Welch's (D-VT) chief of staff, who said he would tell Welch about my call. I once again left a message with Senator Gary Peters's office. I again called Senator Ron Wyden, who I knew way back when he was a young attorney representing poor elderly people in Portland, Oregon. There was no response.

I spoke to Representative Earl Blumenauer, a four-teenth-termer from Oregon who liked the "idea and the list of endorsers," but avowed how incredibly busy he was, working all weekends, but said we would spread the word to those members "in tight races," and would try to have a staffer attend.

Getting closer to the big day, Mark and I divided up the twenty-four panelists to speak with them about their presentation and the overall fit with the others on the Zoom call, plus our plans after July 23rd to get the Democratic Party even more receptive to our advice. One of the people on my list was Bill Hillsman, the political advertising specialist concentrating on radio ads as a major medium too often minimized, in his judgment. We talked strategy about GOTV. It was on this call that I realized for the first time the emergence of Hispanic right-wing talk radio that was having a Rush Limbaugh effect on Hispanic workers day after day. Bill related that the Democrats weren't paying much attention to this medium, which was succeeding in slicing off percentages of the Hispanic vote from Democrats to the GOP.

We both had calls into people who might add to our meager budget. David Kelley from Ohio, who reads my columns and listens to my radio/podcast, in between being a voracious reader and successful businessman, found the July 23rd materials "fascinating" and, as mentioned earlier, contributed to our endeavor. He averred he always wanted to be a wordsmith for the Democrats with emphasis on the corporate outlaws running this country into the ground. He volunteered to try to reach anyone we needed, including Tim Ryan and local Democratic

Committee chairs with the help of his daughter, a rising politico in Cleveland. He then proceeded to elaborate on what we
wanted to get done with fervent eloquence and very quotable
phrases.

If all this calling and trying to call sounds tedious, it is
because it was very tedious to me and Mark, hour after hour.
Tedium is part of what we signed up for, with plenty of aware-
ness beforehand. Mark also spent many a day at his computer
refining memos, sending out letters and messages. I made well
over one thousand calls in three months, often accompanied by
emails, most of them either not receiving replies or being han-
dled by subordinates who added our request to the daily pile.
What lessened the daily grind was what we occasionally found
out about people. Two of the most prominent, until recently,
Democratic spokespersons James Carville and Paul Begala, who
used to urge me to support the Democrats and not go off on the
Green Party or any Independent run, were totally incommunicado. They never returned calls or indicated they knew anything
about our broad-gauged effort to snap the Dems out of their
self-inflicted recipes of defeat. We stopped thinking they might
open doors or make public comments attracting some political
reporters they knew well. Why should they? They seemed to
know it all, like so many of the "professional"' Democrats who
observed the lethargy of party leaders as well as anyone.

Well, July 23rd was fast upon us. We had received no media
so far. Our endorsers were House members Jamie Raskin,
Hakeem Jeffries, John Larson, Jim McGovern, Peter DeFazio,
and Carolyn Maloney. The lone senator was Edward Markey.

We were grateful for their signing on to letters, but, except for Jamie Raskin, they left it with their one-time John Hancock. They offered no interviews with the press, nor did they put out any press releases. I think their support was a routine peer-group thing, with John Larson and Jamie Raskin being initiating peers. To be fair, we urged specific political reporters to call them for interviews. To our knowledge, no reporters ever did.

CHAPTER 7

Lights, Camera, Action— or Inaction

July 23rd was anything but tedium. Although it was a Zoom affair, the atmosphere tingled with vitality. Our only regret was that we could not all be together in person. The following summaries of the presentations raise issues of opportunity, some of which are well covered in liberal and progressive political literature. Others are novel either in content or in the way they are expressed—that is, unused, refreshing political oratory. Others are just so close to the nerve of the established power as never to be mentioned either in the Democratic Party's platform or in the deliberations over proceedings for the platform. Unlike the great 1892 People's Party platform—a historic manifesto relevant today—major party platforms are known for their amnesiac effect—the bland sequencing to the bland so as not to upset the party's main mission, which is to raise massive amounts of money for candidates who do not upset the donors of those dollars.

I like to divide agendas for elections as either being *on the table* or *off the table* by the two major parties. In my 2008 Independent presidential campaign, I assembled nearly twenty reforms and redirections that were *off the table* by both major parties but, obviously, on my very modest table. I have kept my campaign website, votenader.org, intact as a reminder of how important issues can be used in a campaign.[1] Some were topics that were taboo. Democratic and Republican Party discipline is impressive when enforcing taboos. These include the military budget, stronger corporate crime laws and enforcement, challenging corporate welfare giveaways, campaign finance reform, or unconditional support for whomever is in charge of the Israeli government. Because the foreign and military policy is mostly composed of bipartisan taboos, and because very little competitive space exists between their policies, we devoted limited but still some declarative time for those subjects by our speakers. The neglectful similarity by the GOP and Democratic Party on such portentous global issues, including upgrading and strengthening nuclear arms control treaties, is one of the most tragic paralyses emanating from the two-party duopoly.

On the morning of July 23rd, 2022, Mark and I were being positioned and technically checked for our Zoom event and Winning America remarks. Seated in my chair, waiting for the opening bell, I looked over the six-and-a-half-hour program once more. It included a pretty impressive range of thinkers and doers, a vision of what our country could become, and proposals for long overdue advances long earned by the American people. I recalled a pithy ancient epigram by Imam Abu Hamid Al Ghazali, an Arab philosopher in the eleventh century: "Knowledge without action is a means without an end and action without knowledge is a crime." (That certainly, as one example, applies to the Bush/Cheney criminal invasion of Iraq in 2003.)

Mark wanted to convey the bigger picture about Trump, Trumpism, and the onrush of autocracy over democracy. In our book, *Wrecking America*, we wrote that Trump would likely "use the 11 weeks from the Election Day to the Inauguration either trying to undo the results if close using some chaotic maneuver . . ."[2] or unprecedented misconduct and, along with Senator McConnell, "hurriedly nominate and confirm a new Supreme Court Justice within weeks or days were there an opening."[3]

Of course, both happened—the violent insurrection of January 6th and the rushed appointment of Amy Coney Barrett, followed by his in-plain-sight disruptive plans for 2024.

WinningAmerica.net was formed in March 2022 to counter the early conventional wisdom that there was no way to stop a red wave in November 2022 due to rampant inflation and the midterm jinx for the presidential party. As if there were no ways to connect the inflation spiral to corporate pricing power, their broken overstretched supply chain from distant nations, and Russia's war on Ukraine. As for the jinx, strong plain language, a public agenda, and an energetic get-out-the-vote movement could supersede the superstition. After all, their opponent was the worst GOP in its history—wearing on its slimy sleeves serially corrupt, violence-prone, anti-labor, anti-women, anti-children policies, as well as being chronically dishonest and authoritarian. Mark asked, "How can a party that would have disgusted Ike, Taft, and Reagan still even be in the running?"

His efforts to lift his morale and overcome defeatism led Mark to something Norman Cousins once wrote: "No one is smart enough to be a pessimist."

He championed an approach of framing the election as being about a party of "dangerous extremists" stealing our freedoms and livelihoods. Then, we would spell out these general charges with down-home specifics. Democrats need to hear from public advocates and civil leaders who are at the intersection of policy and politics ignored by busied candidates foraging for funds. Now they can plug these best suggestions for practical political advantages into the sockets of their campaigns. From Joe McCarthy to Newt Gingrich to Donald Trump—Democrats have failed to adequately punch back, allowing unrebutted conspiracy theories and slanderous slogans to frame campaigns.

What follows are summaries that can be considered "teasers," with more available for the asking at the WinningAmerica .net website.

Our first speaker was Robert Kuttner speaking on "The Economy: For the Many, Not the Few." Kuttner is a prolific author on economic subjects and cofounder of the Economic Policy Institute and *American Prospect* magazine. In 2022, he published *Going Big: FDR's Legacy, Biden's New Deal, and the Struggle to Save Democracy*. He starts with a hypothetical campaign speech to remind people how far today's America has slipped behind in maintaining, never mind increasing, the size of the middle class compared with the middle of the twentieth century up to the early 1970s. He deflates the corporate propaganda of "progress" with the stagnation of "regress" of the past fifty years for the average worker. He made FDR's case: "We can win back America on pocketbook issues." Obvious, you say.

But they've been largely oblivious to the Dems' messaging and actions in Congress.

"I am running for Congress here in Middletown [yes, this is hypothetical] because our government needs to serve working families as it has in the past. Donald Trump got one thing right when he said, 'We need to make America great again.' But my Republican opponent has voted against every measure that might actually make America great again for regular people, or help you and your kids thrive economically. He has voted for every measure that enriches billionaires who ship jobs overseas and treats their employees like so many expendable machine parts.

"When I was growing up, you could buy a house on one income. People had decent pensions. You could go to college without being burdened by debt before your economic life even began. Imagine if some politician forty years ago had said, 'I have a plan on how to pay for college. We will end free tuition at public universities and stick kids from working families with decades of debt.' That politician would have been laughed off stage. But that's just what both parties did.

"When I was growing up, big corporations had unions and a sense of reciprocal duty to repay the loyalty of their workers. Banks and airlines and power companies were regulated in the public interest. Small business was not being gobbled up by big business. You could get medical care without paying a fortune out of pocket or being told, 'You can't see this doctor or go to that hospital or have this procedure.' That's not intrusive government. What's intrusive is today's unaccountable private 'regulation.'

"We once had a kind of compact in this country between the people and their government and between corporations and workers. That's not nostalgia. It's the way things were and could be again. Now, they weren't that way for everybody. There was a great deal of racial discrimination. Women were denied the opportunities available to men. But we were making progress. Today's economy is so productive that there's plenty to go around—if the top doesn't take it all. If working families got the same share of the economy's productivity that they did half a century ago, if wages had risen with productivity, the typical family would be earning around $100,000 a year.

"What went wrong? I'm sorry to say both parties (for the most part) got into bed with giant corporations and with Wall Street. They helped corporations and bankers move jobs overseas where labor was cheap. They cut regulations and taxes on the very rich, while working people were hit with higher payroll taxes, while private regulation by employers and insurance companies invaded our lives. Things don't have to be like this. We have a climate crisis and a crisis of collapsing roads and bridges and electricity grids that need investments that could create jobs right here in Middletown. We could end the kind of globalization that serves billionaires and instead bring jobs and economic development home.

"So I hope you will give me your vote. Thank you."

Progressives like Sherrod Brown have shown that you can get elected in unlikely places with this kind of appeal. Progressives today complain about the original gerrymander—the US Senate—as if rural people were hopelessly and irrevocably conservative. When I was working for Senator Proxmire in the 1970s and the Senate was very solidly Democratic, you could literally drive from Washington State to Pennsylvania without passing through a single state that had a Republican senator. Why? Because the Democratic senators of that era in rural states, as well as urban states, delivered for working people. It can be that way again.

The long-term problem is the capture of economic policy by neoliberalism, deregulation, privatization, globalization, the shift in who pays taxes with catastrophic results for the distribution of income and wealth and for the weakening of unions. I have a piece in the current *New York Review of Books* going into the details—and there are more in my own book *Going Big: FDR's Legacy, Biden's New Deal, and the Struggle to Save Democracy*—but here's the basic story. There was a long shift away from the legacy of Roosevelt and the New Deal model, and three successive Democratic presidents who were by no means progressive: Carter, then Clinton, and then, I'm sorry to say, Obama.

Thanks to the long legacy of Roosevelt's tangible help to working people as late as the 1996 presidential election, counties that were below the national median income and at least 85 percent white split evenly between Bill Clinton and Bob Dole. In the 2016 election, however, the same counties went 658 for Donald Trump and 2 for Hillary Clinton. That's the legacy of going Right on economics and thinking that you can come compensate by going Left on cultural issues. On the contrary, you buy the running room to make progress on divisive social issues by being the champion of all working class people.

We need to be persuasive on a long-term progressive economic vision, while having a strategy for surviving short-term. The long term requires a lot of public investment with jobs—especially production jobs—front and center. We need to use the climate crisis as an opportunity to shift to a productive, equitable green economy rather than a command that working people tighten their belts. And we need a kind of New Deal for the young. They're in an economy where you are more likely to have gigs than payroll jobs. And Democrats need the young to turn out, because when the young turn out, they vote for Democrats.

If this election is about people's frustration with the price of gas, we lose. But Biden is not on the ballot, and a lot of good people are on the ballot down-ticket. Trump and the Supreme Court have given the Democrats a kind of gift—Trump inserted himself in the process to get all kinds of unelectable Republicans nominated; he reliably keeps reminding voters how crazy he is; and of course the January Sixth Committee has done a superb job of filling in the details. The Supreme Court has given Democrats a gift by showing how at odds it is with public opinion on everything from kids being massacred in classrooms to women being criminalized for trying to pursue their reproductive rights.

Justice Thomas also handed the Democrats a political grenade to use against Republicans when he wrote in his concurring decision in the *Dobbs* abortion case that the Supreme Court could also reverse three earlier decisions: overturning criminalization of sodomy, allowing same-sex marriage, and even permitting contraception. So the House took the first step by passing the Respect for Marriage Act—which codifies the court's 2015

Obergefell decision protecting same-sex marriage—and forty-seven Republicans voted for it. It split the GOP beautifully.

Bottom line, we can win back America based on pocketbook issues. The best analogy is to the 2018 election when, because Democrats and moderates got organized (they were all appalled by Trump), Democrats were able to pick up forty-one House seats.

There is a decent chance if Democrats play this right—use wedge issues against Republicans and then bring it back to the pocketbook issues where there's a forty-year frustration that we can tap into, this will not be the typical first midterm election of a new president. We have a very good chance of holding the Senate, even picking up a couple of seats, and we might even hold the House. So don't mourn. Organize.[4]

Next up is the self-taught, leading investigative tax reporter in the country, Pulitzer Prize winner at the *New York Times*, David Cay Johnston—a whirling, nonstop force of nature. Johnston was early on reporting the corporate crimes committed by businessman Donald J. Trump and is the author of *The Making of Donald Trump* (2016).

It's absolutely critical in an election that you talk to people on a level that they understand and that's not the policy wonk talk that probably all of us are deeply invested in. You need to talk to people where they live. Keep in mind Upton Sinclair, when he wrote *The Jungle*, expected that it would lead to revulsion by people over the treatment of meatpacking workers. Instead, as he put it, "I shot an arrow at America's heart, and hit its stomach."

Let me bring up a word that you should never, ever, ever, under any circumstances, unless you absolutely must, say again: that word is "spend." It scares people. When Joe Biden said he wanted three and a half trillion dollars for his so-called Build Back Better bill, that's all you heard on Fox, *"Three and a half trillion dollars!"* As if it would all be spent in one year. Instead, here's the best way to make the point: "We want to invest in a wealthier future for everyone."

And, by the way, the three and a half trillion dollars is over ten years. That's less than three dollars a day per American. "Would you be willing to invest three dollars a day so that you and your children and your grandchildren will be prosperous? Well, that's what was proposed." By the way, after I wrote a column about this, Biden used my language for *one day*, and then he went back to talking about spending with no context.

I'll tell you another thing I know from talk radio: no one believed or had heard that the Biden plans included tax cuts for everybody who made under $400,000 a year. Nobody. They thought, "Oh, my goodness, the Democrats are gonna raise our taxes. We're going to have to spend three and a half trillion dollars in one year, whatever that number means." Million? Billion? Trillion? Meaningless numbers. Scary numbers. But you can reduce things down. People get "three dollars a day." Biden's American Families Plan: at least four years of college education at no cost, childcare, family leave, sick leave. The cost of that plan was less than a dollar and a half a day per American. That is, Biden wanted to invest less than a dollar and a half to make all of us better off. "$1.50 a day."

Here's another thing to think about: What's happened to wages? I can give you numbers off the top of my head all day, none of which you'll retain, but perhaps this will be effective. In 2020, the median wage in this country went up by twenty-six dollars. That's fifty cents a week. Would you notice if your income went up by fifty cents a week? Would it make any difference in your life compared to the year before? So imagine twenty-six dollars is one inch, or the height of the heel of a man standing outside of Trump Tower. Now look at people who make over $1 million a year, how did their wages do? If that typical increase of twenty-six dollars was one inch, the increase for the one in nine hundred workers who make over $1 million a year would go all the way to the top of Trump Tower, plus another 315 feet. It would be more than nine hundred feet high. A skyscraper of money.

The average increase in pay for people who make over a million dollars a year from their job—only including salary and bonus—was $330,000 in 2020. Under the radical Republican Trump plans, we were accelerating the conversion of our country from one where we reward people for their work into a system to transfer that money to the richest people in this country. That's why we don't have the revenue to invest.

Also: right now the bottom 99.9 percent of Americans are being burdened with hidden tax increases to support the super wealthy—the richest 1/1,000 families. How? The Trump tax cuts were financed with borrowed money. That is, the government is borrowing money so that the wealthiest people in this country don't have to pay as much in income taxes. And at the very same time, Republicans want to cut the programs that benefit the vast majority of us—like ending Social Security and abolishing the Affordable Care Act (or "Obamacare").

So number one, most important: Don't talk "spend." Talk "invest." We want to invest in a wealthier future for all Americans. If we don't have a better educated workforce, we will get left behind by the rest of the world. We need to invest in our workforce, not in super rich people. There are people in the United States with daily incomes of over $5 million a day, and some of them pay zero income tax; all of them pay a lower income tax than someone making $100,000 a year. Why? Because they got Congress to put in provisions to benefit them.

We also need to recognize that this system is getting worse. In 2020, the average person saw their income go up by nearly nothing. But of all the pay raises handed out in America that year, 82 percent went to people who make over $1 million a year—one of nine hundred workers. You could point to a crowd that's gathered and say that's just the leg of one man sitting in the front row—that man's leg got 82 percent of all the pay increases. That's what we're doing in this country. We are creating a system in which the people at the top are taking more and more and more of the income and the productive capacity of this country for themselves, and they are holding back other people.

You will hear about the price of gasoline. There's something called the Baker-Hughes rig count. With oil prices going up to over one hundred dollars a barrel, you might think that the oil drillers would be out there [drilling] for more oil. Nope. The drill count's hardly gone up at all, and I look at it every week. Why would you go invest and spend money to drill for more oil—which will lower the price of oil—when you can simply sit around your living room drinking your seventy-five-year-old Scotch and collecting superpremium prices for the oil you're already producing?

You're better off *not* producing, and that's something to hit the Republicans with. Republicans have created an economy and want to have more of this strategy of mining the interests of ordinary people, so they can move money into the pockets of people who are already so rich that they can't spend [most of] the money that they have.[5]

The third speaker in the section "The Economy: For the Many, Not the Few" was Thom Hartmann, the most erudite nationally syndicated talk show host in the country. Hartmann's books[6] on corporate history and corporate power abuses are unique and educationally eye-opening. His focus here is on *Unions and Energy*:

I strongly argue that we need to be promoting unions as democracy in the workplace, and both the key to reaching the middle class and the tool that *built* the American middle class. All but probably the youngest people are able to remember a time—or at least know of a time—in America where dad or grandpa was able to get a good union job with a high school diploma and lift himself and his family into the middle class. But somewhere along the line, in the 1980s, when Reagan declared war on the unions and on the American working people, the focus of the GOP became the "Corrupt Union Bosses." And, of course, Jimmy Hoffa didn't help that—we actually had some corrupt union bosses, but they're long gone. Nor did they ever dominate the union movement the way that the Republicans tried to spin it.

It's time to renew the union movement in the United States.

If you believe in democracy, you should believe in democracy in the workplace. In 1947, the Republicans rolled out this phrase: the so-called "right to work" with the Taft-Hartley Act, which was passed over the veto of Harry Truman. For years now, I've referred to it as the "right to work for less." And now, after a couple of radio panels with a bunch of union leaders in Chicago over the years, I've got many of them now saying "right to work for less." That's the winning phrase.

A lot of anti-union sentiment has to do with what lives on the internet. If you Google "unions," there is just a massive amount of anti-union information about "forced unionization" and "forced dues paying," including corruption around these issues on Wikipedia. Here's the right approach: "No, unions are a democracy within the workplace that represents you. And you have a *right* to work for a reasonable wage. And what the Republicans are promoting has led to wages stagnating. We've seen good jobs vanish. We need to bring strong unions back."

So number one, there is a strong case for unions and unionization.

You can also tie these issues into energy—since we want *American* energy manufactured in *America*. Now, that is another catch phrase that the Republicans and the fossil fuel industry have been using: "All-American energy. Oil and gas." Well, aside from volcanic activity and the heat and energy from the core of the earth, literally all energy on this planet came from the sun. Plants captured that energy. Those plants died and rotted and over millions of years became peat and then got crushed under the earth and became oil and natural gas—but that was *all* sun-light that was captured by plants.

I realize that's not a bumper sticker that's going to win any elections. But I think it's an important point: Why are we going through this inefficient process of trying to dig two-hundred-million-year-old sunlight out of the ground and burn it and poison our atmosphere, when we can simply catch the sunlight that's falling on the earth *right now*? There's a massive amount of sunlight falling on this planet. And the Chinese are way ahead of us on this, as are most other highly developed countries.

Let's go to the source and start getting our energy from sun-light. This then disconnects us from the control of people like "Mohammed bin Bonesaw" and Vladimir Putin. Fossil fuels are the essential infrastructure that are supporting these autocrats. America has absolutely no energy shortage because such a mas-sive amount of sunlight falls on the United States, as well as in most of the country there's fairly reliable wind. Hence, we are see-ing shifts to renewables now: Utah's over 20 percent renewable-source energy, and it's nearly that in Texas. This is energy that we can collect without having to beg Saudi Arabia for anything, without having to be afraid of Putin or other despots.

I would portray the fossil fuel industry as a threat to our future and our economy. They have been lying to us since the 1970s about how they know that these fossil fuels are going to destroy our environment and in the process also destroy our economy, our country, and the future of our children. I think that that is a very powerful selling point. You've got Republicans all across the United States who are going into school boards and going on the media talking about "the Children"—"We've got to protect the Children against feeling uncomfortable that we're going to talk about race, or having to wear a mask" for God's sake. Yet *this* is real and the future of our children and our grandchildren.

When you do opinion polling, you find that among people under thirty in the United States, which includes children, the number one political issue in America today is climate. Because it's *their* future that's being disrupted. They're very cognizant of what's going on, and how terribly it is going to hit them. So if we combine this message of "we need to protect our vulnerable young people and provide them with the kind of future that we old farts had: a stable climate," that's a minimal obligation of citizenship, of parenthood, of being a human being.

So number one: talking about young people and their future is gonna get you a lot of attention from young people and it's gonna get you concurrence from older people. I think that there's also a message that "this will save money for the average American." Republicans are constantly BS-ing us, telling us that gasoline is the most efficient form of fuel. No! I saw a report a couple of days ago suggesting that to recharge a car with a two-hundred-mile range in many parts of the United States costs as little as six dollars. I drive an electric car, and my guess would be that it's probably closer to eight or ten dollars, but still—two hundred miles! That's pretty damn good.

It's appealing to talk about how this would save us money, save our planet. This will preserve the future of our young people's health and—if we manufacture wind turbines and solar panels in the United States—will also provide us with millions of good jobs.

This message needs to be boiled down to a very simple and very straightforward statement: We need good union jobs in the United States to recreate the middle class. In the United States, 55 to 60 percent were in the middle class when Reagan entered the White House. In 2015, NPR reported that we dropped below 50 percent and some estimates today suggest it's around 45 percent. So we need to bring back unions and provide ourselves with the energy for a twenty-first-century society and economy. And that energy can come at a low cost if we get it from that free nuclear fusion reactor ninety-three million miles away—the Sun.

Then, the following facts that campaigns can use when speaking of the economy:

- Because of the expanded Child Tax Credit, child poverty dropped by a third in 2021. It's rare for a government policy to work so unambiguously well, yet the GOP wouldn't continue funding it. "The oligarchy didn't want to pay for it."—Robert Reich

- Republicans often attack Democrats for "Socialism!"... even after Trump handed farmers $30 billion because his trade policies were bankrupting them.

- Fox reporter John Roberts to Sen. Rick Scott, "Your plan would raise taxes on half of Americans and sunset things like Social Security, Medicare, and Medicaid. Why would you do that?"

- **Taxation:** Last year, fifty-five large corporations made $40 billion in US profits and paid *no* federal income tax. Other companies paid less than 10 percent. The current IRS commissioner, Charles P. Rettig, says the sum of uncollected taxes last year was a trillion dollars.

  Firefighters and teachers should not pay a higher tax than a billionaire. "The party that can appeal to a multi-ethnic working class will be the majority party for the next generation." (Mike Madrid, *New York Times*, March 23, 2022)

  The GOP had cut the IRS budget by 20 percent below its 2010 level, inflation-adjusted. Audits of large companies plunged by 58 percent between 2010 and 2019. Congress was turned into a recidivist enabler of massive tax evasion—which if done by ordinary people would constitute a crime.

  Trickle-down economics has never gotten billionaires to spread the wealth. That's what unions are for.

- **Michael Kazin:** The following aggressive pro-worker, anti-corporate message moved voters five points in a poll in the fall of 2021:

  People are living paycheck to paycheck and struggling to pay their bills and taxes. They need a government that looks out for the middle class, working families, small businesses, and the vulnerable who work hard. They don't need a government that jumps whenever the biggest corporations send money and lobbyists. My approach is blue collar. We should bend over backward for those who work hard so we create jobs in America and grow the middle class again.[7]

The next panel was on healthcare, led by Dr. Steffie Woolhandler, who has taught at Harvard Medical School and Hunter College and is cofounder of Physicians for a National Health Program (PNHP) and coauthor of the leading Medicare-for-All proposal embodied in H.R. 676—the gold standard legislation for single payer. Candidates want talking points that grab people's attention and support, Dr. Woolhandler provides the feast.

Let's start with Medicare for All—although that's not the issue of the day, it will be the issue going forward over the long term. While there's a lot in healthcare that we can do in the short term, it's useful to at least review the key arguments around Medicare for All since the majority of voters still endorse it . . . as do organizations like Physicians for a National Health Program, Public Citizen, the Nurses Union, and many other great organizations.

There's a crisis in America's health and longevity. You probably know that Americans have higher death rates than people in other developed countries but may not know just how bad it is. We just issued a report about what we call the "missing Americans"—the number of people who die each year in this country who would still be alive at the end of the year, if we had mortality rates as low as other developed nations. Even before the COVID pandemic, five hundred thousand Americans went "missing" every year, that is who died unnecessarily because of our poor mortality. During the COVID pandemic that number has gone up to one million deaths annually—one million people going missing who would still be with us if we had the same death rates as other developed nations. And it turns out that half of all deaths below the age of sixty-five in this country are these "missing Americans." (See Ed Young covering our work on the "missing Americans" in the *Atlantic* in July.)

The other price of our healthcare system is cost. Americans are paying twice as much as people in other developed countries for healthcare—20 percent of GDP—and of course the electorate is paying for that directly through their payments and indirectly through their taxes. Access and affordability are huge issues—thirty million uninsured Americans, tens of millions more who have insurance that they can't afford to use because of high co-payments, deductibles, and services that aren't covered. Then there's major problems with medical debts—more than half of all the bad things on your credit report are medical bills. And research we've done with Elizabeth Warren when she was at Harvard shows that medical illness or medical debt play a major role in personal bankruptcies, contributing to more than half of them.

How do you fund Medicare for All? We're not supposed to say "spend," but consider taking all the money that's now being wasted on overhead and bureaucracy—which we estimated at $800 billion a year (the Rand Corporation and the Congressional Budget Office have similar estimates of the quantity of administrative waste)—and investing it in *actual* healthcare, such as doctors, nurses, drugs and preventive care.

Beyond Medicare for All, there's what we in academia call "financialization." In the electoral sphere, you may call it "the Wall Street takeover of American healthcare." Amazon, for example, just purchased Medical One, a major provider of primary care and employer of primary care physicians. So *Amazon* now owns your doctor. That's what we mean by financialization, which is a problem in two ways. One is just the surveillance fears. Amazon—which already knows the books I read, the stuff I buy, and the movies I stream—will now also know my personal healthcare and that of my patients.

That's scary. But add to that the false assumptions that greed is good, that profits are good in healthcare, that whatever is profitable is somehow acceptable. We've already seen that with the insurance companies now going feet first into providing Medicare through the privatized Medicare Advantage plans and providing managed Medicaid plans. More than half of the private insurance industry's total revenues come from the taxpayers through the Medicare Advantage or Medicaid managed care programs, which are privatized programs.

Those insurance companies are ripping off taxpayers. According to MedPAC—Congress's oversight agency of Medicare—the price of Medicare Advantage is 104 percent of the price of traditional Medicare. So they're raising the price to everyone by charging taxpayers for their very high overhead and profits, which is in the range of about 15 to 19 percent overhead. How do they get those profits? Well, they "upcode"—the payment to private insurance firms from the government is based on how sick the patient is. So the private insurance companies just exaggerate how sick the patient is in order to cause the government to pay them a bigger capitation or premium payment.

Well, some of you who are familiar with health policy may be saying, "But wait, isn't there a limit on how much overhead profit they can get? Didn't the ACA say only 15 percent of the premiums from the government or the premiums from anyone can go to overhead and profit?" While the ACA does say that, insurance companies have gotten to be experts in what I call "overhead laundering." They make these giant overhead and profits, and then, rather than computing it as insurance overhead, they just push that money over to provider organizations that they own.

For instance, United Healthcare, our largest insurance company, owns sixty thousand doctors; if their overhead starts to look too high, they just shift those profits over to their subsidiary that owns doctors—then it's out of their overhead and they get to hang on to the profit. Which means they're profiteering at the expense of the taxpayers and at the expense of sick patients.

I needn't spend a lot of time on drug company profiteering since most people understand that we're paying twice as much for the same medicines here in the US as people can buy in Canada. Physicians for a National Health Program explained all this—along with drug company profiteering—in the *British Medical Journal*. But I would like to conclude about the new kid on the block: private equity, or what we used to call "leveraged buyouts." Private equity vulture capitalists go in and extract value from productive industries, like doctors' offices or hospitals. Wanting to get their money out in three to seven years, they load these providers, hospitals, nursing homes with giant debt. They hive off the real estate, put that in a separate company, or sometimes sell it for money.

Consider two egregious examples. The closure of Hanuman Hospital in downtown Philadelphia, a venerable safety net hospital, actually was closed and its downtown real estate sold off because it was more valuable as condos than it was for patient care. The nursing home industry puts it in a separate subsidiary, which means that the nursing home just becomes an operating company that has to pay rent . . . which in turn means they have to reduce staffing. This raises the death rate. But if patients try to sue the nursing home about a loved one being harmed or dying, the nursing home is then judgment-proof since they're just an operating company that doesn't own any property.[8]

Mark Green: If a voter says to a candidate, "I hear that if the Republicans are back in control, they want to end Obamacare." That true? And what would that mean for average Americans?
Dr. Steffie Woolhandler: That would mostly affect folks who are newly eligible for Medicaid since 2010, and there's a lot of those. There'd be at least ten million people who would lose their health insurance which would harm the health of low-income people all over the country.

The topic of COVID-19 was broadly and specifically covered by Dr. Irwin Redlener, cofounder of the Children's Health Fund and founding director of the National Center for Disaster Preparedness at the Earth Institute, Columbia University.

First of all: the Trump Administration *did* have a role in stimulating the development of the COVID vaccine. But he also then undermined his own modicum of proper judgment by politicizing this situation to a point where it's become unmanageable as a public health problem.

By now, we've had multiple waves of COVID and, as most voters are aware, initially in early 2020 it was a lethal killer that was filling up hospitals with patients on ventilators in ICUs—and there were very high death rates. Then Joe Biden happens to have taken the vaccine idea and expanded it in ways that have saved— in spite of the fact that people are still dying of COVID—many millions of lives by the use and promotion of vaccines. And we would have saved more lives if, in fact, the incentives and motivations to get vaccinated hadn't been polluted by misinformation and politics.

One of the things we could say about COVID right now is that people, generally speaking, are tired of it. We've had it with COVID and we want to move on, and we want to make believe this is over. And it's not over. By the time November comes, it is likely or at least very possible that we will be seeing another surge of COVID infections occurring in all parts of the United States.

Our language in dealing with this has to be consistent and strong: "You must get vaccinated. Period." We may have vaccines at that point that are more likely to suppress it even if you don't have the latest vaccine. So from a public health point of view, and if we had nothing else to think about other than the public health issue here, the desired message is clear.

We have 65 to 67 percent of Americans now vaccinated. "Fully vaccinated" at this point in 2022 is two shots and two boosters, and that's what we have to be pushing for. And we have to talk about this as if we understand that the science means that we're not going to be curing COVID any time soon, but we can control it. Individuals can't stop getting infected, but they can control how likely it is that they will be admitted to hospitals or die from the disease. That's the grown-up reality of what we're talking about.

Whether we get drawn into the politics (as Republicans would like us to) about what we need to do depends on how we handle this. We need to be straightforward and clear—Get vaccinated. Wear masks. Are we going to mandate masks in indoor situations? We probably should, but we probably *won't* because it's become so politically fraught.

The misinformation that's being constantly put out—which is that we are violating people's freedom of choice by forcing them to get vaccinated or forcing them to wear a mask—requires simple language to correct. Government has a responsibility to protect lives to the extent possible, without overly interfering with individual freedoms. That's why we have clean water and clean air regulations, and OSHA in workplaces. And, similarly, this is why we ask children to be vaccinated when they go to school to prevent a host of infectious diseases to which they would otherwise be susceptible.

Democratic candidates have to be prepared to say, "We don't do more than we have to. But we do what we need to do as a government to save lives." In other words, if you want to go skydiving, if you want to do cliff climbing, be our guest. But we cannot do something that can infect an elderly person or a person who is immunocompromised. That's one of the things about a civilized society that we have to be able to understand. We're in this together—all of us—and need to avoid risks that can harm others. It's why you can't drive drunk or without wearing seat belts.

That will likely come up in debates. "Are you trying to force me to get vaxxed?" *Force you?* Because I don't want you to infect my grandma—or your grandma, for that matter? The price of civilization is mutual agreement not to harm others based on rules enacted by democratic vote.

Here Democratic candidates have a strong and popular argument. Part of the deal about living free in America includes keeping each other safe and healthy as best as we can. That's why you can't drive drunk or without a license. And why your children must get the routine vaccines of childhood and why pilots and doctors must be qualified to practice their craft.

Donald Trump, however, has poisoned "the general welfare" (to quote the Constitution) with erratic, unscientific, extreme politics. But really, Democrats just want to protect grandparents, young kids and anybody who may be at great risk from getting COVID. I'm sure you must realize that a million people died from COVID in America and five hundred more are lost every single day! Many older and vulnerable Americans listening to us right now want to be reassured that we'll protect them from further COVID and the next pandemic.

Candidly, here's the report card as of the fall of 2022: The Biden administration has widely distributed vaccinations saving Republican and Democratic lives alike. The Trump administration repeatedly underplayed the danger of COVID, a deception that led to hundreds of thousands of preventable deaths, or more than World War I, Vietnam, and Iraq combined. Only the Democratic Party was pro-life, as defined by saving post-birth lives.

HEALTHCARE—COVID NOTES

- Life expectancy fell under only one president—Trump—because of the rise in "deaths of despair"—drugs, guns, suicides, COVID.

- A Health KFF survey found that 60 percent of the unvaxxed were Republicans. Democrats were 17 percent.

- It's crazy that so many in GOP complain that it's tyranny when the government tells people to wear masks during a once-in-a-century health emergency but ordering pregnant girls to carry their fetus to term—even if due to rape or incest—isn't.

- Dangerous reactionaries fight pro-health measures like masks and free, miracle drugs to save lives. Yet we accept laws prohibiting drunk driving and requiring seat belts be worn without complaints about Big Brother infringements on our liberty . . . and, unlike COVID, neither is contagious.

- "Excess deaths" were worst in states with low vaccination rates and Republican governors.

- When it comes to death rates, there's still a clear and dramatic correlation between how much of the population has been two-dose vaccinated and its COVID death rate since last May. The least vaccinated decile has a death rate *3.3 times higher* than the most vaccinated one.[9] Given the short-term profit motives of vaccine drug companies, their taxpayer subsidies, and their protection from full liability, constant vigilance and healthy skepticism must confront them and the Food and Drug Administration (FDA) heavily lobbied by the drug companies which fund much of its regulatory work.

The next panel was on "Crime & Corruption" with the opening talk by Richard Aborn on the topic "Crime and Guns."

Crime obviously is an issue candidates hear a lot about.

First, approach it with balanced language so prospective voters understand that we will do everything feasible to drive it down. Indeed, the good news here is that we have reduced crime dramatically for the past eighteen years.

However, we're now experiencing a sharp uptick in many categories of crime. One awful response is "defunding police," a provocative phrase that most people reject since police are rightly regarded as the front line of defense when it comes to violent crime. And it obscures essential and achievable reforms that center around three urgent areas: excessive aggressiveness, implicit bias, and over-policing. If we then layer accountability on top of police conduct, we would go a long way to having the kind of police forces in America that we need.

Ultimately, all reforms and accountability requires police working hand-in-hand with the community in a partnership, since people there know what they want, often know who's driving crime, and very often understand the best ways to reduce crime. An antagonistic relationship between cops and communications communities is self-defeating.

Historically, control was prescribed with a bludgeon. "We use the same tool against all types of crime" is like using the same kind of drug against all kinds of disease. Of course, in the medical profession, you have to have the right medicine for a particular disease. Well, that's true in crime, too. So I'm going to break this down into two broad categories—how we treat nonviolent crime and violent crime.

Nonviolent crime should not lead to prison. If we start incarcerating young nonviolent criminals, we are simply going to give them a college-level education on how to commit and live a life of crime.

It's the very reverse of what's smart. It's best treated by the broad matrix we now call prevention, which largely operates at the intersection of mental health and criminal conduct. It's now increasingly accepted that early mental health treatment can deter nonviolent criminals from getting into a life of crime . . . which over time lowers crime rates. The flip side, however, is that if you don't, young people may graduate toward more violent crime.

As for violent crime, classic deterrence should not mean *aggressive* policing or *overly intrusive* policing. Instead it's putting police where the crime is—which is called "precision policing"—so the public actually sees uniformed police officers out there, whether it's in transit systems or on the street.

Would-be criminals—like all of us in civilian life—engage in an economic theory called "behavioral risk analysis." We gauge the risk associated with an intended course of conduct versus the benefits. And if a potential criminal sees cops, there's a decent chance he's not going to commit the crime.

Should someone be arrested, incarcerated, and convicted for a violent crime, what do we do while they're in prison?

Our prisons are too violent in this country. In my view, the greatest exercise of governmental power is when the government takes away the liberty of an individual. If we're going to exercise that power, we better do so in a responsible, humane, and safe way. That means our prisons have to engage in actions that prepare inmates for when they reenter society . . . which requires that we invest heavily in *reentry* in order to reduce *recidivism*.

Let me go on now to the next topic—excessive bail. For many years it fell disproportionately and unfairly on the backs of young men of color. This system put young men of color in jail prior to conviction, that is, preventative detention. But it's now also being done for low-level offenses as well as high-level offenses. The former need not be sent to jail or prison (jail is less than a year, prison is more than a year), since there's little correlation between that confinement and recidivism. Remember, the core purpose of bail is to make sure that individuals show up to court, not to punish them.

For high-level or violent offenses, the data is a little bit different. It shows that if adequate bail alternatives are not given to the court, there are many violent criminals released who may well end up reoffending. But part of that reality is that the vast number of crimes are committed by a very small number of offenders. It's the 80/20 rule of economics applied to crime—the vast number of violent crimes are committed by a small number of people. So we should focus on those individuals ideally before they commit additional violent crimes.

Finally, the thing that really drives both crime and the fear of crime is America's addiction to guns. If you look at the rates of interpersonal violence in other Western countries, you will see that it's essentially the same, except when it comes to gun violence—and America is far and away the most gun-violent country, certainly in the Western world, and perhaps in the entire world, excluding active war zones. So both to drive down the fear of crime and the reality of crime, it is very important that localities be hyper-focused on guns. That means the police working hand in hand with the district attorneys and the courts. In New York City, we did carve out resources to accelerate gun cases through the judicial system. No curtailment of rights, no curtailment of discovery, every single constitutional right honored, but done so swiftly.

What just happened in the Supreme Court is a disaster. They ruled that the Second Amendment extends to the right to carry concealed guns. The 2008 case called *Heller* concluded for the first time that people had a constitutional right to have a gun in the home for self-defense. The NRA will now use that case to challenge every single gun law we've passed in the last twenty years, although the *Heller* decision itself, written by Justice Scalia, carved out exceptions from a discretionary licensing process so we can still push assault weapon bans and large magazine bans.

There is also a relatively new concept of "red flag" laws, which allow police to go into somebody's home in response to a call from the community, and—if there's a sufficient showing of imminent harm—take guns out of the home. We have one in New York and they're very effective. They can help stop mass shootings by keeping guns out of homes with disturbed youths, like the one who killed twenty-six in Newtown, Connecticut.

Nothing we have ever proposed interferes with a law-abiding citizen's ability to get firearms. The NRA talking-point that "the gun safety movement is out to ban all guns, and it's just a slippery slope," is just nonsense. The Second Amendment as interpreted by the Supreme Court establishes a constitutional right to have a gun at your home. Federal and state gun safety laws are not about law-abiding citizens but rather about stopping criminals from getting guns that lead to some $280 billion in costs annually—and over forty-thousand gun-related deaths (homicides and suicides).

Last, I helped write and enact the 1994 congressional ban on assault weapons through the Congress. We were forced to take a ten-year sunset, and here's the data: in the ten years before the ban on assault weapons and large magazines went into effect, there were 25 percent more mass shootings than during the ten years the ban was in effect. In the ten to twenty years since the ban lapsed—and the Republican Congress chose to put those guns back on the street—mass shootings have gone up 400 percent.[10]

The vast corporate crime wave is almost never discussed in the major parties' campaigns, even though the people they are shaking hands with on the hustings suffer from effects of it every day of the year. Russell Mokhiber, publisher of the weekly *Corporate Crime Reporter* for over three decades and author of *Corporate Crime and Violence: Big Business Power and the Abuse of the Public Trust* did not have enough time for a summary of the categories, so he decided on an intriguing way to get the voters' attention.

For the past thirty-six years I've been editing *The Corporate Crime Reporter* newsletter from our office in the National Press

Building. But during COVID, I've been working mostly from West Virginia, a 70/30 Trump state.

People around here have a keen understanding of street crime from family members and the media. But pretty much they don't have an understanding of law and order for corporations, even though they are often victims of corporate crime and violence. So let's go back to Election Day—November 3, 2020. Our family votes at a local state park two miles away. I went and voted there, and then went fishing at the lake right next to the polling booth. And next to me also was a man fishing whom I'd never met, who had just voted for Trump. He spent about a half hour telling me about his troubles during COVID, how his dad died from working at a brake lining facility in nearby Maryland, how his nephew was hooked on opioids, how his cousin died from a cancer he believes he got from being sprayed with chemicals in Vietnam, and how he was trying to get his aunt out of a local nursing home due to, in his view, elder abuse in the nursing home.

I told him about my work on corporate crime, and that pretty much everything he just described were corporate crimes that I've written about over the years, beginning with my 1988 book *Corporate Crime and Violence*. We both sat quietly and resumed fishing. I guess we both understood that no matter who we just voted for, no one was going to take the corporate crime epidemic seriously. No matter the administration, corporate crime continues undeterred.

For example, some nursing home deaths are criminally prosecuted as reckless homicides, but very few. There never was a criminal prosecution of the chemical companies for dropping the toxic herbicide Agent Orange on Vietnam and exposing more than four million Vietnamese and tens of thousands of American soldiers, causing cancers, diabetes, and birth defects. Nor has an asbestos company ever been criminally prosecuted for the tens of thousands of workers exposed and sickened with the deadly asbestosis.

The opioid epidemic could have been slowed if the Justice Department had listened to its own prosecutors in 2006 and brought criminal charges against Purdue Pharma and top company executives—those federal prosecutors, working in the heart of Appalachia in West Virginia, saw the devastation that opioid addiction was having on their own community sixteen years ago and wrote out a one-hundred-page memo to their supervisors at the Justice Department calling for strong criminal response to the damage.

Had they been listened to, tens of thousands of American lives could have been saved. But high-powered corporate criminal defense attorneys went over their heads and limited the range and scope of the prosecution. And if you want a nice summary of this, the *New York Times* put up a mini-documentary entitled "A Secret Memo that Could Have Slowed the Epidemic."

My friends and neighbors here in West Virginia are for the most part decent, hardworking, religious people who strongly favor law and order, family, and country. A "law and order" message, "Fund the police. Crack down on crime," resonates with them . . . whether the message is directed at street criminals or corporate criminals. But the criminal justice discussion in this country has been focused almost exclusively on street crime.

Here's two examples taken from podcasts by the *New York Times*. Jane Kosten has one called *The Argument*, and she puts on these public intellectuals to discuss issues of the day. Last month she put on one titled, "Is Crime that Bad? Or Are the Vibes Just Off?" and she opened with "Republicans say Democrats are soft on crime. Democrats say Republicans are over-policing with no accountability. And what do voters think? What's clear is that crime—or the perception of crime—is driving our political conversations." Yet the conversation is focused almost exclusively on street crime.

There was a throwaway line by one of the panelists about "white-collar crime," which usually refers to individuals committing crimes like insider trading, often against the market or against the corporate state. But "corporate crime" should include illegality *by* powerful institutions themselves, committing crimes against human beings. Another example is from Ezra Klein at the *New York Times*, who put up a podcast recently called "Violent Crime Is Spiking. Do Liberals Have an Answer?" Again, no discussion of corporate crime, even though corporate crime and violence inflicts far more damage on society than all street crime combined.

So, for example, the FBI tells us that twenty-four thousand Americans are murdered every year. Compare that to fifty-four thousand Americans who die every year from on-the-job occupational diseases like black lung and asbestosis, and the other tens of thousands who fall victim every year to pollution, contaminated foods, hazardous consumer products, and hospital malpractice. The FBI puts out its yearly "Crime in the United States" report—no talk about corporate crime. We've been calling for years for a "Corporate Crime in the United States" report, to no avail.

The problem is that the mainstream media and political elite focus on street crime and violence. There's an exception from this year's election cycle in Missouri that may show a path forward—a Democratic Senate candidate named Lucas Kunce. He's a Democrat and thirteen-year veteran of Iraq and Afghanistan who's running for the U.S. Senate. In May he wrote an opinion piece in the *Joplin Globe* entitled "They Are Guilty of Corporate Manslaughter. Prosecute Them." He addressed the corporate crimes committed by the baby formula companies. In a nutshell, a whistleblower from Abbott's Michigan plant sent the FDA a thirty-four-page document outlining contamination and sanitary issues at the plant. The FDA sat on it for three months. By then it was too late—two babies who drank the contaminated formula had already died, and more were hospitalized.

Kunce called for breaking up the baby formula cartel, but added, "We prosecute everyone at Abbott who helped hide the unsanitary plant conditions from the FDA. They killed two babies."[11]

STREET CRIME & SUITE CRIME NOTES

- Do *not* "Defund the Police." Instead, *fund* the police and reform bad practices (choke holds, don't shoot misdemeanants running away). According to a 2021 analysis of police budgets in the nation's fifty largest cities by Bloomberg CityLab, law enforcement spending as a share of general expenditures rose slightly, from 13.6 percent in 2020 to 13.7

percent in 2021, even as many cities cut spending in other areas as a result of the COVID pandemic.

- Despite stereotypes, eight of the ten states with the highest murder rates voted for Trump in 2020. The Third Way compared murder rates in Trump and Biden states and found that they were 40 percent higher in red than blue states. Red states on average had lower education levels, higher rates of poverty, worse healthcare, and less economic opportunity.

- Gun-related deaths cost the United States $280 billion a year. The greatest cause of death of children under sixteen is not cars or drugs but guns.

- Former Chief Justice Warren Burger: "There is absolutely no reason why a civilian on the street should be carrying a loaded weapon."

- Governor Abbott said, after twenty-one children were killed at the Uvalde massacre: "It could have been worse."

- If a "good guy with a gun" is the answer to "a bad guy with a gun," how come four hundred armed cops couldn't stop one person killing so many children in Uvalde, Texas?

- If laws can't stop criminals with guns, why did the two eighteen-year-old murderers—in Buffalo and Uvalde—wait until exactly their eighteenth birthdays to buy their AR-15s?

- Politico-Morning Consult poll: Requiring background checks on all gun sales: 88 percent strongly or somewhat support. Creating a national database with info about each gun sale: 75 percent support. Banning assault-style weapons: 67 percent support.

- The NRA says that more guns will make us safer. We now have more than one gun per American—do we feel safer?

Criminologist Emma Fridel found that mass shootings are 53 percent higher in states with more gun ownership.

- CDC estimated 45,000 gun-related deaths in 2020, a surge of 35 percent from prior year, a historical increase.
- The issue with guns is not the much-disputed Second Amendment but rather the public health of millions of Americans per decade.[12]

The next panel was "National Security," led by William Hartung, who discussed the military budget. He is the author of *Prophets of War* and for many years was the director of the Arms & Security Program at the Center for International Policy. He is now at the Quincy Institute.

As most Americans know, we're at a critical moment for the future of our country and the world. And we need to devote time and resources to the most urgent challenges—that especially includes the huge and ever-growing Pentagon spending that takes away from other needs. Unfortunately, at the moment, we're going in the wrong direction.

The House this year voted to add $37 million to the Pentagon's request—more than the Pentagon even asked for—and that'll push the budget for the Pentagon and nuclear warheads at the Department of Energy together to $850 billion. Now that's far more than we spent at the height of the Korean or Vietnam wars, more than a $100 billion more than at the height of the Cold War. This kind of spending can't continue.

It's hard to adequately describe what an enormous sum that is compared to competing problems—more than a million Americans have died from COVID, we've been inundated with fires, floods, droughts related to climate change, and Americans are struggling just to put enough food on the table to live an active, healthy life. So put simply, we need to set our priorities straight if we want to make America safer, fair, more prosperous.

Here are some other few comparisons to show us just how huge the Pentagon budget is. In a time when we need creative diplomacy more than ever, the Pentagon gets fourteen times more money than the State Department and the Agency for International Development combined, and our $850 billion annual military budget is seven times the annual cost of the [renamed] "Inflation Reduction Act," which Republicans previously blocked because they said it was too expensive.

Consider the proposed annual budget for just one item: we have thirty-five combat aircraft larger than the annual budget for the Centers for Disease Control. The cost of one new aircraft carrier—$15 billion—is more than we spend on the Environmental Protection Agency. The $20 trillion we spent on the Pentagon since 2001 . . . just a quarter of that would be needed to decarbonize our electrical grid—i.e., no dependence on fossil fuels for electricity anywhere in America.

So unless something changes, we're poised to spend a good $8–10 trillion on the Pentagon over the next decade yet we can't afford to do that given all our other problems.

Now, a lot of Americans might say, "Well, we need to spend this to defend the country, and also most importantly to support the troops," but unfortunately that's not the case. More than half of the Pentagon budget goes to corporations. Just the top five: Lockheed Martin, Boeing, General Dynamics, Raytheon,

Northrop Grumman split over $150 billion a year. That's almost 20 percent of the Pentagon budget going just to those five companies. And Lockheed Martin itself gets $75 billion a year, which is larger for that one company than the State Department and USAID combined. I can't think of a more dramatic example of misplaced priorities than lining the pockets of that one contractor when our diplomacy is suffering.

Overall, the Pentagon employs more than half a million private service contract employees. If you cap that and cut it by 15 percent you'd save $26 billion a year—over a quarter of a trillion over the next decade. And that can easily be done. They cost more than government employees; they often do redundant tasks; and they're much harder to control and supervise. To make matters worse, we can't really calculate how much money the Pentagon is wasting because they've never had or passed an audit—the only Federal agency for which that's the case.

It's not as if this money showered on the contractors is giving us value for the money. These big companies run tens of billions of dollars and cost overruns to deliver weapons that are years behind schedule and often don't perform as advertised. Sometimes they even put our troops at risk because they're so shoddily put together. And then you've got companies that gouge the government for spare parts—charging 10,100, in one case 38,000 percent more than the thing actually should have cost. People like Senator Warren and others are trying to crack that problem.

Of course we need a strong national defense. But that's not what our current strategy is providing. For example, the focus on China involves a huge amount of threat inflation. The United

States spends 2.5 times what China spends on its military; we have thirteen times as many nuclear weapons; we have a more capable Navy and more capable Air Force. And unlike China, we have strong allies in East Asia: Australia, Japan, Korea, Taiwan, and we're building relations with India. So the idea that the United States has to carry some huge military burden to "win a war with China" (which is not possible in a war between nuclear powers) should not be a goal of our policy. Our goal should be to defend our allies in the region, and for them to participate heavily in that undertaking.

On the other side, we need to cooperate with China to deal with climate change, pandemics, and the global economy. These problems cannot be solved without some sort of US-China cooperation.

Also, we shouldn't overplay the capabilities of drone systems and certainly don't need thousands and thousands of tanks . . . don't need thirteen aircraft carriers . . . and don't need intercontinental ballistic missiles which are redundant and put us at risk of an accidental nuclear war. In fact, the Pentagon, the Air Force, the Navy are trying to retire some old systems that aren't relevant to dealing with China, or much of anything else. And members of Congress from the districts where those things are built are pushing back, saying, "No, we need this ship that's got a cracked hull, that can't defend itself in combat. We need an airplane that's less capable than the prior generation of planes and costs dramatically more."

Something like the military reform movement that Senator Gary Hart pursued would have a lot of promise because it asks the right question: What's the most effective way to defend the country? Even people who view themselves as somewhat hawkish could be open to that kind of approach as long as we don't put all our faith in technology.[13]

Mr. Hartung's presentation flowed smoothly into Ret. Col. Lawrence Wilkerson's talk about the "Disaster of Empire"—another two-party taboo that the voting public deserves to have ended once and for all.

Bill's already told you about the disaster that is the defense budget. The related disaster I want to tell you about is the disaster of empire.

That is what America is today. In fact, I would assert that we are not the "new Rome." We are the new empire in the world that history has never seen. We are not merely the "new Rome" but outdo Rome in historical-relative terms by a large magnitude. We have 750 and counting outposts in the world. The rest of the world—to give you some comparison, including Russia and China—has less than ninety.

In addition, we maintain some 150 "installations" and "bases." Take Norway, for example, where the people are basically opposed to having US military bases in their country. But given situations like the present crisis in Ukraine, the Pentagon simply builds the bases on *existing* Norwegian bases . . . and then doesn't categorize them as military installations or bases. They will be "military facilities" that the US maintains on Norwegian bases.

As a military professional for thirty-one years—and having served at the top of the military structure, if you will, with Chairman Powell for four years—I can tell you we could cut that entire overseas base budget by 75 percent tomorrow and not reduce our ability to project power or to maintain the security of the United States in any serious way.

Another emerging problem is something that the Pentagon is only now recognizing and something I've been working on, so far to no avail—that is the dissolution of the all-volunteer force, by which I mean the way we populate our military is falling apart. Recently, the Pentagon has acknowledged that recruiting shortfalls are so dramatic that they currently lack plans for how to find service people in the near future. For now, it's paying bonuses up to $50,000 in order to sign up an instrument or a mortarman; the Air Force is paying $25–$30,000 in order to get people. As for the Navy, the idea that we could have a 355-ship fleet is ludicrous. We could build the ships, but we wouldn't have the men and women to people them, to command them, to sail them.

Here's some simple arithmetic: every year the Pentagon must recruit approximately 150,000 new service members in order to stay viable in its armed forces. Every year, approximately four million Americans turn eighteen years of age, 23 percent of whom can meet the minimum standards for military service (taking into account obesity, intellectual incapacity, criminal records, and so forth). That's about 920,000 people.

This deficiency has only gotten worse with these endless, stupid wars we've been prosecuting. One major negative impact is on military families themselves, who previously have been the richest environment from which to recruit. They are now increasingly recommending that their children not serve—do not enlist, do not take that bonus. That's really hurting recruitment. Of those 920,000 then, only 9 percent are motivated to serve, leaving approximately 83,000 both able and willing to serve. That's a shortfall of 67,000 troops a year. . . .

At the same time that the all-volunteer force is becoming unsustainable, no one appears to be confronting this situation *and* foreign policy has become increasingly militarized. In fact, along with sanctions, military force is about all the United States has offered the world in the past twenty-plus years. But a new emerging threat might ironically energize recruitment to combat what is coming at us like a freight train—the climate crisis. We're going to need recruits for all manner of missions from fighting forest fires that have dramatically increased, to dealing with inundated coastlines, including military installations, and to delivering medical care across our own country and the globe. We're the only country in the world that can project that sort of power to move medical care, whether it's a hospital ship or a disaster relief operation by the Marine Corps.

We're also going to need them for refugee control—some of the simulations we've run have shown 500- to 600-million-plus refugees in the world by mid-century or earlier; we already have 175 million refugees in the world right now, so a half-billion refugees is not improbable. So we're either going to have to have a Civilian Conservation Corps like the one set up by Roosevelt, or we're going to need to have the military vastly increase but with a totally different mission: not killing people on behalf of the state but ensuring our own survival, perhaps our own existence.

To put the current need for some twelve million recruits over ten years in context: in 1944–1945 we had twelve million men under arms from a population of 140 million Americans. We have 330 million Americans now, so twelve million might sound plausible. But it's probably just a starting figure in order to deal with the crisis. I'm a member of the Climate and Security Working Group, which is retired DOD, DHS, and NASA professionals, and we all see this as a very serious issue that we're going to have to deal with urgently. Do we have the courage, plans, concepts, or even the stamina to figure this out for a military that is falling apart?[14]

Immigration has become a national security issue in part because Trump has persuaded millions of Trumpsters to believe it to be so and because the impoverished countries of the South are coming to the United States in record numbers after decades of US support for right-wing dictatorships and oligarchs and in part due to severe US sanctions on countries such as Cuba and Venezuela. Marielena Hincapié, Director of the National Immigration Law Center, made the following remarks:

First, I'm going to share some framing thoughts about where we are on immigration. Second, I'll share what our polling shows that voters want from Democrats in terms of solutions. And third, I'll focus specifically on the border and the urgent need to protect immigrant youth with DACA—so-called Dreamers—so that Democrats can be on the *offense* on this issue.

To begin with, immigrants and immigration have been essential to who we are as a nation and a source of strength for our future. I was just listening to Colonel Wilkerson, and there's a lot of what he is saying which is critical for the solutions on immigration. Immigration is a global phenomenon. And we're experiencing record numbers of people moving across the globe due to climate crisis, a rise of authoritarianism, xenophobia, and war—as we've seen most recently with Ukraine, for example.

At the US-Mexico border, we're experiencing the crisis and chaos that was left behind by Trump's cruel policies, including family separation and weaponizing public health policies, like Title 42, that were created back during the Second World War to essentially block Black and Brown immigrants from legally seeking safety and freedom through our asylum system. So we need to understand Republicans' anti-*immigrant* agenda as actually being an anti*democratic* agenda that is dangerous, and that the attempt is really to block future voters from becoming citizens.

We need a paradigm shift that sees immigration not only through a domestic-policy lens, but actually through a national security lens, an economic and foreign policy lens . . . and also the lens of climate justice, racial justice, and economic justice.

We are expecting record numbers of refugees around the world and we don't have laws to handle that. What's needed is a regional approach—as well as global and Western-hemispheric approaches. Title 42 focuses on people's freedom to stay in their home country, so they are not forced to migrate. And for those who arrive at our borders and at our airports—or those who are citizens-in-waiting (like immigrant youth who are popularly known as Dreamers), or the essential workers who have kept our country running—we need to ensure that we have a humane immigration system that provides legal pathways for people to become full participants in our democracy.

Republicans are convinced that immigration politics are in their favor, and the media at times echoes that by amplifying false narratives. But Democrats, even in frontline swing districts, should know that they should confront Republicans about their dangerous extremism on immigration and border issues. In poll after poll, a strong majority of Americans agree that the nation's immigration system is in desperate need of reform since we have not had a comprehensive reform since 1986 under Ronald Reagan. What voters want is a fair and equitable immigration policy and candidates who defend those policies.

The National Immigration Law Center and the NILC Immigrant Justice Fund have spent a considerable amount of time and resources to better understand the best way to engage swing voters on these issues. Last year we conducted voting research in Arizona, Wisconsin, North Carolina, and Georgia, and found four core messages. They want:

- messages that are anchored in shared values;
- information about the harms of the complex immigration system;
- candidates to lift up the contributions and amplify the contributions that immigrants provide; and
- an aspirational vision of what our candidates are in favor of, not simply against.

These top-line frames will appeal both to base voters and persuadable voters across a range of states and districts. They should enable Democrats to feel comfortable speaking from a position of strength.

To focus on the border to begin with, several developments over the past year have thrust border politics to the forefront. And Republicans are certainly trying to weaponize that into a political game. Contrary to conventional rhetoric about "open borders," remember the Department of Homeland Security was just created in 2003, after 9/11; since then the United States has spent over $381 billion on border and interior enforcement—more than all federal law enforcement agencies combined. So the border actually has been secure.

What's happened, though, is that the Trump administration decimated our refugee-resettlement system and asylum system. In a survey this past May that we conducted of six battleground states—Arizona, Colorado, Georgia, Nevada, Pennsylvania, and Wisconsin—we found that 58 percent of likely midterm voters would prefer a candidate who favors allowing people to legally request asylum at the southern border over a candidate that opposes that. Separately, two-thirds of those surveyed believe that people fleeing violence and oppression should have an opportunity to have their asylum cases heard and fairly considered. That is central to our tenet of being a nation of laws and the rule of law.

Just like the Trump Supreme Court began rolling back fundamental rights like abortion, it's poised to strike down DACA in its next term. But again as with Choice, 60–75 percent of voters support Congress protecting Dreamers.

I'll close by saying that voters want solutions. They want to hear that Democrats will ensure that people have the freedom to stay in their home country; that a fair and functioning immigration system processes migrants at the border, that it creates legal pathways for people, and that people can be processed in their home country throughout the Americas. And finally, that it provides Dreamers with permanent protection, so they can continue contributing to their families, communities, and our country.[15]

The next panel featured who I believe is the leading children's legal advocate in the country. Robert Fellmeth is a professor of law at San Diego School of Law and founder and director of the Children's Advocacy Institute. A former assistant district attorney and prolific author, Fellmeth has caused the passage of many child protection laws through the California legislature and won many basic lawsuits reverberating throughout the country. The GOP has a terrible record against the needs of infants and children—a key vulnerability the Democratic Party has not seized upon as a left-right supportive agenda.

> Children of course are our legacy. They're what we leave behind and what should be a leading frame in this year's campaigns.
>
> They lack political power. They don't vote. They don't contribute to campaigns. Lobbyists for children are 1 percent of the lobbyists for other interests. Even AARP spends ten times more than all children's advocacy lobbyists.
>
> We prize our forebears who risked everything for us in the eighteenth century. How are people two hundred years from now going to view us? That's what all candidates should be talking about. "We've got the future of our children and country at stake here."

First of all, we want to have children be properly attended to by their parents. If children get that, a lot of other problems will go away.

Second, [we've] got to reduce child poverty—the rate in the United States is now 18 percent. That's one of the highest of all developed countries. If we had an expanded child tax credit, we could cut that by 30 percent. We did have an expanded child tax credit in force for a while, but it was sunsetted by congressional Republicans. It should be restored.

Third, we should make sure we have coverage for childcare, as well as tax benefits for childcare expenses. We've got to have parenting education in schools—I took trigonometry in high school and I've never used it, but almost every student is going to have some parental role, or uncle, or aunt, and we ought to provide that education. (We got a bill passed in California to do that and the governor vetoed it.)

Fourth, we've got serious problems with foster kids and with child abuse in this country. We've got a system of foster care—and representation of these children—which is inadequate and defective. There are asset caps for foster children's benefits, so these children cannot receive any benefits if they have assets of $2,000 or more, which is ridiculous. This "lookback policy" means that any child coming from a family earning more than the poverty line cannot get federal assistance for their foster care costs. Keep in mind that it's even worse than that because the poverty line of 1996 hasn't compensated for inflation—so now over half the kids [who] were taken into custody, and who are removed from their home for their own protection, cannot receive federal funding.

Children in foster care do not have counsel—the court judge in the Dependency Court is their legal parent, and they decide everything about those children: where they'll live, what school they'll go to, who can visit them, everything about them—and yet they don't have attorneys in many states,

Of course, we've got programs like social security, SSI for disability, SSDI survivor benefits that are supposed to go to children. But these benefits are often stolen, embezzled by the states and the counties. We've issued a report on this issue and are now trying to litigate the [matter].

Every child who is in foster care should have a trust created to help them when they [reach] eighteen years of age, because when foster kids hit eighteen they fall off a cliff. These protections need to go up to twenty-one, and then you need to have a trust fund to sustain them up to twenty-five.

And as all young parents know, social media is a serious problem for children. The corporations running these platforms are trying to addict our teens and our children . . . and they're succeeding. We've got a bill right now in California—A.B. 2408—that will allow district attorneys and the attorney general to bring actions to stop purposeful addiction of children. These teens who are being addicted are committing suicide at unprecedented rates.

Mark Green: Bob, for a while under Biden, we had a children's tax credit that alone reduced children's poverty in America by a third to a half. Why don't Democratic candidates say, "Oh, don't you want to vote for *halving* child poverty?"

Robert Fellmeth: Absolutely. "Don't you think we ought to have a better child-poverty rate than Australia or Canada?" Finally, children should also have complete medical coverage. We have to campaign on funding IDEA (Individuals with Disabilities Education Act) and CAPTA (Child Abuse Prevention and Treatment Act) systems. They've got to be fully funded—they're not. Last, states ought to be providing community college education at age eighteen so that our youth can obtain jobs that are significant and important. California did that years ago, and it has a major positive impact.

CHILDREN NOTES

- Frederick Douglass: "It is easier to build strong children than repair broken men."
- Only 23 percent of American workers have access to paid parental leave.
- America needs a coordinated family policy—childcare, universal pre-K, expanded child tax credit. Only thing holding us back is a reactionary, anti-government party insistent on keeping taxes low to the wealthiest which robs children of what they need.
- 2021 UNICEF Report reported that the United States ranked fortieth of rich nations in providing child care to young parents.[16]

Next there was a break in the panels for a Q&A on *Donald vs. Democracy* between moderator Mark Green and Representative Jamie Raskin, former professor of law and recently a leading member of the House Special Committee on January 6th. He is the author of *Unthinkable*.

When we're talking about defending democratic institutions and the democratic process, make sure that people understand that the heart of authoritarianism and autocracy is corruption. Which brings me to Donald Trump, who got into politics purely as a moneymaking and business-promotion opportunity. He was probably as shocked as anybody else when he actually won. Then he became the first president in our history to reject the idea of giving up more than 150 businesses around the world and several trademarks.

It is the fault of Democrats that we did not more aggressively pursue the Emoluments Clause violations. That was the source of his determination to stay in office at all costs, which led both to the Ukraine shakedown and then also to his attempts at a political coup and a violent insurrection against the Union. I mean, why was he so eager to stay in office? Was it because he had such important public service he wanted to render to the American people? I don't think so. Nor is it true of other autocrats, kleptocrats, and tyrants like Putin in Russia, Orbán in Hungary, and al-Sisi in Egypt.

They're moneymaking operations that convert government into an instrument of self-enrichment. So make sure that voters understand that, whatever our flaws as a party, we are the party of democracy and the one that uses the government as an instrument of the common good, and not of private self-enrichment.

Mark Green: If a candidate merely says "our democracy is failing," I find voters don't connect to that. That's a word that's highfalutin and abstract. Talk about how you can connect that issue to the personal needs of voters—e.g., if you don't have democracy then the oligarchs will cut their own taxes even more and big "fossil fool" donors will make sure that the air is more polluted.

Jamie Raskin: I think in precisely the way you just described it. There's a clear economic cost to society when you allow a billionaire like Trump, his family, and his corporations to dictate economic policy. If Trump justices have their way, they'd overturn the constitutional right to privacy—at least as it relates to abortion—and are aiming to create a corporate state without basic public regulation. The Supreme Court that dismantled *Roe v. Wade* in the *Dobbs* decision also tried to sabotage the ability of the EPA to regulate greenhouse gas emissions.

Mark Green: A lot of smart people—Jeff Greenfield, David Brooks, and David Axelrod—all initially opined that the January Sixth Committee has already failed, they won't reach a lot of people, and Trump voters won't change their mind. What do you think of those predictions months later?

Jamie Raskin: Yeah, there was this rather obnoxious reception to us, saying that it's already failed, it's "too partisan." But that's just Beltway harping and sniping. We're beyond that— we're literally in a struggle for the survival of not just our democracy and our people but also our planet, given the rising cost of climate violence. At the same time, we have to fight right-wing authoritarianism . . . Proud Boys, Oathkeepers, and local imitators. So, now is the time for every self-respecting pundit to get off the couch and to get into the struggle to defend democratic institutions.

I have found it very convenient to keep going back to the phrase "dangerous extremists," because it unifies what Alito and the gang have done on the Supreme Court with what the cowboys in the Oathkeepers have done, with what Roger Stone and Michael Flynn (we call them the Flynnstones) have done on the ground, and with Donald Trump's whole governing model. "Dangerous extremists" puts us where we need to be, which is in the moral center and the political center.

Mark Green: We're told that Trumpsters never change their minds. That's certainly true for most of them, but obviously we don't expect most Trump voters to vote for Democrats. But if only 5 percent of soft Trump voters and independent voters shift from their 2020 vote then a Democrat can win the Presidency by fourteen million votes, rather than seven million. So, after your January Sixth hearings and the Trump Court's radical rulings, can you yet detect any movement against his party? Or is it too early to tell?

Jamie Raskin: Well, we know that about 66 percent of the independents now reject the Big Lie and hold Trump accountable for what happened on January Sixth, which, of course, he is. I mean, imagine if Donald Trump had said, "You know what, I'm tired of all this. I'm just gonna retire to Mar-a-Lago and play golf," none of it would have happened. There was nobody else pushing it.

Many of those Trump voters were like Obama voters—we don't live in a society with a well-developed political and constitutional and moral ideology, so people float around and almost everybody is vulnerable to anti–status quo, antiestablishment appeals—so Obama gets in, and he got in on voters' reform impulse. But if you don't quickly crystallize that impulse into a hard-core policy program, then you're going to be the victim of that same reform impulse. . . .

Those are voters that we have to get to, and we need a strong, fighting Democratic party that will engage with people. The little part I've done to try to help on this has been with my Democracy Summer Project—which is getting college and high school kids to come out and learn about the history of social and political change in the country, to understand the history of the civilizing movements and where they fit in, and then give them some concrete political skills in terms of voter registration and conducting canvasses and online organizing. That's what we need to do—the *opposite* of a political party based on lies, propaganda, and disinformation is a political party based on education, and that's a much harder thing to accomplish. When people say, "You guys suck at messaging," I'd say "Okay, we can do better at messaging. We need more Mark Greens to help and more help like the speakers today." But it's a much tougher project to get people on the side of enlightenment and progress than on the side of hatred and scapegoating. You need to educate them.

Mark Green: Finally, you have a choice of answering either of two questions. First: What question would you like me to ask you? And second: Why do Democrats have such good policies—provably—but are so awful at punching back hard at Republican slogans? I won't name senators, but I can't remember one thing many have said in ten or twenty years. What are they doing? Why do so many Democrats appear to be weak tea, unlike say you or Elizabeth Warren? Where are the rest of them?

Jamie Raskin: I'll turn it around, and I'll collapse those two questions. You're absolutely right that most of us are not taking political rhetoric seriously, which is a huge mistake. So when people say to you: "How come the Democrats can't get their messaging together? What's the message?" What is your answer to that? I would agree that many of them are just trying to survive, instead of trying to build a winning program that will sweep the country.[17]

DONALD vs. DEMOCRACY NOTES

- Trump's lava of lies keep coming—one supporter said, "I can't say that a word he says is true but I trust him"— either because Trumpers (a) like his middle-finger personality (30,000 reportedly turned out for Bonnie and Clyde's funeral) or (b) are credulous dupes who root for him like Philly fans for their home team. Also, "Humans are hardwired to believe what they are told by other humans, who they perceive to be like themselves" (Katherine Dykstra in *New York Times Book Review*). Hence the success of Ponzi schemes and street-corner three-card monte.

- For one twenty-four-hour period—January 6th to 7th, 2021—Senator McConnell thought that Trump would and should be held accountable for the crimes and violence on that day. "We have a criminal justice system in this country. President Trump is still liable for everything he did while in office." Then McConnell fell silent for eighteen months about Trump's culpability.

- Federal District Court Judge David Carter in a civil suit involving Trump: "Dr. Eastman and President Trump launched a campaign to overturn a democratic election. An action unprecedented in American history. . . . It was a coup in search of a legal theory."

- Dick Cheney on Donald Trump: "In our nation's 246-year history there has never been an individual who is a greater threat to our Republic than Donald Trump. He is a coward. A real man wouldn't lie to his supporters. He lost his election. And he lost big. I know it, he knows it, and deep down, I think most Republicans know it."

- Trump's natural autocratic impulses only hardened when he was not held accountable for his actions (a) in the first impeachment trial concerning his "perfect" phone call trying to extort Zelenskyy into investigating the Bidens (thanks to a smoke machine named Bill Barr) and (b) in his second impeachment trial for his role in inspiring the attack by his supporters on the Capitol seeking to stop Vice President Pence's certification of the 2020 electoral count.

- Later came the Department of Justice's raid of his country club estate for possession of classified materials endangering national security. The question now hovers around the 2022 midterm elections: Is only Donald Trump above the law? . . . Do we believe in the rule of law or the law of rule?

- Books by former allies nearly uniformly belittle Trump (okay, not counting Jared, at least so far). Appointees such as Esper, Barr, Omarosa, Bolton, Michael Cohen, Fiona Hill, Col. Vindman, and Deborah Birx condemned him in their memoirs—also, Mattis, Mulvaney, Tillerson, and Barr are now openly hostile. Most recently, his own ex-counsel, Ty Cobb, called him a "deeply wounded narcissist [who] acted in a criminal manner" and who should be "barred from future office." *His own lawyer.*

Were there any similar tell-alls by those around Obama or Clinton? No. Why not?

Trump's Lifetime of Lawlessness and Scandal:

HUD won cases against him in 1973 for racist policies excluding Black tenants in his company's rental housing. In civil cases brought by the New York attorney general years later, he was personally fined $25 million for fraud against students in Trump "University" and another $25 million for violating the NY Philanthropies Law with his Trump Foundation—leading the attorney general to conclude that the latter was "little more than a checkbook to serve Mr. Trump's political and business interests [in a] shocking pattern of illegality." The incorrigible Trump was also investigated for fraud by the attorney general and Manhattan district attorney. The New York Supreme Court ruled in favor of the attorney general finding that Mr. Trump engaged in a conspiracy with top executives at his company to deceive banks and insurers about the size of his wealth and the true value his of his properties. The court ordered Mr. Trump and the Trump organization to pay more than $450 million in total, which represents $363.8 million in disgorgement and pre-judgment interest. In a separate case, Manhattan District Attorney Alvin Bragg is prosecuting Mr. Trump for falsifying business records in a scheme to conceal a payment to an adult film star.

Trump team lost sixty of sixty-one cases arguing the 2020 election was stolen from him. Wrote one judge, "A president is not a king" (Appeals Court Judge Ketanji Brown Jackson!). As his former national security advisor John Bolton has said, "For Donald Trump, obstruction of justice was a way of life."

Spurred a violent attempt to overthrow the US government.

His misinformation and incompetence about COVID cost several hundred thousand lives, according to Dr. Deborah Birx.

CREW (Committee for Responsibility in Washington) has identified forty-eight likely crimes he committed as president ("he's a walking crime scene").

Was "Individual–1" in payoffs to porn star Stormy Daniels (he wrote $130,000 in checks for her while *in his White House office*) that sent his lawyer Michael Cohen to jail.

He used his pardon power repeatedly not for mercy but for donors and cronies.

Told generals he wanted them to be as loyal to him as Hitler's generals were.

The first . . . time that Trump was deposed under oath as president, he pleaded the Fifth 440 times; Hillary testified before a House Committee under oath in public for eleven hours on Benghazi . . . and answered every question.

Told 34,000 plus lies or falsehoods—or twenty-two a day by his last year in office, according to the *Washington Post* fact-checker. That's a lot, right? Is there another human being in the world who's lied an average of twenty-two times a day for a year?

When asked about possible Hatch Act violations by his White House staff, he said, "And who decides on Hatch Act penalties—me. Do what you want."

When informed that his suggestion to border patrol agents was illegal, Trump told them not to worry because he'd "pardon them."

There is the emoluments scandal of America's first for-profit presidency. CREW has listed over three thousand conflicts of interests in his term in office, including his middle finger to the Hatch Act prohibition on using government resources for political purposes, as when he commandeered the White House lawn for his RNC Convention speech.

His stolen confidential files from the White House are currently being criminally investigated, including ones with nuclear secrets (according to the *Washington Post*).

Ex–US Attorney Geoffrey Berman reports in his new book, *Hold the Line*, that AG Barr "put in people to do his bidding by targeting Trump's enemies [Clinton, Kerry, Craig] and helping Trump's pals [Flynn, Stone, Manafort]. It was a disgrace." . . . in what will likely go down as the greatest scandal in the Department's history, a multiple of what Mitchell and Kleindienst did.

After some sixty women accused him of abusive conduct—one alleging rape—he simply called them "all horrible, horrible liars."

George Conway: "Sooner or later if you're behaving illegally, it catches up to you."

Trumpian Violence:
Trump incited and later defended a violent mob that attacked the Capitol which led to five deaths and 139 injuries to Capitol Police.

When Bill O'Reilly asked whether Putin was "a killer," Trump replied, "We got a lot of killers—what, you think our country's so innocent?"

During the George Floyd protests in the summer of 2021, he said "when the looting starts, the shooting starts." After suggesting the imposition of martial law, he seriously asked Defense Secretary Esper, "Well, can you at least shoot them in the legs?"

Whenever someone criticizes or questions Trump publicly—like Cassidy Hutchinson before the January Sixth Committee or the judge who issued the warrant for the FBI search at Mar-a-Lago—they're inundated with threats of violence by the MAGA Mob.

Greg Sargent: "In late August, 2022, Trump shared an article comparing the FBI to the 'gestapo' while citing the shootout at Ruby Ridge. That was a key radicalizing event for Oklahoma City bomber Timothy McVeigh. Worse, Trump propagandists are now using similar martyrdom tropes."

Trump's silence over nearly six years on hate speech is taken as a permission slip for violence, anti-Semitism, and racism.

Atlantic Magazine: "The new era of political violence is here. The danger is not a Civil War but individual Americans of deep resentments and delusion" who believe in what they call "our Second Amendment rights."

President Biden, on the other hand, repeatedly condemns violence and hate speech. His "United We Stand" summit against political violence planned for this fall is an excellent way to try to un-normalize threats, which FBI officials worry is reaching a level of chatter akin to that preceding the 1995 Oklahoma City bombing.[18]

The next panel was "Rhetoric and Debate" starting with Mark Green's "War of the Words: Big Government Republicans Want to Destroy Our Freedom and Democracy." Mark Green has written or cowritten twenty-six books, including *Losing Our Democracy.*

Is rhetoric passé?

Traditional media consider the economy, abortion, crime, and immigration as key 2022 variables. Can Democrats still find messages that elevate the possible death of a working Democracy—access to voting, majority rules, rule of law, transfer of power—to become a tiebreaker in a tight election?

Those who discount political slogans as a sideshow have overlooked "The Rail Splitter," "Blood and Soil" in 1920s Germany, "I Like Ike," Reagan's "Morning in America," and of course MAKE AMERICA GREAT AGAIN—all provided a strategic lens to focus target audiences.

As the clash between democracy and despotism hurtles toward November, American politics now has become a contest between governing Democrats trying to enact policies for families and GOP insurgents running on faux populism to blur their radicalism. Trump Republicans largely just rotate loaded culture-war words—"woke, cancel, fake news, socialist, trans, open borders, critical race theory"—in order to slyly scratch the itch of anxious white voters and to villainize Democrats. (Earlier iterations of manufactured threats to panic tribalists included death taxes, death panels, war on Xmas, migrant caravans, Dr. Seuss—the opportunities to spread hysteria are nearly endless given the ability of social media to trigger the confirmation biases of the GOP base.)

Yet such language has indeed managed to steer much of the national conversation due to voters with five-second attention spans, smash-mouths at Fox and talk radio, as well as the rhetorical reality that hate can attract more eyeballs than positive policy. Adding to the problem has been the reluctance of above-the-fray Democrats to return fire. "Democrats Deliver . . . For the People . . . Build Back Better" were nice homilies but drowned out by far-right polemicists. . . .

In this Age of Rage, Democrats need more muscular language to contrast the values, views, and ethics of the two major parties. President Biden did launch a strong counterattack with his "Democracy" speech in Philadelphia in early September. While that alone won't sway any significant number of Trump cultists, the goal is more modest—if even 5 percent of Independents, soft-Republicans, and nonvoters understand that extremism isn't patriotism, then a seven million-vote win in 2020 will grow into a twelve million margin by 2024 and make any attempt to sabotage democracy appear treasonous.

Early evidence—Democratic successes in six of six by-elections since 2020 and the 60 percent Kansas vote for reproductive choice—hint that may be happening. Whether Democrats can continue their momentum will depend on their willingness to stick to three strategies—stay on offense, keep tattooing an unstable Trump on the back of Republicans, and show how anti-majoritarian rules—e.g., about dark corporate money, gerrymandering, and the filibuster—have consequences, like screwing millions of workers out of a higher minimum wage.

- **Contrast I:** *"Mainstream, Not Extreme."* Most voters know at some inchoate level that a party now dominated by theocrats, corporatists, and white nationalists is fundamentally different from one led by Joe Biden and Nancy Pelosi.

  But simply attacking "extremists" may fall short since the MAGA playbook will simply find some hyperbolic reference as a flimsy rebuttal—what about AOC and that guy who considered killing Justice Kavanaugh? Or they will pout that calling them "extremists" is like Hillary implying that all Republicans are "deplorable."

  No, not all Republicans, but many. Here are the receipts:

  Team Trump tried to violently overthrow our constitutional democracy by stopping the peaceful transfer of power; promised, if reelected, to pardon those convicted of Insurrection-connected crimes; misled the public early in the COVID pandemic destroying tens of thousands of lives; openly conspire to rig the next election; want to criminalize all abortions; enforce new state laws making it harder for minorities to vote; invoke the parlance of war to inflame MAGA mobs who then threaten local officials; and separated thousands of children at the border from their asylum-seeking parents without due process of law or any tracking system to later unite them.

  This already malevolent list only grows as the news and a slew of books (except Jared's) invariably (a) further incriminate—never exonerate—the ex-president and (b) GOP presidential contenders continue their near-gravitational race-to-the-bottom to see who can out-incite the Far Fright.

According to multiple polls, some half of registered Republicans doubt Obama is an American, associate pedophilia with the Democratic Party, and believe that white people suffer more discrimination than Black people . . . while 60–70 percent embrace The Big Lie that Biden stole the 2020 election. This QAnon-level insanity provides an array of material for powerful messages: e.g., *Big Brother Republicans are Dangerous Extremists*.

- **Contrast II:** *Whose Side Are You On?* Since at least the robber-baron era, Republicans exploit patriotic poetry during campaigns ("the Exceptional Nation") and then prosaically deliver lower taxes and deregulation to their wealthy donors once in office. But events such as January 6th and the *Dobbs* decision put Democrats in a position to win the age-old election question—*Whose Side Are You On?*

Look at the history of social progress from FDR to Biden *opposed by Republicans*: Social Security, Medicare, Medicaid, labor laws, Affordable Care Act, Americans with Disabilities Act, all civil rights laws, environmental/consumer protections and agencies, the new infrastructure law and Inflation Reduction Act. Imagine America without them.

Why wouldn't proud Democrats daily compare that history of delivery to the 2022 plan of Sen. Rick Scott, the head of the National Senate Campaign Committee, to sunset and risk repealing the social safety net? Democrats can now provide Scott's party with a slogan they can run against: *"Let's Make America 1922 Again."*

- **Contrast III:** *"The Party of Corruption."* Despite a long run as the party of "law and order," today's GOP is compromised by violent militants and lawless leaders. When the majority of a party in polls call the January 6th mob "Patriots" and its leaders warn of "riots in the streets" if Trump is charged, it should be impossible to pose as sentries of safety.

  Worse, the far right so often talk up a "coming civil war" within the context of their "Second Amendment Rights" that they appear indifferent to the impact their incendiary words have on millions of armed and unstable followers, such as the gunman who attacked an FBI office in Cincinnati after Trump called them "thugs." The unwillingness of Republican officials to condemn violence can only be seen as coaxing more of it. And any organization that opposes bans on AR-15s, the weapon of choice for slaughtering children, can effectively be called "soft on crime."

  Indeed, there's so much illegality in TrumpLand (the Center for Responsibility and Ethics in Washington estimates that Trump committed fifty-five crimes in office) that perpetrators ironically benefit from scandal fatigue as frequency normalizes corruption. When one law or norm appears to be broken, Trumpers can always conjure up some excuse for *that* ("hoax, witch hunt . . . Fake News, only joking". . . whatever).

  But explaining away any single scandal ignores how MAGA's whole is greater than the sum of their parts. Trump himself is now the subject of at least six criminal probes, surely a record for an ex-leader in a Western democracy.

Politifact reports there were 142 people indicted over eighteen years in the Nixon, Reagan, and Trump administrations; in the twenty years under Carter, Clinton, and Obama, there were only three. One hundred forty-two versus three. That math overpowers "Where's Hunter's laptop?"

Recall when a few "influence peddlers" in 1948 and the gift of a vicuna coat to Ike aide Sherman Adams in 1956 made corruption a big issue in both those election years. From the vantage point of 2022, to quote Dustin Hoffman in *Wag the Dog,* "That was *nothing.*"

Since Sen. Joe McCarthy gleefully called the Democrat Party the "Party of Treason" when it wasn't, it should be kosher to call today's GOP the "Party of Corruption," which it is.

- **Contrast IV:** *Freedom or Fascism?* Anat Shenker-Osario of ASO Communications has attracted much notice for showing how the GOP embraces the language of freedom while trying to ban abortions, books, masks, transgender kids, marriage equality, and (some) voters. Leading Democrats like Speaker Pelosi, Governor Gavin Newsom, and Pat Ryan, the newly elected member from upstate New York, have all embraced this winning formula.

It used to be seen as an epithet to call the GOP "fascists" (or "semi-fascists" in Biden's telling). But if their unapologetic assaults on freedom and democracy are not an American version of fascism—by a party forever calling Democrats "communists" and "socialists"—what would be?

To take one example, "critical race theory"—which is taught in zero grade schools—should lead Democrats to reply: "Stop exploiting hatred. Parents want educators choosing books, not politicians banning them."

- **Contrast V:** *50 Percent More Economic Growth.* Worldwide inflation is high (due largely to the pandemic, Putin's war, and market power). Yet Democrats also deserve polemical blame for allowing Republicans to be seen as better on the economy by 14 points in a recent NYTimes/Siena poll.

  If you add up economic growth for every president since 1961, it rose *50 percent faster under Democratic administrations*. Trump and Bush 43 each bequeathed Americans deep recessions that cost trillions of dollars and millions of jobs. According to analyst Simon Rosenberg, 96 percent of all the jobs created since 1989 occurred during the eighteen years of Democratic presidents (Clinton, Obama, Biden) rather than the sixteen years of the Bushes + Trump. Biden's economy has returned to pre-pandemic employment levels.

  We're reminded of Jon Lovitz on *SNL* who, in the role of Michael Dukakis watching George H. W. Bush stumble through a debate, thinks to himself, "How am I losing to this guy?" Today, Lovitz-Dukakis could campaign on *"Vote yourself a pay raise."*

- **Big Lies:** Whenever a Democrat says, "Trump lies," skeptical voters reply, "Well, they all lie." Which may be true. What's a unicorn, however, is an ex-president who nearly *always* lies (as Steve Bannon has privately marveled) while his political enablers silently squirm.

  Again, quantity counts. Never before in our history has a president made 34,000 plus lies/falsehoods in one term (or twenty-two times *a day* in 2020), as the *Washington Post* has documented, or claimed he won an election he lost by seventy-four electors. Or pretended that "voter fraud" cost Trump key states when scores of judges and his own attorney general say otherwise, not to mention that nearly all voter impersonation cases this election cycle were committed by **Republicans.** *A Democracy relying on a minimum of mutual trust cannot survive a Pinocchio Party.*

- **Trump is a poisoned chalice:** At every opportunity, Democrats ought to hang Trump around the neck of all GOP opponents. They may protest "but he's not on the ballot," except he is the top dog insisting on [and receiving] fealty in a party they chose to run in.

Democrats associated the disgraced Nixon with all Republican candidates on the 1974 ballot, winning forty-nine House seats. It would be political malpractice if Democrats don't make them now pay for their active or silent embrace of a politician who two recent national polls (NBC and Marquette) show has fallen to his lowest popularity since leaving office—34 percent. Or ten points below Biden, who's invariably called "unpopular" in the national media due to his numbers. Looks like being a one-man crime wave is not a political plus.

The elections of 2022 and 2024 will turn on substance *and* slogans. A party not believing in fair elections, the rule of law, climate violence, and the science of vaccines cannot be trusted to govern a modern society.

Democracy is priceless . . . and on the ballot this Fall.[19]

Jim Hightower, one of the great speakers for progressive policies of the past two generations, grew up in Texas and knows how to talk to all folk but especially rural Americans. He was elected Secretary of Agriculture twice by Texans and is the editor of the popular monthly Newsletter, *Hightower Lowdown*, now available on Substack.[20] Hightower's presentation was titled "How to Talk Like a Populist":

My overall suggestion for Democrats, rhetorically speaking, is that you not try to memorize the phrases and the language and the stories you're hearing today. Instead, take the essence of them, then make the words your own. Oscar Wilde said, "Be yourself—everyone else is already taken."

It's you that the voters want to hear from, and it's only you that will create the legitimacy behind the message you're trying to deliver to folks. With that core premise, here are a couple of pointers to help you deliver a strong democratic message.

First of all, humor is the politician's very best friend—especially self-deprecating humor—it's the key to unlocking the audience's mind. Use whatever humor you have—it can be huge humor, it can be very subtle humor, it doesn't matter. Whatever kind of humor, you've got to turn that little sucker loose every time that you speak. And I'm not talking about telling jokes, but adding memorable punctuation points to the message that you're delivering.

For example, if you're talking about inequality, you can say a briefcase full of statistics—and too often Democrats do—and/or use all sorts of experts. But that can be overdone. You could use some of that—Bernie Sanders, for example, did it well for the most part. Sanders pointed out that there are three American billionaires who have more wealth than half of all Americans combined—that's a powerful point. Then you can add that Republicans promised that Trump's trillion dollar tax cut would benefit everybody—in effect, "Everybody was gonna get a seven-course meal." Well yours and mine turned out to be a possum and a six-pack. That says it about as well as it's gonna be said, and more memorable than any number of statistics we could cite.

Humor lets us say strong things that sting better than vitriol can. My friend Molly Ivins once described a member of Congress from Fort Worth, who was particularly stupid, and she could have gone on about that. But instead, she said, "If he gets one digit dumber we're gonna have to start watering him twice a day." Nice. Mark Twain once referred to a fella who he had no appreciation for at all who had died. Said Twain, "I was not able to go to the funeral, but I did approve of it." That nailed the guy about as well as it possibly could.

Now, my second point is to *be Democrats*. Not pusillanimous Democrats. Don't hold back—if you believe in the Democratic message then, by God, speak it! That's what people wanna hear. They're not gonna agree with every one of your points, but they'll at least figure, "Well, the guy or woman has got some integrity to be able to say what it is that they are thinking."

People are ready for genuine Democrats . . . and don't assume that rural and red state voters are all just a bunch of rubes and right-wing nutballs. In my first campaign for office here in the state of Texas, I was campaigning over in Tyler, an old bastion of the Southern Confederacy period in our state. I went to a very ornate courthouse to visit a judge who I was told was "very very conservative, so don't dump your whole load on him." Well, I go in, and sure enough, I try to pull back a little bit of my message. But I say for example, "George, I'm running on an issue about gas utilities, and how they're very high and they're really squeezing consumers and squeezing businesses, etc." And then, in a compromise conclusion, I said, "Judge I really just think that they're not quite being fair with us."

The judge then suddenly lunges forward at me right in my face. And he said, "Hightower, in your private moments wouldn't you say they're fucking us?" "Well, yes, sir, I would." And I did, and I will do it some more, because people who might be called *conservative* are not conservative when we talk about justice, when we talk about equality, and when we talk about power in our society.

The polls show this. Celinda Lake and Mike Lux with the Consortium recently did an important survey of rural voters, and George Goehl with People's Action, too, talked to them about what they thought really mattered. And the most common response they all get from voters who have switched from Obama to Trump is: "Where are the Democrats? Why aren't they on our side? Why aren't they standing with us against these monopolies? Why didn't Joe Biden go to one of those meatpacking factories in the crisis that they were facing during the COVID period. Where the hell are the Democrats?"

And you can also see it from the initiatives that are passed in our country. That's as big a symbol of what voters are really thinking as we can have—better than polls, because initiative after initiative on minimum wage, on monopoly power, on Mother Nature itself, overwhelmingly favor the Democratic position. Big-time. I've been a supporter of the rights of nature—that nature itself should have a right, the lake, the river, the trees, the forest, ought to have a right to legal action, to live and to sustain.

People may say, "Now that seems like a kind of environmentalist concept, isn't it, Hightower?" Well, the people of Orlando, Florida, put it up to a vote. They had an initiative there to give the rights of nature to water systems in their area, and even the supporters didn't think that it would carry and it was going to just be an educational sort of process. But in fact, 87 percent of the people of that county, including Disney World, voted for this rights of nature initiative, and that includes beaucoup Republicans and independents.

We don't have to fear the people—we have to get with the people. And, in fact, if possible, get out in front of them. But at least follow them when they're taking these powerful positions. People *are* looking for FDR-style Democrats to stand up to the corporate elites and the CEOs, the powers that be who are knocking down the middle class, who are holding down the poor, who are tearing down our democratic rights in this society.

And when I say "the powers that be," here's something to consider in your messaging: *say who they are.* I'm talking about what I call the six Bs: the bosses, the bankers, the billionaires, the big shots, bastards, and bullshitters who are running roughshod over us. These are people who have no concept, and they're as confused as goats on Astroturf when it comes to actually standing for the principles of America, including that notion that we're all in this together.

When I say all the people, I mean *all*. We should always have a message of unity. You don't have to draw out every ethnic group in society, but just make the point that we're all in this together. Jesse Jackson was powerful on this. I was with him in Wisconsin in his 1988 presidential race when he talked to two thousand farmers on a farm in the northern part of Wisconsin. Jesse made the point that the Wisconsin farmers who were fighting monopoly power squeezing them have the same interests as the poor people across the country who are trying to be able to afford the food.

Here's how he put it: "We might not have all come over on the same boat, but we're in the same boat now." That was a powerful political reality, and that is a Democratic powerful political reality. There are many more of these phrases and stories. But remember the stories. Don't forget your Bible and don't forget your Woody Guthrie. Don't forget the cultural icons that spoke with stories that related to people. The stories you tell are the message itself.[21]

Next was an outlier—a political consulting firm—ASO Communications that develops messaging for progressive campaigns and was founded by Anat Shenker-Osorio.

This will be midterm messaging guidance based upon reams and reams of different studies, with all sorts of different folks that I will highlight in my slide deck.

When debating messaging, and in particular electoral messaging, we get told that there is this perennial debate between persuasion and mobilization—are you focusing on the swing voter or are you focusing on the base? This is a false binary. If your words don't spread, they don't work. And so by definition, if the middle does not hear your message, it does not persuade them—something no one heard couldn't possibly persuade them.

We need to remember that a message is like a baton that needs to be passed from person to person to person, and if it gets dropped anywhere along the way it is by definition not persuasive. That is why effective messaging is built out of a credible theory of change and a recognition that it's really hard to break a signal through the noise. And to get people to actually listen to what you're saying.

Our messages must first engage our base. You need to make sure that the choir wants to sing from the songbook you're handing them, and if you speak the language of milquetoast, then your base won't carry your message and then the middle isn't even gonna hear it. Of course there's not enough of our base to win—we need to also persuade the conflicted. To do that, you need to actually stand for something, have something to say, and create a polarity.

That's why effective messages are actually gonna turn some people off, because there are people who fundamentally disagree with us. Happily, they are the minority. If the opposition likes what you're saying, what are you saying? You're either producing blandly ineffective milquetoast, or you are accidentally parroting the tropes of your opposition, which we do all the time.

The first rule of messaging is: say what you're for, say what you're for, say what you're for. I like to joke that if the Left had written the story of David, it would be a biography of Goliath because we like to talk about our opposition all the time, or send a message that's essentially some permutation of, "We're the losing team. We lose a lot. We've lost recently. You should join us." Or, "Boy have I got a problem for you." Well, it turns out that the average voter does not want your problem.

At the same time, we need to remember that politics isn't a game of solitaire. Our voters don't just hear from us, unfortunately, they hear from the unrelenting scapegoating and race-baiting wedge issues of the other side. Race-neutral isn't a thing—if you choose to be silent about race, the debate about race does not go away, because the other side is pumping it out twenty-four hours a day.

The same is true of attacks on trans youth, as with other kinds of attacks on gender. They will always sing from the same songbook—because they only have one thing to say, which is to make voters blame some imagined "other" for their ills—to escape from the fact that they are taking out of our pockets and making life difficult for all of us. This is simple divide-and-conquer, the oldest trick in the book. And so when we try to counter that by saying nothing at all, what our voters still hear is this unrelenting race-baiting with no rejoinder.

Over years of testing, we've found that messages that work have a particular architecture. They begin with saying what we're for. Then they get into the problem, not as the opening salvo but rather as the second point. And they talk about those villains who deliberately divide us in order to rule for the wealthiest few. That ties together specific racialized harms with the class-economic argument that many people are feeling. They then emphasize unity and collective action to solve the problem with some sort of call to action—a vision that people want to get behind.

I'll finish up by describing what moves people both on vote[r] choice and on various mobilization metrics. The first is that we have to tell a story and cast this election as a clear crossroads between two opposing forces. On the one hand you have either MAGA Republicans or Trump Republicans—there are advantages and disadvantages to using each term—who want to take us backward by overturning the will of the people, controlling our lives, and ruling for the wealthy few. And on the other side you have the protagonist: the voters. Remember that voting isn't a belief, it's a behavior. It's a thing that we need people to do.

And because of the despair and the despondency of our voters—and the dangers that they will defect, not to the other side but rather to the couch—we need to make them the heroes of our story and remind them how, through collective action of voting in 2018 and 2020, we were able to defeat Trump, and how we will do the same with Trumpism in this election.

What we're seeing right now is that among all the ads we tested, ads that either are about or reference *Roe*, are the most persuasive, hands down. We are in a persuasion window around *Roe*, so tying it to other issues is activating to our voters and is also persuasive. Freedom is another incredibly effective frame to connect across issues. It's a way both to make our demands and to call out the opposition . . . because freedom is a core American value. This is true in the American Values Survey, it's true from Gallup and Pew. Across time, when Americans are asked what value you most closely associate with this country, "freedom" is number one across races, ages, geographies, etc.

We cannot afford to let the right wing pretend that they can claim freedom as their idea. Freedom has been integral to our progressive narrative and to our victories—from the Freedom Rides to the Freedom Summer to FDR's Four Freedoms to the freedom to marry—that rhetorical shift from the "right to marry" to the "freedom to marry" was a very deliberate choice. In particular, we see in testing that using "freedoms" in the plural is more progressive than the singular "freedom."

So how do you do this? It opens with the shared value: "Americans value our freedoms," then names the villains second: "But Trump Republicans want to take away freedom and rule only for the wealthy few, from freedom to decide if and when we grow our families"—that incorporates abortion, *Roe*, references to freedom to vote, to freedom from gun violence—"Trump Republicans want to overturn the will of the people and block the policies we favor, just as we turned out record numbers." This is reminding voters of their agency, "Americans must join together across race, place, and party to remove them from power, or to vote for us." Obviously you make this modular to your own purpose.

Contrasting voters' concerns, our underlying values, and just our basic needs—kitchen-table stuff—demonstrates to our voters what's at stake in a way that's both persuasive and mobilizing. We made an ad that does that: "What side are you on? Americans who believe liberty and justice are for all? Or traitors inciting violence against our country and trying to take away our freedoms? Which side are you on? We work for a living and care for our

families, while the Trump Republicans would block everything
our families need. This November, it's time to show which side
you're on. Vote for Democrats."

And then, finally, when you are talking about abortion, you
want to engender empathy and create agency. It is a useful tool
to activate loss aversion in people—that's why we talk about how
"they are taking away our freedoms. They are taking away this
and taking away that." Loss aversion is very motivating for people, but you need to be careful that you don't go all the way
into "it's over. You're going to be bleeding out on a table," or,
"They've done it. They've taken it away," because remember
there are three people running in every race: you, your opposition, and "stay at home," which has the home-team advantage
because people are already home.

You need to actually motivate people toward feeling like their
participation could create change. And what we find is that airing
personal stories and raising up the *specter* of this projected future
loss is effective. We've made one more ad that does that, and
we call it "Someone You Love": "Someone you love may struggle with a pregnancy. A pregnancy they longed for that couldn't
survive. That would endanger providing for the children they
already have. That comes too soon after giving birth. That they
were too sick to carry. That wasn't right for them. Someone you
love might need an abortion. Someday you can help ensure that
when the day comes, they can get the care they need. Support
someone you love."[22]

Then we moved on to Bill Hillsman on "Memorable Advertising,"
Founder of North Woods Advertising in Minnesota. He has

won 150 "Pollies" (Oscars for ads) and is the author of *Run the Other Way*. His winning underdog candidates included Senator Paul Wellstone and Governor Jesse Ventura.

I'm going to talk first about how you actually craft a good ad or evaluate whether the ad is any good, then I'll talk about how to make media plans, and maybe save money on them.

When you really think about it, any political communication needs to do three things. First: it's got to get the attention of the audience. Second: you have to provide the information they need to persuade them. And third: you want to produce some type of an emotional response so they'll be motivated to go vote. If there's one thing I've been convinced of in all these years in politics, it's that most political communications people think voting is a logical act. It's not. You don't *really* reason somebody into voting the way you want. Voting is an emotional act, which is something that Republicans understand much better than Democrats do. That's why they've been able to sell this big lie to enough people to put Democrats on the defensive and make Democrats respond to Republican framing of the issues rather than set their own agenda.

It's very important in the 2022 elections for Democrats to confront their opponents. Make them uncomfortable. Put them on the defensive. Every Republican candidate should have to answer whether or not Joe Biden is the duly-elected president of the United States. Every Republican candidate should have to answer for the thousands of MAGA people who stormed the Capitol. Don't miss an opportunity to remind voters that, in fact, Joe Biden won the election by seven million votes—that's pretty much a landslide.

When it comes to targeting your audience, remember that there's more of us than there are of MAGA Republicans—quite a lot more as a matter of fact. And especially if you're involved in a close election, remember that most swing voters, especially self-identified independent voters, are the people [who] decide every close election. They deserted Donald Trump and the Republicans in droves in 2020. So the more you can tie your Republican opponent to Donald Trump and the attack on the Capitol, the more these swing voters are going to come your way.

Republicans are going to want to talk about inflation and crime in this fall's election. The truth is that both of these are aftereffects of a worldwide disease. Pandemic inflation is a function of supply and demand, and when supply chains are disrupted, there's a shortage of goods. Then combine that with immense worker shortages and absenteeism caused by COVID, and you get major price hikes for less-available goods and services. This is not brain surgery.

Worker shortages result in more criminal behavior as well, because there are fewer patrols on the street, and there's a criminal justice system that's delayed by or shut down by COVID. So the Democrats kind of blew their chance in late 2021 and early 2022 to anticipate these attacks and frame that message that you can't control inflation or crime until you control COVID. Doing this successfully would have really altered public perception going into this fall's elections. But this is where we are.

So what are we going to do? I agree with previous speakers who said that Democrats should talk about their accomplishments, especially the ones that affect people's day-to-day costs of living. Hopefully, there'll be a prescription drug plan passed before the November elections [a month later, there was] that Democrats can merchandise. Remember, one of the reasons that Obama won reelection in 2012 was that Americans, regardless of their party identification, really liked his healthcare plan—that alone was able to overcome many other issues and problems they might have had with a potential Obama second term.

Republicans understand that fear can be a powerful emotional motivator, and we shouldn't be afraid to use it either. And it needs to be aimed at the swing voter audiences: independent voters, moderate Republicans, suburban women, and older lapsed Democratic voters, especially union members, who voted for Trump at least once, if not twice. The message has to be couched in what's traditionally seen as a Republican value: *personal freedom.*

So the fear that we want to talk about is not somebody breaking into your home, but rather the fear of these government intrusions into personal liberties—your right to take care of your own body, your right to vote, your right to marry and raise a family as you see fit, your right for your kids to have quality public education. When you really expose what Republicans are up to, swing voters who don't pay that much attention to politics are really shocked.

Here are some good guideposts to follow, whether creating communications for yourself or evaluating the work of consultants. Number one is: be direct. Number two is: know what the one point (and I do want to emphasize *one point*) that you want the audience to remember. Too many political ads and communications try to make five or ten different points in a limited time and space, and consequently they fail to make any of them.

Number three: use conversational language. A good political ad is not a speech and it's not a treatise, it should sound like a conversation. Know your audience. Think of one person in the particular group of voters that you're trying to persuade, think of what that person's daily life is like and what's important to them, and then write your communication directly to that one person.

Think about *benefits*, not features. Political ads are full of facts and figures and positions on issues and attacks on opponents, and these are all what we call an "advertising feature." None of them have very much to do with the voter's daily life. So make your communication about *benefits*—how is this person's life going to be improved by *voting you or your candidate* into office?

Then try to use something out of the ordinary to grab attention. It could be humor, it could be an emotional appeal, it could be a shocking statistic or a fact, and it should be aimed at swing voter audiences: independent voters, moderate Republicans, suburban women, and these older lapsed Democratic voters. You could also use a production effect—a sound effect, or a video effect—to grab people's attention. But remember, if you don't grab their attention right away, your message is doomed to fail from the start.

The final guideline is: argue from *the specific* to *the general*. We worked with Ralph Nader when he ran for president in 2000, and I couldn't believe every time I saw him speak in a local area— he started with some problem that was unique to that particular constituency of voters. So you want to talk about something specific that's going on in a voter's actual life, and then work your way out to how your election or your candidate's election can help solve that problem and make life better.

Here's a quick word about media plans and media buying. Everybody thinks media plans are science and math problems, but they're not. They're kind of an art. If you've done these things as long as I have, you realize that if you have experienced media buyers doing these things rather than just computers, they can overlay information about the audiences that you're trying to reach that computers just aren't really capable of. And when this is done effectively, it saves you money, and then you can use that money to do other things in the campaign like voter identification programs or get out the vote programs.

Nearly every mass-media plan that we've analyzed of late is spending much more than would be necessary if the media buy was worked harder by experts. Most of them are called programmatic buys, so consultants put a few basic spending goals into the computer and ideally the computer spits out what it determines to be the most cost-effective media plan. Yet we're seeing that these plans have ridiculous frequency levels that are ineffective and show commercials far, far more times than voters can stand. That makes the overall buy incredibly cost-*in*effective, but highly lucrative for the consultants—so that's why people are seeing ads repeated with frequency levels of twenty or twenty-five, or something like that, which to me is just nonsense. If you've got a commercial that works, it shouldn't take that many repetitions of the ad to get the point across.

I do have a specific example of a media plan that we looked at recently in Pennsylvania. There's a new communications company in Washington, D.C., called Victory Margins that I've been working with for the past couple of years. It focuses solely on reaching the swing voters in any given election. They brought me an analysis that they'd done on all the pro-Biden spending done in Pennsylvania in 2020.

The pro-Biden forces spent approximately double what Trump was spending in Pennsylvania in 2020. So if the ads and the media planning and buying had been effective, Biden should have beaten Trump by a lot, not by a little. As we looked at the data, it became clear to me that the most important imperative in the plan was to amass a common amount of gross rating points— or GRPs—which is just the shorthand term for media buyers. What this plan did in essence was very little skewing or balancing based on audience data intangibles among the various media markets. It had all the refinement of a meat cleaver when using a scalpel would have saved the campaigns and the donors tens of thousands, if not hundreds of thousands, of dollars.

Last, I like to make a strategic pitch for target audiences. The current fascination for the party and Democratic donors with only funding communications designed to expand and turn out the Democratic vote could turn into a long-term disaster. As mentioned, every close election is decided by swing voters, not base voters. Mainly, these are self-identified independent voters, but four years of President Donald Trump and its immediate aftermath have brought in this audience considerably. So in 2022, women voters, lapsed Democratic voters, suburban voters, moderate Republican voters are looking to go someplace else, and Democrats would make a serious mistake if they don't make a concerted effort in 2022 to win them over—if they're lost in 2022, I think they're going to be lost for the next two to four election cycles.[23]

RHETORIC & DEBATE NOTES

- Never use "climate change" (a pablum phrase invented by Frank Luntz) but rather "climate violence." Never use "extremists" when you can say "dangerous extremists" . . . which is far more evocative of abortion bans, gun massacres, and insurrection denialism.

- A Republican will oppose everything Biden proposes and then call him a "failed president" when many of his proposals are blocked by unanimous opposition from GOP members. "Don't confuse the victim for the culprit—the GOP is the 'Party of No.'"

- Presentation can be as, or more important than, content, especially given the default monotone when a candidate repeats a talking point the fiftieth time. Using genuinely emotive language or evocative imagery can make even standard talking points inspiring.

- Don't repeat a smear or falsehood in a response ("I don't want to defund the police"—unhelpfully spreads it).

- It's best in a debate to remain calm and confident. So avoid sophomoric eye-rolling or jaw-clenching. *But* if your opponent says something really really wrong/nutty, then be ready to pounce not more than one or two times in a debate and say a version of, "Are you kidding me? Seriously? You think voters are fools?" This will get viewers' attention and help drive the issue under discussion to become the news story post-debate.

- If a rival overuses "woke," call it out rather than be bludgeoned by it. "You invoke 'woke' like Joe McCarthy sneering about 'Communists'—you use it as a smear against anyone urging fair treatment for all by assuming the speaker's insincerity. I think that insulting people because of their race, orientation, or gender is wrong. You don't?"

- If you're repeatedly hectored or interrupted during a debate, one good response: "Sorry to speak while you're interrupting me. May I finish?" Also: Call your party the "Democracy Party"—which is better than "Democrat Party" and at the same time highlights the GOP's assault on our freedoms.

- "Stop Stealing Our Freedoms and Rights." The GOP is coming for your Social Security, your Medicare, your right to marry who you choose, your right to use contraceptives, your right to control your body (if you're a woman), and your right to participate in free and fair elections.

- Why be subtle if trying to make the GOP pay a price for Trump? "He's the worst traitor in US history since Benedict Arnold." His campaign DID coordinate with Russia in 2016 (according to a 1,000 page bipartisan report by the Senate Intelligence Committee); never criticized Putin in his term as president; stole classified documents when he left office; spurred the only assault on the U.S. Capitol to steal an election based on the Big Lie that he had won . . . and, in a first, put the life of his vice president in jeopardy. Need more evidence?[24]

The next panel covered three areas not often discussed together. As Cornel West has written: "Race Matters but So Does Class Matter."

Heather McGhee started the presentation. She is a past president of Demos, author of *The Sum of Us: What Racism Costs Everyone and How We Can Prosper Together* and chair of the Color of Change.

> I've spent twenty years working to address inequality in our economy and in our democracy, first from the think tank world, then advising campaigns and candidates, and then, about four years ago, I decided to leave what was in many ways my dream job—running Demos, an amazing think tank—in order to go out in the country. I spent three years on the road traveling from California to Mississippi to Maine and back again, multiple times, talking to ordinary people, talking to organizers, talking to people who had lost faith in politics.
>
> What I came back with was the basis for my book *The Sum of Us: What Racism Costs Everyone and How We Can Prosper Together*. My goal was to understand why it seems like we can't have nice things in America—I'll save you the four hundred pages, the answer is racism.
>
> Racism in our politics and in our policymaking is so pervasive and so undermines our sense of being in it together, that it imposes a cost for everyone. Now, this is a pretty radical idea to put forward—it runs contrary to the liberal orthodoxy to hear from a Black woman, who descends from enslaved people on both sides of my family, to say that racism isn't just a great thing for the people at the top of the racial hierarchy, but ultimately it is the weapon

that the plutocrats use to divide and to conquer. For if we ever were to have a broad multiracial working- and middle-class solidarity in this country, the billionaires would be on the run. And they know that. Which is why they have pumped an incredible amount of money into us-versus-them, zero-sum politics, the demonization of people of color for an economically anxious white audience, a 24/7 social media and cable news white nationalist ecosystem.

At its worst, it leads to things like January Sixth, the massacre in Buffalo, both of which were animated by the so-called Great Replacement Theory—the existential fear that people of color are replacing white Americans, and that America is for white people to begin with. So at worst it risks the entire project of democracy and becomes a trigger for political violence.

We all know that this country has had a civil war in its short life. But since then, it should be clear how racism is used in our politics and policymaking to undermine our ability to come together to win public justice and public goods. The kinds of racist stereotypes that, for example, would persuade a senator to refuse to renew the child tax credit because he's heard that people use it for drugs . . . which effectively killed the renewal. It's the racism that produces the demonization and stereotypes and biases that make us punch down in our society, and that cut the cord of empathy.

So what does that mean for candidates who are trying—by necessity and hopefully by their inclination—to create a multiracial, winning coalition? That means that we've got to speak about race and class not only in the same speech, not only in the same ad, but as inextricably connected. I want to give you a few examples.

There's a man now running for the Senate who is a former state legislator in Kentucky, named Charles Booker. He is, of course, an authentic son of the working class—that authenticity matters. But he also developed a message and a story that is explicitly trying to connect what he calls "the hood"—Black disinvested neighborhoods—to "the holler"—white disinvested neighborhoods. And by explicitly making the connections between the ills that face "the hood" and "the holler," he is calling for a bigger *Us*—an *Us* that includes everyone who struggles.

In his telling, the term *Them* in white audiences doesn't become people of color and immigrants, *Them* becomes the corrupt politicians and the billionaires who pay for them who are trying to pit us against one another. This is a turn that is frankly not always comfortable for white progressive politicians to take—i.e., to say that racism is bad for white people, too. What's interesting is that it's been people like Jesse Jackson in the Rainbow Coalition and Charles Booker who are really able to make that connection so clear. But I want to invite all of us who are trying to build a multiracial coalition to attack inequality, to release the stranglehold that the corporate power and the billionaires' greed have on our people and our planet.

We need to get smarter. There is *no* option to avoid talking about race, even if we do have the most populist economic message we possibly can (as Warren and Sanders and, of course, Ralph Nader did). In this day and age, when race is the ecosystem, it's the oxygen of politics, of people's neighborhoods, of people's anxieties, Black, white, and Brown, we have to have a story that includes how race fits into the country we are in and the one we want to be. Who's on your side? Who is the enemy? Who do we need to organize against? Who do we need to organize with? Who is to blame?

If we're not answering those questions in our political storytelling, then we're not actually telling stories. Anybody who has a child knows there's always a good guy and there's always a bad guy—and we need to not be afraid to fill in the answer of who that is. Because if we don't, a much louder and more coordinated right wing will make each other the answer to that question.

What does that mean in the context of some of our current political debates? I want to raise what I—if I were a candidate— would do if attacked on the idea that my book is critical race theory. If I were running for Congress right now, the RNC would be thrilled to be able to throw the critical race theory *ad hominem* at me. And here's how I would respond: first, we're a great country, and we are great enough to not be afraid of our own truth and our own history. Second of all, this is not Black history—this is all of our histories. Both the good and the bad. And over 80 percent of Americans believe that we need to teach the best parts of our history and the parts we never ever ever want to repeat.

Ultimately, we are a country that has, from the beginning of our history, had an organized force of concentrated money and concentrated power that has been willing to exploit human beings, to rip apart families, to pit us against one another for their own greed. That force was alive in the days of plantations, and it's alive today, and we need to be united against it.

Politicians are worried about what our children are learning at school but they should also learn how to spot those people who want to pit us against each other today. Our children need to learn empathy and civics to be great citizens. Yet most Republicans want to defund public schools in order to scare parents away from them.

Democrats should contrast that with our goal of equipping our children to live in the multiracial twenty-first century and in a global economy, and to understand that the most important things that matter in life are those things that we have to do together. And in the country that we're becoming, that includes what we must do across lines of race . . . which is nothing to be afraid of but rather something to cheer.

So what I just did briefly was to make sure that candidates explain that the enemy is not teachers trying to teach *Beloved* in high school but rather a right-wing cabal that wants to keep us divided from one another. That the enemy has always been afraid of integrated education. The enemy has always been afraid of public goods. Why? Because a government that's strong enough to help us meet our basic needs and have a shot of fulfilling our dreams is also a government that's strong enough to stop them from cheating on their taxes, poisoning our air and water, and destroying small businesses and small farms.

Usually left out of the talk about schools being "woke" but instead about politicians who should be making an economic argument and a public goods argument simultaneously, as we are making an argument about racism and depression of people of color. Answers need to always include "Each Other"—about "turning to one another." Paint a picture of an America where we solve big problems together, feel strong and courageous because we have each other's backs and can defeat the forces that want to keep us afraid of one another.[25]

Next came Rob Weissmann, president of *Public Citizen* and author, with Joan Claybrook, of *The Corporate Sabotage of America's Future And What We Can Do About It.*

Since it's impossible in my limited time to fully explain today's "War Against Democracy," let me stipulate this: Donald Trump and his allies have unleashed neo-fascist forces that are aiming to sabotage the very functioning of our electoral system, introducing electoral and political violence in ways that we really haven't previously seen in American history (excepting the Civil War). The core of the Republican party (not just the Trumpers) embraced a policy of voter suppression designed to exclude people of color—young people, in particular—and they have adopted an extremist gerrymandering agenda that is designed to rig districts to give them control of the Congress as well as state legislatures. Let's also stipulate that big money dominates elections among both parties, often determining who wins primaries, what candidates feel comfortable saying, and ultimately what they do as candidates.

To begin with, democracy is actually popular. Americans believe that we should have a democratic system, but there's one huge caveat: people like democracy and accountability, but they're not passionate about it as an abstract concept. Democracy reform lacks emotional appeal. But if you tie it to policies that people *do* care about, you can bridge that divide because people fundamentally understand that the whole system is broken due mostly to big-money dominance and political corruption. Now, if you tie that to issues they do care about—like drug price reform, education, expanding healthcare, raising the minimum wage—you have a winning package.

Foundationally, polling shows public sympathy for democratic norms. By large margins, people do oppose the Insurrection. In even greater numbers, they oppose the use of political violence. The work of the January Sixth Commission is extremely popular. There is pretty strong political support across the country for prosecuting Trump. *Safe and accessible elections* is a winning theme and phrase—the idea we want to ensure that every voice is heard. That speaks to a wide array of issues, but particularly the idea that state legislatures should not have the power to overturn election results, or have the final say in determining who won a contested election.

Assuring voting rights and prohibiting extreme gerrymandering are essential. They are included in the Freedom to Vote Act and John Lewis Voting Rights Advancement, both of which were put on hold when Manchin and Sinema refused to fix the filibuster. All that changes *if* Democrats hold or even expand their House and Senate majorities this fall.

Due to the Trump Court's evisceration of voting rights (see its judicial activism in *Shelby County*), essential reforms include imposing penalties for voter intimidation, providing funding for election administration, and shifting toward affirmatively making it easier to vote in the ways that were so successful in the context of the pandemic—with more early voting, more voting by mail, and the use of drop boxes.

On gerrymandering, the key is to move *away* from partisan control over redistricting and *toward* lodging redistricting authority in independent redistricting commissions. That's something you need federal legislation to do, since some states have reformed their redistricting procedures on their own, but at least half have not.

While those policies are all well-liked by the American people, there is one counter-narrative that works well for the Republicans, which is the idea of voter fraud. Voter fraud is a total fiction. Letting yourself get drawn into the argument over whether it's fiction or real is probably not a winner. You're better off *affirmatively* making the case for stopping states' anti-voter legislation—here you can see strong support in swing states for Congress to act and prevent states from making it more difficult to vote. There is comparable support in swing states for Congress to act to ensure that eligible voters are able to cast their ballots.

You can be very confident in talking about these popular policies—stopping voter intimidation, protecting local officials, supporting election audits, and so on. Some caveats: the traditional term of "voting rights" doesn't do as well across the political spectrum—the "Freedom to Vote Act" was named that way for a reason. In terms of "addressing voter suppression," we find that "voter suppression" is not the right term—"stopping anti-voter bills" is a winning formulation. You want to talk about "voters getting to choose their leaders, not leaders choosing their voters."

Let's conclude with the issue of money and politics. Here the core reform is to replace the big-money funding of elections with small-donor funding and public-matching money; then comes the disclosure of all outside money—ending dark money is super popular; overturning *Citizens United*, which is resonant and popular now. There's a lot of recent success with candidates running on the idea of rejecting corporate PAC contributions. According to a poll from Pew, nearly everybody thinks the system is corrupt, everybody thinks that big money dominates, everybody thinks corporations and the superrich have too much sway over elections and politics.

There's also overwhelming support on whether there should be limits on the amount that individuals or groups can spend on campaigns; unfortunately for now, however, the Supreme Court has ruled that to be flatly unconstitutional. As a workaround, the Freedom to Vote Act, which advocates small donors and public funding to help assure more competitive elections, is actually much more modest than what the American public wants—the public is willing to go *far* when it comes to clamping down on big money dominance of our politics.

The elements in that bill that push transparency (ending dark money) poll at between 90 and 94 percent support—you're talking really really high numbers when you're over 90 percent. One of my favorite counter statistics is that only 80 percent of people believe that the earth revolves around the sun. So when you get to 90 percent and higher, you have something that's really extraordinary.

Anything about stopping big money dominance of our elections resonates with people. There are conflicting views about whether "political corruption" is the right way to talk about this stuff, but there is no conflict in the polling on this. Surprisingly, just a basic simple formulation of preventing billionaires from buying our elections—people go for that, too.

But to close the deal electorally and substantively requires linking the democracy discussion to substantive comments—persuadables are more favorable to pro-democracy reforms that are tied directly to underlying policies that people care about. You talk about democracy and the need to address political corruption. You establish your bona fides with people as someone who gets it—that's actually one of the things that Trump was able to do in the "Through the Looking Glass" world in which we live. You talk about political corruption. You say you want to take it on. You offer meaningful solutions for doing it. You're establishing your credibility as someone who's on the side of people, and you're talking to them in ways that they care about. If you talk about taking on corporate power that blocks essential reforms at this nexus of big money dominance of our politics, you are reaching people in both their minds and their hearts.[26]

Following that, Ruth Ben-Ghiat addressed "The Authoritarian Template." A professor at New York University, she is the author of *Strongmen: Mussolini to the Present*.

I'm an historian of fascism and right-wing authoritarianism all the way up to Putin. When Trump came on the scene, I started looking at my country with great alarm, watching the same stuff happening that I studied abroad. And so I wrote *Strongmen: Mussolini to the Present* to warn Americans. I kind of predicted that Trump would not leave quietly, because authoritarian-minded people don't believe in the transfer of power, and leaving office is like psychological death for them. They're also afraid, of course, of prosecution.

Think about what Trump has managed to do as somebody coming from outside—he domesticated a major party and made it his own personal tool. January Sixth was like a kind of leader-cult rescue operation and why the congressional hearings are so very important.

The Republican Party has really become a kind of extremist entity. The *Washington Post* had a study showing that one in five GOP lawmakers at the state and local level have sympathy or affiliations with some kind of extremist beliefs or organizations. Some Proud Boys and Oath Keepers are running for office at the local level.

Unfortunately for us, Trump has the same personality as Mussolini and a lot of the other guys I study. The outcome is different at different periods, so it'd be silly for anyone to say Trump is Hitler. Yet at the same time, it's very important to recognize that authoritarians like Trump only have allegiance to themselves, and they use and discard everybody in their pursuit of *Me, Myself, and I*. So while it's unbelievable that Trump risked having his own vice president killed, *it's totally normal in the history of coups and inherent in the logic of coups.*

In my political newsletter Lucid on Substack, I interviewed Representative Swalwell—he emphasized that the essential question is, do you believe in violence or do you believe in the rule of law? The Insurrection showed that the party has embraced violence as a way of doing politics and as a way of solving problems. January Sixth was an attempt both to keep Trump and his people in power and to keep the "wrong people" like Kamala Harris out.

Trump has been able to bring the authoritarian playbook to our country—polarization, hatred, civic strife, of course building on existing racism, radicalization, the Tea Party, creating a crisis, and then saying, "I alone can fix it." There's a myth that the strongman leader is "good for business." So, it's very important to talk about the way that it's *not good for* business and not good for society.

This extends to guns, and I wrote a *Washington Post* op-ed in 2021 saying gun violence primes us for authoritarianism by creating a culture of fear and suspicion. But talking about guns can be a difficult topic because people start with this: "You want to take our guns away." So it's important instead to talk about outcomes, very calmly: "$280 billion a year, which is the cost annually of gun violence, is that good for society?" No, it's not. Recent polls show that there's an uptick in low-level violence since January Sixth, there's an uptick in every single group that suffers hate crimes. "Is civil strife good for society? Is this good for the economy?" No, it's not.

Democracy is also about accepting differences in society, including different opinions, which goes with the principle of mutual tolerance. So far better than "I alone can fix it" is: "We fix it together." We can do that in town councils and school boards, the sites of everyday governance. Here it's also important to talk about the denigration of previously respected and beloved figures in our communities like librarians and teachers—this is not the American way.

And it's been very effectively done, starting with anti-mask and anti-vax crusades as part of the larger picture of trying to ruin public schools. Consider the current anti-LGBTQ phase where teachers and librarians are being attacked as "groomers." This is how the GOP is transforming its political culture to prepare for autocracy.

The next point I'll discuss is freedom. Something that isn't stressed enough about authoritarianism (or antidemocratic behaviors and policies) is that it's not just about restricting the rights of people or taking people's rights away—voting rights, abortion rights, marriage equality. While some people lose rights, other people have their rights expanded, which removes checks on abusive and corrupt behavior—the plunderers win, the exploiters win.

So if you look broadly at what Trump did, he did a hell of a lot in his four years. It's wrong when people say that he's incompetent. He was incredibly competent at the things he cared about. His administration, for example, eroded professional ethics in civil service, rolled back environmental regulations so that natural resources could be plundered. Authoritarianism tries to immunize crime. Historically, we've had a regional form of authoritarianism with Jim Crow in the South. Now there's another stage on the national level. The issue of giving shooters, people who run over protesters, and rapists forms of immunity is why accountability must be stressed.

Today, elections are not actually the measure of the difference between democracy and dictatorship, since rulers like Orbán in Hungary and Putin in Russia do have elections. They're just fixed. So it's important to stress accountability and transparency. Related is the issue of indecency. When you discard the rule of law, it has a ripple effect into workplaces, into schools, into all the places where there are these little Trumps. This imitative bullying and harassing is not good for profit, and it's not good for the soul. Decency might sound old fashioned, but I still stress it.

The final point is that it's important to not allow far-right Republicans to claim patriotism. One of the most disturbing things that Trump did was a kind of emotional retraining of people so that they saw violence as having a positive value and even being patriotic—"saving the nation." And that's a continuity with all these strongmen—any violence, whether it's a coup or fascist takeover, it's always to save the nation. It's always patriotic.

Infinitely better is to celebrate the American dream in terms of celebrating the successes as a multiracial democracy, as a society that has allowed immigrants like my dad to prosper. Candidates can cite all the businesses and products that Republicans and swing voters also use every day and that are helmed by immigrants. That celebration of possibility should also include people who were born here but lived in poverty and who in the space of one or two generations enjoyed huge gains in the standard of living for their whole family.

I think stories like that, whether they're immigrant stories or class-uplift stories, are very important. They require a different kind of narrative to reclaim the concept of patriotism from the right.[27]

Mark Green: Talk about the different kind of language a Democrat can use in the pursuit of votes. Earlier we discussed the phrase "dangerous extremists," but your analysis includes other phrases that might work to attract the swing voters and Independents who decide elections.

Ruth Ben-Ghiat: I've written three books on fascism, yet I don't use the word "fascist" very often in describing domestic affairs. I don't actually call Trump a fascist, even though he's got tons of fascist things. The reason: it turns off the people you need to reach, and it conjures up an older style of one-party states which doesn't describe how it works today. "Extremist," however, is very important, because the January Sixth Insurrection showed everyone what "dangerous extremism" looks like.[28]

DEMOCRACY NOTES

- GOP Extremism: American Democracy is "hanging by a thread," according to the *New Yorker*'s Jane Mayer. An original hatred of monarchy has somehow evolved 246 years later into a reactionary hatred of democratic government itself. Bill Clinton had a useful phrase here: "In a democracy, you can't hate your government and love your country." We Democrats have to defeat this antidemocratic minority to save Democracy *in order to* stop climate violence, gun massacres, attacks on women's health, and gross inequality.

- Tom Friedman column in *New York Times*, April 18: "As long as we can still vote out incompetent leaders and maintain information ecosystems that will expose systemic lying and defy censorship, we can adapt in an age of rapid change—and that is the single most important competitive advantage a country can have today."

- It took one hundred years from the end of the Civil War to enact the 1965 Voting Rights Act. Then in 2013 the Roberts Court in the 5–4 *Shelby County v. Holder* stripped away key sections, notwithstanding a 98–0 vote in the Senate reauthorizing it in 2006. Why? Because, asserted Roberts—who frowns on "judicial activism"—"things have changed in the South." Within the month, however, several southern states began enacting voter suppression laws. (Has Roberts apologized?)

- Voting rights are essential to secure all other rights. GOP claims that new state laws that make it harder to vote—e.g., not allowing mailing out absentee ballots to all eligible voters, fewer drop boxes—are "voter integrity" laws responding to "voter fraud." But all studies show that that's less likely to occur than being hit by lightning. Attorney General Bill Barr concluded in December 2020 that "there was no significant fraud" that changed the result in any state. The fraudsters are those who cite "voter fraud" to claim that Trump won and who then openly try to steal the next election.

  The Associated Press studied 25.5 million votes in six swing states and found a negligible number suspicious. The reason is clear if you think about it—why would any person risk fines and jail time to cast one vote when it can only make a conceivable difference if part of a larger conspiracy, which itself would risk easy exposure? So-called voter fraud rarely occurs since it's already a crime *and* a staggeringly inefficient way to rig elections.

- And like Elmer Gantry denouncing sin, voting fraud is not only minuscule but usually employed by *Republicans* to help win elections despite their unpopular positions:

  Mark Meadows registered to vote in 2020 using the address of a mobile home that he never lived in;

  A Trump supporter in Arizona who voted in her dead mother's name during the 2020 election—Tracey Kay McKee—was sentenced to two years of probation;

Matt Mowers, a former Trump aide running for the House from New Hampshire, voted twice in two different states;

A 2016 House race in North Carolina was actually rerun because of massive GOP political fraud;

Two Trump supporters in The Villages in Florida cast multiple ballots for Trump; and

The Michigan attorney general urged a special prosecutor to investigate how the state GOP got election officials to take and rewire voting machines.

- Since the last election, GOP legislatures passed thirty-four laws in nine states that limited access to voting and put partisan operatives in charge of running elections.

- How can a GOP losing the popular vote in seven of the past eight presidential elections still win elections with unpopular views? Here are six ways they sabotage democracy in America: reducing access to voting in blue areas; an electoral college tilting to low-population/rural interests; a severely malapportioned Senate; Dark Money and *Citizens United*; extreme gerrymandering; the Senate filibuster.

Possible remedies: matching public funds for small donations; ranked choice voting . . . national popular vote to replace the electoral college; restore key elements of the Voting Rights Act (by Congress or the next SCOTUS); ban extreme gerrymandering and establish national standards for independent state redistricting commissions; add new "states" to the Senate (D.C., Puerto Rico); require large federal contractors to disclose their large political contribution annually; and establish term limits and age limits for justices and perhaps expand the Supreme Court to rectify McConnell's court packing.

- Right-wing Big Brotherism: "They want freedom of speech but only if it's their speech. They want freedom of religion but only if it's their religion. They want government out of their lives but want to govern women's bodies. They want law and order, but they think they're above it. They want families first but only their families. All that has been gained over so many years is being chipped away. Margaret Atwood was prophetic back in 1985. Yes, it could happen here and now." Susan Pfaff in the *New York Times*.

- Five of nine SCOTUS justices were appointed by presidents who lost the popular vote (Bush 43 and Trump). Three were appointed by a corrupt president who lost the popular vote and were confirmed by a bloc of senators who represent less than half the country.

- The Court in *Roe v. Wade* in 1973 voted 7–2—the majority included five Republicans—to make abortion legal. Fifty years later, the Alito Six reversed, saying it was "egregiously wrong" because (a) abortion is not in the Constitution (neither are "corporations") and (b) abortion "is not deeply rooted in our traditions and customs." Which means laws in 2022 should be constitutionally evaluated based on guessing what was in the minds of the fifty-eight (all male, all white) authors at the Constitutional Convention of 1787.

- Also, the First Amendment's prohibition of "the establishment of religion" could in a future case make it unconstitutional for government to allow one religion's definition of when life begins to prevail over others (all six justices in the majority were raised Catholic).

- The Supreme Court has no soldiers to enforce its rulings, depending instead on public trust in the Rule of Law. Instead, McConnell has packed the Court with right-wing justices when it comes to our freedoms and our rights—which has led to a stunning decline in public esteem for the Court from 44 percent to 19 percent favorable in January 2021 (+25) to 35 percent to 42 percent in August 2022 (−7), according to an NBC poll. An astonishing 32 point collapse. And the 60 percent Kansas vote for reproductive rights after the *Dobbs* decision was a clear rebuke.

- SCOTUS let stand a Texas Law (call it "The Snitch Law" or "Bounty Law") that permitted people—neighbors, coworkers, family—to inform on women seeking abortions and be paid $10,000 by the woman or her doctor. This radical law was allowed to take effect by the Court on its "Shadow Docket"—previously reserved for small, procedural disputes—which does not require full argument or briefs.

- Professor Laurence Tribe: The Alito Six are "seizing power for themselves against everyone else in the game of life and law. When enough people see what's going on, SCOTUS will lose its unique power."

- Bill Kristol: "Self-government requires a minimum amount of social trust to succeed. With every tweet that spreads cynicism and lies, and with every call to arms that welcomes civil conflict, Trump Republicans are poisoning the Nation they ostentatiously claim to love."

- The 24 states that banned abortion tend to have the weakest social services and the worst results in several categories of health and well-being, such as child and maternal mortality and teen birthrates," a *New York Times* analysis found.

The Republican Party wants to force girls to give birth who are not even old enough to babysit for other children. They value an embryo in a girl over the girl.

We need to talk about what overturning *Roe* and *Casey* means for women who are in abusive relationships. Men will be able to hold abortions over a partner's head or threaten to report them for reproductive healthcare or miscarriages. Which makes the state a party to domestic violence.

Columnist E. J. Dionne in the *Washington Post*: "The best path toward reducing the incidence of abortion is to offer far more support to women, both during pregnancy and as they raise their children. By walking away from child credit, expanded child care, and paid parental leave, our nation has signaled its indifference to their struggles."[29]

Annie Leonard, codirector of Greenpeace USA, and a practitioner of effective language for people, attended to the subject of climate violence and "Winning Language on Climate."

I actually have some really good news about climate: it's not too late, and leadership on climate—if it is done well—can be an electoral winner.

We are in a very different place than we were even five years ago on climate—both in terms of the physical reality and in terms of public opinion. On the physical reality front, in terms of the actual world, we are dangerously close to tipping points where we will cross limits that are going to be impossible to recover from. We are entering a period in which humans have no experience and are poorly equipped for the extreme impacts that are already descending upon us—impacts on health, on the economy, on security. It's truly an emergency.

It is important to not *just* tell people about your problem, because everyone has their own problems. But climate change is more and more becoming *everyone's problem*. Last year, one in three people experienced an extreme weather event, and we're on track for it to be much higher this year. Last week, I was visiting a friend in Sonoma, and I parked and went inside, and he actually came outside and turned my car around so it was facing out. And I asked him, "What are you doing?" And he just said casually, "Oh, we always park facing out now, in case we have to flee."

Our reality now in California is that we are constantly ready to flee. And it's comparable everywhere in different forms, and getting worse. That's why we are seeing huge change in the public perception. A majority of people in the United States are concerned about climate change and want action from elected leaders. The gap now is between where the science is, where the public is, and where the elected leaders are.

Based on our research, here is the best clear language on climate violence to close the gap. "Ninety-nine percent of climate scientists are convinced that carbon pollution is heating our planet, threatening our health, safety, economy and security. . . . Industry has created a blanket of pollution around the earth that traps heat and is dangerously heating the planet. The good news is we know how to solve this—by switching to cleaner and cheaper energy."

Best words to use: "pollution" or "carbon pollution" (not "emissions"), "heating" (not "warming"), "industrial activity" (more so than "we" or "humans").

And here are the strongest three "messages" to shift the debate.

Message 1: Investing in a clean economy creates jobs now.
The counterargument that fighting climate change will cost jobs is wrong and needs to be repositioned as both holding back innovation and growth, and threatening the health and safety of all Americans. But we shouldn't say "fighting climate change doesn't kill jobs," which subconsciously puts the false argument in people's heads. Rather, we should say this assertion is the key to America's future and an opportunity we can't miss. We should name specific new jobs and who will get them. For example:

- "There are millions of EVs to be built. I want to build them in Ohio."
- "American workers should be building the industries of the future, owning the clean, renewable energy, and car markets. Why let China get an insurmountable lead?"
- "Inaction on climate change is damaging the economy with extreme weather." Best words to use: "good jobs" (name them), "innovation," "prosperity," "American manufacturing."

Message 2: Investing in a clean economy saves families money.
Americans are being told that clean energy is expensive. In reality, it has become significantly cheaper in the last decade (solar prices

are down 90 percent), yet fewer than one in five people know this. Clean energy is now often cheaper than fossil fuels. This is the most persuasive argument for building clean infrastructure because it affects every family. Hence: "Clean, renewable energy is not only healthier, it is now cheaper than fossil fuels like coal, oil, and gas. Solar and wind are now the cheapest sources of energy. They will never run out and will only get cheaper. This switch saves everyone money, forever."

Best words: Couple "cleaner" with "cheaper" every time.

Message 3: Big polluters are the enemy, not climate change.

We need to move from "fighting climate change" to "fighting the polluters who are causing climate change." This is consistently the most effective message in our research. We need to create sides: you are either anti-pollution or pro-pollution. Nine out of ten Americans agree that polluters should pay for their pollution. Dirty industries are un-American and unjust, and frontline communities and people of color and rural communities are the ones who suffer the most.

We should frame those standing in the way as "pro-pollution" candidates, politicians, and organizations. Best words: "Climate change is caused by pollution, plain and simple. Big polluters hurt our economy, health, and communities. They need to be held accountable for this damage. Big polluters are the elite few protecting their profits over the health and safety of all American families."

Best words: the "pro-pollution lobby," "big pollution," "make polluters pay."

Here's our strongest sequence of thoughts and words: Burning fossil fuels is creating a pollution blanket around the earth that is trapping heat in our atmosphere that would otherwise go back to space. That trapped heat causes stronger storms and downpours that wipe out farmers' crops and lead to food shortages. It means hotter temperatures that fuel wildfires and cause crippling heat waves, where our kids can't play outside. It causes Arctic ice to melt, raising the sea level and causing millions of American homes to flood every year.

So in sum: This tested, simple language and imagery should be repeated, repeated, repeated every time climate is discussed with the public. Doing so will change the opinion playing field to win. With the bully pulpit, the issue can be simplified and explained in a way that significantly grows support.[30]

CLIMATE NOTES

- Columnist Greg Sargent: Now that Dems have enacted their big climate bill, "They have unilaterally launched the biggest response to our planetary emergency in US history, without the participation of a single Republican."

- The SEC in March required public companies to disclose climate-related risks. And those that have made public pledges to reduce their carbon footprint will need to detail how they will do that. (The UK and Japan are also doing it.)

- Bill McKibben: "Reducing reliance on fossil fuels helps clean the planet, adds to our wallets, and undermines the power of dictators and thugs."

- When discussing climate violence, federal spending or tax credits should be described as investments that create the opportunity for millions of new jobs while protecting our health. If you care about justice, our children's future, or the stock market—whether you live in a big city or a rural area—you should demand renewable energy *now* . . . at speed and scale. Demand an end to coal-fired power. Demand an end to all fossil-fuel subsidies.

- Most of the obstacles to decarbonization are not technological but political.[31]

Joe Madison often talked about the need to mobilize the 120 million non-voters. He outlined how reaching non-voters could be the road to victory all by itself in the swing states. Mr. Madison worked on getting out nonvoters in Detroit and Philadelphia and other cities and was a national daily radio talk show host for forty years.

One of the lessons that I've learned from my good friend and mentor Dick Gregory is that there's always a difference between a *moment* and a *movement*.

All *movements* require sacrifice. And one of the things that motivated me to go on my hunger strike was that there were demonstrations—most of which weren't effective—and I just felt that I had to bring it up a notch. And although my hunger strike, too, wasn't successful, one thing it did was to wake up a sleeping giant and mobilize young people. When you sacrifice, the first thing most people ask is "Why?" And this is when you have the opportunity to explain the issue and to educate people.

When I used to participate in civil disobedience, one of the things people didn't realize is that when you go into a lockup many of the young people there—if they recognize you—one of the things they'll do is to ask you, "What are *you* doing in here?" That's both personal and educational.

Now, in terms of getting out the vote, I'm going to go back to when I was the political director for the NAACP, and there was a fascist mayor in Philadelphia by the name of Frank Rizzo. He was dealing with term limits as mayor and wanted to change the city charter so that he could run for consecutive terms. I was sent in by Benjamin Hooks to do a major get-out-the-vote and voter registration effort.

Since I thought that Democrats weren't doing enough face-to-face advocacy, first thing we did was to identify the low-voter-turnout areas and then did some old-fashioned recruiting. We recruited one person a block, or one person in an apartment building or a condo building, who would volunteer to go door-to-door to find out who's registered to vote. That's what Democrats should be massively doing right now, not in late September or October. Then if they're not registered, leave them a voter registration form or information where they can get registered to vote.

Once we registered them, they became part of what I refer to in military terms as our infantry. Now, today everything is virtual, but you use the virtual as backup. You don't stop doing the virtual piece, but this face-to-face work is extremely important. Then, three to five days out, we started putting up door hangers and pamphleting information saying, "This is where you go to vote." And then on Election Day, that same block captain is knocking on doors.

Now, this may sound old-fashioned in this virtual environment we live in, but nothing beats this shoe-leather, face-to-face approach. And then you use texting and phone banks to back up what you're doing.

One other thing that few people now discuss: we should be hitting the campuses in August and September with voter registration. My alma mater, Washington University in St. Louis, was one of the universities in 2020 that had a record voter registration and turnout, and that should start when students arrive on campus. Make sure that they are registered to vote, and then you also have to start deciding on what is the best time to distribute absentee ballots on campus. Now that's what I came to this Winning America effort to tell you. Keep in mind that in 2018, 120 million eligible Americans did not vote. That's the target group. And we've got the technology to identify them.[32]

While the other speakers were addressing their social concerns, I took the opportunity to conclude the session as if I were addressing an audience who wanted a wrap-up of what can work to "crush the GOP" and Trump's Fascism. The candidates could compare this free content with what they were given by their political media consulting firms.

The Democratic Party must make it vibrantly clear that they own the answer to the perennial voters' question—"Whose Side Are They On?" Here are some substantive and tactical ways to do that:

1. Democratic candidates need to turn the tables on the GOP and sharply describe *how Republicans refuse to protect the safety and lives of the American people.*

    The GOP, for example, says *no* to expanding the tiny budget and authority of OSHA (60,000 work-related deaths from trauma and diseases a year). The GOP says *no* to expanding the budget and regulations of EPA against lethal toxics (cancer, respiratory illness, 65,000 air pollution deaths a year). The GOP says *no* similarly to stronger auto safety, food safety, water pollution prevention and drug [safety] standards, aviation and chemical plant safety, protection of children from pesticides. And, despite nightly news of wildfires, droughts, floods, hurricanes, and sea level risings, not one GOP senator supported the climate mitigation efforts within President Biden's "Inflation Reduction Act." Under Trump, even the phrase "climate change" was banned at the CDC. *Don't Look Up* was both a movie and the reality.

More. The GOP blocks full health insurance that would save over one hundred thousand lives per year, is against elevating Medicaid in Republican states even when paid for by the federal government, and denied the seriousness of the COVID Pandemic in early [2020] causing a huge number of preventable deaths. What do you call a political party so dangerously extreme to all the people? A death cult? At the least, this is a brutish party which despoils "patriotism" while trying to repeal the enlightenment of the American Revolution. [Look at the livelihoods and rights of GOP-run red states compared to Democrat-run blue states. Many useful comparisons.]

2. *Corruption* is in the news and on the minds of many voters, which is why some 80 percent of Republican voters oppose the Supreme Court's *Citizens United* decision on unlimited campaign contributions by corporations. The Obama administration over eight years hardly had any public political

corruption scandals. Yet for the four years of the Trump regime, corruption was a regular occurrence, with a record number of resignations and regulatory violations, all with the concurrence of the White House and Justice Department.

Trump's obsession with self-enrichment, along with those of his nominees, set historical records. Serial law violations, such as constantly using federal property to promote his reelection violated the Hatch Act, a federal criminal statute. The GOP generally has no problem with disobeying laws, whether they are regulatory laws, civil service laws, or election laws. Trump's 2019 monarchical [impeachable] declaration— "With Article II [I] can do whatever I want as President"—would have disgusted our Founding Fathers.

3. Displaying a morbid consistency, *the GOP also wants to destroy the social safety net.* The party has blocked the Democrats' legislation to upgrade Social Security and expand benefits frozen for over forty years, to expand Medicare and neonatal care and renew the $300 a month support for sixty million children in poverty that expired in January 2022 . . . despite having reduced childhood poverty by one-third! The GOP cruelly opposed paid child care, paid family leave (accorded by just about every country in the world), paid maternity leave, and just about everything else now provided people in other western democracies.

But then, this GOP historically has been the bastion for the superrich and corporate powers—virulently opposing FDR's social security, unemployment compensation, consumer and labor protections, minimum wage, and crucial public works programs in the 1930s Depression.

Senator Rick Scott (R-FL), a former corporate felon, heads the Senate Re-Election Campaign Committee this year. He issued a fifty-page report so vicious that his boss Senator Mitch McConnell backed away from it. Scott refused to withdraw it. The Democrats every day should use Scott's repulsively cruel positions—including five-year time limits on Medicare and Social Security as Exhibit One.

4. *The GOP has never been so anti-labor.* They oppose any increase in the federal minimum wage, now at $7.25 an hour—the same as 2009; some GOP politicians want to repeal the minimum wage entirely, as they block the $15 minimum wage earlier passed by the Democrats in the House. This overdue bill would raise the wages of over 25 million workers and should be daily discussed on the hustings. That's why Democrats should exhort them, "Vote Yourself a Raise—You've Earned It."

When Trump Republicans took power, they turned the National Labor Relations Board into a pro-corporate shill. The party backs the notorious Taft-Hartley Act of 1947— the most anti-worker law in the western world—and is today blocking House-passed legislation to give workers a decent chance to organize unions and protect their workplace rights. They are blocking pay equity for women and the ERA. Their overall war on women is not surprising since most GOPers still pay tribute to the worst serial sexual predator and disrespector of women ever to reside in the White House, and have refused to call him out on these crimes.

The GOP has no problem giving huge tax breaks to CEOs who make anywhere from $12,000 an hour (on a forty-hour week) to over $833 a *minute* (Tim Cook of Apple), while the party makes sure that these corporations' capitalist owners—the shareholders—continue to be stripped of their authority to hold accountable their out-of-control hired bosses.

5. *Whose values?* Unable to run on their record, the GOP runs on "Texas values" or "Kentucky values" or "Missouri values." Democrats should take this manipulative phoniness head on! In my article in the *Louisville Courier-Journal* on October 24, 2014, I showed how Senator Mitch McConnell's positions were directly contrary to ten Kentucky values—"Rewarding Hard Work, Honoring Your Elders, Practicality in Addressing Problems, Respecting Women, Being Forthright, Responsibility, Love Thy Neighbor, No One is Above the Law, Defending the Constitution, and Patriotism."

This approach of politically flipping the power of values can be applied in essentially any red or blue state.

6. *Do not buy into the polarized voters' trap.* Strongly emphasize that many reforms are favored *by both conservative and liberal voters*—reaching over 70 percent in the polls. They include raising the minimum wage [raising taxes on the under-taxed wealthy]; finally enacting universal health insurance; upgrading public facilities—roads, schools, public transit, drinking water safety, community health clinics; cracking down on business crooks; reducing corporate

welfare—subsidies, handouts, giveaways and bailouts; expanding the right of taxpayers to sue the government for corruption with their corporate buddies; legislating pro-democracy clean elections; protecting consumers and children from commercial exploitation via direct marketing and the internet gulag; revising trade agreements bad for American workers; protecting pension rights; extending civil liberties; and—when explained—ending corporate personhood and having the people actually control more of what they own—the commons (public lands, public airwaves, pension and mutual funds, etc.) (See *Unstoppable: The Emerging Left-Right Alliance To Dismantle the Corporate State* by Ralph Nader).

While the GOP gears toward its extreme "base," it's essential that Democrats come across as working for all the people under the motto "We all bleed the same color." These policies can be assembled under umbrella names such as [a] Freedom for Women Platform to Protect Our Children, etc.

As mentioned above by Mark Green, for too long the GOP has won the war of words. They took away from liberals—regardless of their unctuous hypocrisy—the Bible, the flag, blue-collar workers, the trade issue, the very words "populism," "freedom," and "liberty." They haven't managed to take away the word "justice"—yet. (Nor do they appear to want to.)

The GOP has been better at slogans, nicknames, lawn sign placements, and labeling (remember the party of "Acid, Abortion, and Amnesty"). They prevail in part because Democrats have hardly contended—a big mistake. Indeed, when Trump had fun with his sticky pejorative nicknames repeated everyday verbatim by the mainstream media without even allowing rebuttals, they created a one-man mass-media machine without having to take his own medicine, despite the many openings for such [Trumpian nicknames].

7. Democrats have to make the GOP *voting record* and proposals in Congress front and center. Representative Jamie Raskin issued a "Roundup of 20 Outrageous Things the GOP House Majority did in My First Term" (before the November 2018 election). The House and Senate Democratic party structures need to immediately compile these terrible GOP votes and proposals right after Labor Day and end a drought on conveying such an obviously powerful campaign message to the people affected.

8. Democrats *must confront the mass-production lying machine* that has overtaken most Republicans as a daily practice. The GOP lies about election fraud as it seeks to win elections by fraud. It lies about history, lies about the natural world, lies about the laws of the land and, of course, lies about the Democrats. Voters must understand that they would not tolerate their coworkers or neighbors lying daily and still associate with them. It would be too unstable [and treacherous]. The GOP has far more power over their lives [than their neighbors].

This is what fascism is built on: perilous scapegoating, racism, bigotry . . . and then to reliance on masters of the "Big Lies" to impose their own supremacy over their indentured followers. Ignoring these "believers" or dismissing them as "ignorant" only intensifies the liars' takeover of these voters, driving them into ever more extreme beliefs and behavior.

This is just what has been happening in recent years. Remember that fascist regimes often start with elections, with minority footholds overtaking the . . . majority. The GOP extremists have far more messianic energy than their Democratic opponents of all stripes. Derision and haughty aspersions are traps to be assiduously avoided by the Democrats.

9. Democrats could use more ground troops and less airpower. Given the record of avoidable election losses and close calls (less than 100,000 votes in 2020 in several swing states would have given Trump four more years, and not many more would have lost the Congress to the GOP), candidates and their staff *have to think more independently of their present outsourcing* to political and media consultants. This "permanent government" is conflicted with corporate clients and a 15 percent commission of electronic media ads.

Such Beltway consultants are often inexperienced or averse to installing a decisive ground plan for GOTV since resources will have to be redirected away from consultants' sweet spots—expensive TV ads. Budgets have to be shifted to GOTV in neighborhoods, projects, and other distinct low-turnout communities through highly personal gatherings, motivational mobilizations, and respected "influencers" in these locales. Consulting with and understanding voters and nonvoters in specific self-explanatory ways will also tether regular political advertising to be more memorable and less repetitiously irritating to targeted audiences. Here are just a few specifics:

- Produce in volume a simple two-sided Voters Guide Card, with one side polling the voter with six issues "yes or no," and on the other side place the "yes or no" positions of the candidate and your opponent. The voter first registers his/her position by checking the box yes or no and then turns the card to find out on whose side the candidates are on.

- Make transporting voters to polls a *festive occasion* by having lunch or dinner afterward and nearby, as they do in Australia. Food trucks are perfectly legal. Indeed, corporate lawyer Lloyd N. Cutler, who was White House counsel to Presidents Carter and Clinton, [once] said lottery tickets handed out to exiting voters as an inducement to vote is perfectly legal as well. A supportive car dealer or popular restaurant can issue these lotteries.

- Be attentive to the many workers on *the midnight shift* who almost never receive contact from candidates. As workers in hospitals, nursing homes, hotels, all-night drugstores, eateries, factories, police, fire, etc., they keep the country going while we are asleep. Announcing several "midnight campaigns" in front of the midnight shift change of a large hospital can reap good word of mouth and elicit respect from these stalwart staffers.

- Convert Labor Day and beyond into gatherings of workers *to unite them as a working class* with similar interests for their families, their economic security, health and safety, regardless of their political labels. Abstract ideologies and their word games fade when you get down to where workers live, work, and raise their families, take care of their elders, and want less GOP-inspired anxiety, dread, and fear in their lives. These meetings can find volunteers and enhance voter registration.

- How do you show that you identify with ethnic and racial groups who feel they are being taken for granted by the Democrats? Announce, with their representatives, *Ethnic Days* where you get to know each other more personally and they display their traditions in music, food, customs, and achievements for a more tolerant society. It is an important way to listen to and consult with people of different identities and learn about their common necessities and aspirations.

- Pay *rigorous attention to language—words and phrases.* Look what Trump did with his *mouth*—what else did he have? The GOP paid Frank Luntz—their wordsmith—to come up with "death tax" to better excite anti-tax sentiment and with "climate change" to replace the more alarming "global warming" or "climate crisis."

- Inject some new words and issues to avoid the rut of repetition. For examples, embrace words that the GOP almost never uses such as "justice," "fair play," or "billing theft"—at least $1 billion a day just in the healthcare industry—or "wage theft" estimated at *$60 billion* a year, or "harmful junk food/drink and other dangerous products" pitched directly to our children[,] radically bypassing parental control and guidance.

- Some other suggestions—don't use "white-collar crime" when you are referring to "prosecuting corporate crooks" (poll ratings very high). Don't use the word "provider" when you're referring to gouging drug companies and hospital chains. They are "vendors" or "sellers." "Providers" sounds philanthropic. Never use "entitlements" to describe Medicare and Social Security which are paid into by the people. "Entitlements" should replace "incentives," which is used to describe corporate bailouts, subsidies, and handouts into which the companies have paid nothing.

- The driving force in all societies is unbridled profiteering greed seeking maximum power over the people. Every major religion warned its adherents not to give much power to the merchant class because its driving commercial motive destroys other crucial values.

10. Finally, some suggested *rebuttals* to GOP *accusations*:

- *"Socialists!"*—All your political career you've been pushing socialism for the rich and unregulated capitalism for the poor. Didn't the GOP always bail out Wall Street crooks? The GOP [in red states] supported many billions of dollars down the biggest US corporate rathole for the unfinished nuclear power plants whose reckless owners are demanding more taxpayer dollars. "Socialism?" Maybe that is why you have Social Security, Medicare, the Postal Service, public drinking water systems, the VA, all of which you want to have corporations control [or abolish].

- *"Defund the Police"*—Name one Democratic candidate in a serious contest who has supported that. You're defunding the federal cops on the corporate crime and violence beat. Since 2011, your GOP has starved the IRS budget, aiding and abetting tax evasion by your super-rich buddies and giant corporations. Some of these big tax-evading profitable corporations pay zero federal income tax, which means just one of their workers sends more dollars to support our public services and infrastructure than the entire company does.

- *"Critical Race Theory"*—Name me any school that teaches that. Another GOP lie. Why do you repeat this falsehood? Because you want to cover up parts of American history just as you are covering up your own party's crimes and wrongdoing right up to [Der Führer] Trump. [What] Republicans always push [for is] corporate control theory in schools to indoctrinate these youngsters.

- *"Open Borders"*—Only Wall Streeters want open borders for holding down wages. We want borders that stop smuggling, pollution, gun trafficking, child trafficking, yet allow longtime US laws of asylum and legal immigration to continue. [If] the United States had stopped backing dictatorship and oligarchs in these countries [over the decades], impoverished and oppressed people would not have had to flee their native lands.

Last, in a not dissimilar situation in 1948, nearly all commentators were sure that president Harry Truman would lose. Then he began his "Do-Nothing-Congress" whistle-stop train tour, telling one audience of 90,000 Iowa farmers that Republicans are "gluttons of privilege, cold men who want a return of the Wall

Street dictatorship. How many times do you have to be hit over the head before finding out who's hitting you?"

Remember: winning elections is about authenticity, empathy, and deep energy levels to get people's attention, excite them to *register* to vote, and actually vote for their own legitimate interests and for the country and world that their descendants will inherit.

NADER NOTES

1. *Wrecking America: How Trump's Lawbreaking and Lies Betray All* by Mark Green and Ralph Nader. https://WinningAmerica.net/WreckingAmerica

2. Kentucky Values vs. McConnell by Ralph Nader, *Louisville Courier-Journal*, October 24, 2014 (These can be values in every state). WinningAmerica.net/KentuckyValues

3. For policies and messages that resonate with both liberal and conservative voters, see my book *Unstoppable: The Emerging Left-Right Alliance to Dismantle the Corporate State* (2014), especially pp. 65–66 for many examples to which you can add. Nader.org/2014/04/27/Unstoppable-25-Proposals

4. Excerpts from a January 2018 memorandum, which I wrote titled "An Invitation to a Conversation" about neighborhood-by-neighborhood socializing, registering, transporting to get nonvoters out to vote. You can pick and choose what seems reasonable for your campaign requirements for [2024]. WinningAmerica.net/An-Invitation-to-a-Conversation

5. Representative Jamie Raskin's "Roundup of 20 Outrageous Things the GOP House Majority Did in My First Term." Such

a list must promptly be compiled by the House Democratic Caucus, as it did in 2014, together with a comparative side-by-side list of what the Democrats Did Do. WinningAmerica .net/RaskinRoundup

6. Rebuttal to the ongoing use of "socialists" to describe all Democrats by the GOP. This attack is ludicrous when the Democrats present the vast "Corporate Socialism" giveaways and bailouts supported by the GOP. WinningAmerica.net /DemocraticSocialism

7. One-page Candidate News Release on Midnight Campaigning. WinningAmerica.net/MidnightCampaigning

8. For state elective office, an excellent timely refund owed most owners of motor vehicles is described by actuary and former Texas Insurance Commissioner Robert Hunter. Injecting a fresh issue like this into campaigns is a good idea. Hunter also explains how California reformed its auto insurance laws (Prop 103) and saved consumers $154 billion since 1988. This is a model for other states. https://WinningAmerica.net /AutoInsurance

9. Suggestions for Successful Elections in 2020 at All Levels.[33] Additional materials are available on the Winning America website.[34]

By the time I finished my remarks, it was about 5:00 p.m. Many people are not used to such marathons, however, it intimately relates to their most essential preoccupation—namely the upcoming election. By comparison, thousands of people stood in the fields listening to the Lincoln/Douglas debates in the 1850s. For our session, there was one lunch break and no music. For public policy aficionados, the narratives of these valiant participants were gripping.

The following week, we thanked these participants and urged them to alert their many members and civic circles to pick up what they believed useful to convey to the candidates in their electoral districts. Civic groups are not accustomed to being so proactive, out of an abundance of caution to avoid being ensnared into an involuntary partisanship. Just having their recommendations either in wonky style or declarative demands satisfied their sense of limits. A major rationale for Winning America is that this self-restraint, having helped lead to exclusion by the candidates' consultants, had to change. Politics requires crying out loud, the more dignified, factual, and broad-based the better.

CHAPTER 8
Before the Fall

In the doldrums of August, we made persistent efforts to reach candidates or their staffs to describe what they missed on July 23rd. Even in an election year, August is not a good month to reach out. It's the month for Congress's longest recess—five weeks until Labor Day when the solons finally return to their Capitol Hill jobs. We used the August period to urge the Democrats to make much more of Labor Day than the brief ceremonies some attended. Labor Day parades, once a mass event in major cities, were nearing extinction. They could have been revived by the Democratic Party as an excellent way to appeal to all workers, regardless of labels. I urged them to have news conferences with workers expressing their grievances, aspirations, and successes in the workplace that would resonate with the working classes who were abandoning the party's historically winning base. Labor Day news on what is usually a slow news day, I insisted, would give the party an occasion to put forward a comprehensive pro-labor agenda with authentic punctuations, such as proposed legislation, readying for the stretch drive to the November elections. I couldn't have gotten a better reception from those I spoke to at the AFL-CIO and its member unions, down to some locals. However, after Labor Day, there were no reports that anything transpired along the lines of my specific communications, either nationally or locally. A grand opportunity had been forfeited. Labor Day sales were brisk, but it was business as usual.

Mark and I planned an all-out last-ditch effort to speak to Nancy Pelosi. As one of the most dominant Speakers of the House of Representatives in modern times, were she to highlight Winning America as a top-level attention for her flock and had campaign staff advance it inside the close races, any consultants who tried to counter her would have had a difficult time renewing their contracts.

On September 8th, I followed Mark's call to Pelosi's political staffer Mary Plasencia. It was a twenty-five-minute call during which I laid out the details of our effort, the range of issues, the endorsers, the available brain trusts, pointing to the fragile campaigns of O'Rourke (Texas), Crist (Florida), and Ryan (Ohio). The estimable value of connecting with the civic groups' many members around the country advances the goal of getting working margins of victory in the House and Senate. Would Speaker Pelosi do this and help us get through to candidates, at least, with a clear, urgent note from her, if not making calls? Mary listened politely and she said she would get our message to the speaker. At the same time, we had supporters of Pelosi calling her from San Francisco and promises at least from a few of her colleagues in the House to second our requests. Whether any of these supplemental aids transpired is not known. Seasoned politicians have very good antennae to distinguish between pro forma urges at someone's behest and serious declarations that the transmitter identifies with strongly. Alas, it seems that the latter was a rare assist for us. I do not know anyone in Congress today who can compare with progressives like Representative Phil Burton and Representative John Moss of California. You knew your message was being delivered with conviction and elaboration when dealing with them.

I was getting close to having the *New York Times* veteran reporter Carl Hulse either do a story on Winning America or place it significantly in a larger story. Instead, his editor in New York sent him to a very humdrum Chicago-area fundraiser featuring the one and only Speaker Nancy Pelosi. I called him to say about his story on this event, "Wow that was an addition to the readers knowledge about the 2022 campaign." He sighed.

On September 14th, Representative Jim McGovern (D-MA), chairman of the powerful House Rules Committee, called to say he was joining with Jamie Raskin and John Larson to endorse our effort. I took this occasion to recognize his early proposal for a Department of Peace that went nowhere but that would help peace groups to rally around a reintroduced bill with a bill number. Imagine not having a Department of Peace as a counterpoint to our Department of Defense (formally and properly called the War Department.) He averred that this proposal "should be revisited."

After July 23rd, Mark put the six and a half hours into a concise print report which we titled *Crushing the GOP, 2022* to elevate the expectation levels of a discouraged, defeatist Democratic Party. Some leadership! It was printed in mid-September, and we sent it all over the place in print form and had it online at WinningAmerica.net

Its contents can be applied to 2024 with hardly a change or deletion. This is the mark of political stagnation.

September was a nonstop month. Mark and I divided up lists of people to call. He took the House Democratic Caucus, Michael Moore (good luck with him), Laurence Tribe, Robert Reich, and the July 23rd participants. I took Jamie Raskin, Amy Goodman, the Labor Day Unions, Bill Hillsman, and various senators to open the closed door to Senator Gary Peters (D-MI) in charge of the Democratic Senatorial Campaign Committee. If anybody could have heard us making these calls, leaving messages on voicemail, or with interns answering the phones, or being told "the box is full," or pressing 1, 2, 3, or 4 whatever buttons to no avail, they would say to us: "Why bother?" To which we had all types of happy talk responses so as not to be too solemn. The real answer would seem pompous: "Hey, we want a just society, a functioning fair-play democracy so people can live with their families and with public institutions in peace, and have prosperity and possibilities for themselves and their posterity."

On September 16th we thought we were getting a break. A Democratic National Committee staffer, Mansoor Abdul Khadir, related that former Congressman and special Assistant to Joe Biden, Cedric Richmond, was sent over to the DNC. He sounded excited. The White House apparently didn't think the DNC chair Jaime Harrison was up to the challenge and sent Richmond to bolster activities there. In 2020, Harrison spent a record $120 million in a hapless campaign against Senator Lindsey Graham in South Carolina. The DNC post seems to be a consolation prize for such a colossal defeat.

In July 2021, after extensive efforts, I secured a thirty-minute telephone conversation with Harrison, essentially going over ways to landslide the GOP. I then asked for his response. A minder cut in, saying the chairman had to take an important call and would call me back to continue the conversation. He never did, despite many reminder calls to them.

In any event, around mid-September, Cedric Richmond, having received our materials, was definitive. He would get the July 23rd report "to all campaigns and was eager to get it to the White House." He worried that Stacey Abrams's campaign for governor of Georgia was too narrowly based on the issues. He wasn't worried about Senator Warnock. He especially liked my Kentucky Values approach to the GOP. I mentioned the difficulty of getting our calls returned, giving examples such as Senator Gary Peters. Hakeem Jeffries's staff earlier had left a message with Richmond about when I could call him. We agreed to talk in about a week to take it to the next stage. He did take a call from Mark, who described Richmond as friendly and focused, and reiterated his sending to all candidates and the White House saying, "They should use these arguments. It's what they all need." I never heard from him again. Follow-up telephone calls, letters, emails, and help from third parties were met with silence. Also, neither candidates nor staff ever said they received anything from the DNC or Mr. Richmond regarding our assembled materials honed for immediate practical use in campaigns. I think that "going dark" after a first enthusiastic call should be studied by social psychologists, as it is a widespread aspect of the internet age.

We did have a small consolation prize of our own, speaking to a Zoom conference of the Progressive Democrats of America (PDA) with their director Alan Minsky moderating. It was like preaching to a very laid-back choir. In the following days, despite our invitation to do so, no one connected to help spread the mission.

David Kelley called to give me the contact for David Brock, the new chair of the Cuyahoga County Democratic Party in Cleveland, Ohio. I spoke with him about getting through the force field around Senate candidate Tim Ryan. He immediately agreed to try. He got the same closed-door treatment that we had experienced. Ryan was really cocooned on his way to electoral doom.

Steve Schmidt, a rebel Republican coming out of the anti-Trump Lincoln Project started with George Conway, emphatically assured me he could get us through to Ryan, who he said he was directly helping against J. D. Vance, whom he disliked almost as much as Senator Ron Johnson (R-WI). He called Johnson an authentic crackpot, a Grade-A certified liar. I never heard from him again, despite a couple of calls.

Dana Milbank, the acerbic columnist for the *Washington Post*, called on October 9th to say he was doing a piece on our supporting the Democratic Party. As expected, his twist was that after opposing the Democratic party on the presidential Green Party and Independent Ticket, I was now backing this once-reviled party. Trying to get a broader vista, I poured the essence of July 23rd into his phone, but he already had his column choreographed. It came out on October 12th and became the only major media story about the Winning America project. But it was his take on my position, not on what we had labored on for months. I thought if he got some reactions he would follow up with another treatment before the election, but it didn't happen. Only AlterNet noticed Milbank's column. Quite stunning though, his piece was the only writeup in all of 2022 through Election Day and the turbulent interregnum. Throughout, we did not stop being vocal. Our entry into active pundit land was not to be. MSNBC, which earlier used to have Mark on, as did Fox News, decided to give voice to a more predictable stable of predictable commentators. The Sunday network talk shows kept questioning the same safe talking heads.

A few times in my innumerable conversations asserting some newsworthiness for our doings to youngish reporters, I'd lighten the tone by saying, "You know I didn't come to Washington over fifty years ago on a UFO." We would chuckle. On second thought, had I arrived on a UFO, I would have received almost as much coverage as the three pandas at the Washington Zoo that year.

My nearest contact with Joe Biden was indirect, through former congresswoman Marjorie Margolies, active in Pennsylvania politics. She was an acquaintance of Jill Biden and sent her observations to Valerie Biden Owens. Marjorie was easy to speak with and receptive. She had often witnessed the party's arrogant ways, "They know it all," she said when it comes to outside advice. She liked my columns and sent them around, but she too couldn't get through to the Pennsylvania Democratic Party. She bewailed the GOP controlling the issues—immigration, crime, and inflation—notwithstanding Senator Scott's fifty-page gift to the Democrats.

On October 10th, Mark and his family went out to dinner and took in a movie. What used to be quite routine was described as a respite from the nonstop pace he was maintaining.

Back from Iceland, Marjorie Margolies called, saying she received copies of the print report *Crushing the GOP, 2022* and would get it to Jill Biden and "everywhere I can." Also, she'd pass it on to Valerie Biden Owens and governor-to-be Josh Shapiro, but it needed someone "big to push it, like Pelosi."

About this time, a reporter from Politico called and wanted to know about any usage of our materials by candidates, or whether it was getting too late in the campaign for a reset of rhetoric and policies. I replied that it is by no means too late, but could not refer her to usage thus far—in any major manner, such as applying the Kentucky Values approach or doing midnight campaigning.

I spoke to NPR's political reporter, Ron Elving, a Berkeley graduate. We had a good exchange, I sent him the package, but nothing materialized. NPR has been going increasingly dark on national civic groups' activities, preferring to quote or interview academics, Washington political corporate think tanks, and their own reporters.

Celinda Lake, after reading our report, said she couldn't agree more, and that the Democrats had no unified economic message highlighting labor. In the view of her polling, the Dems should go vigorously after the huge profits of the oil companies, revoke the Trump tax cuts for the wealthy, and press strongly for extension of the children's tax credit blocked by the GOP from being extended in January 2022. She thought MSNBC's Lawrence O'Donnell should be interested in our campaign. There was no response from him.

As noted, in 2018, Representative Jamie Raskin had put out the "Twenty Most Dangerous Votes" of the GOP in the House. Remarkably, the House Democratic Caucus or its Senate counterpart didn't think of doing so nationally and with vivid contrasts. This is just another example of how unorganized they were to even consider what should be a regular salvo every two years. How could they continue to predict their defeat? Raskin himself seemed unable to get the DCCC or the DNC to do what he did in 2018, when he was tired of waiting for his party to tell the people how the Republicans vote against the people.

The list of futile calls continued. Senator Whitehouse (D-RI) could possibly get us through to Senator Gary Peters, but we couldn't get Senator Whitehouse on the phone. Prominent writers and activist professors concurred on the merits but reflected the same incommunicado they themselves had been experiencing in their work. University of Wisconsin Law School professor and consummate activist Joel Rogers painted a grim picture on October 25th of the race between Senator Ron Johnson and Mandela Barnes, saying, "It looks pretty hopeless." A bigger turnout in Milwaukee was not on the radar. In the final days, Barnes closed to within 1 percent. Milwaukee could have brought him a victory, but enough voters stayed home to secure another six-year term for the Trump-like Johnson. This was his third-term victory due to the same low turnout in Wisconsin's largest city.

The last three weeks leading up to Election Day found Mark and me making nonstop calls and sending hundreds of emails. Democratic pollster Stan Greenberg and Patrick Gaspard, head of the Center for American Progress, wrote an open letter urging the Democrats to go big on the economic agenda. Not a budge. The party was unable to readjust or reset their communications and on-the-ground voter turnout. The Congressional Progressive Staff Association (CPSA) with some one thousand staff members couldn't convince their principals to straight-line the GOP's voting record—a service to a more informed public that they should do as normal activity inside the House, irrespective of elections. Marjorie Margolies conveyed by recommendation that Joe Biden deliver resonating concise addresses on the GOP vs. children, GOP vs. women, the GOP vs. workers, and the GOP vs. a safe environment. A coherent communications strategy requires reminding or informing voters of the enormity of the GOP's unprecedented cruelty and self-serving greed.

Biden's speechwriters were not very good, not very assertive, and their boss was not known for coherent presentations that resonated. However, that doesn't mean you give up on the most penetrating messages that reach people's daily experiences. In these last weeks, campaigns are looking to change two or three percent of the voters' minds and to get out more last-minute voters. The candidates are driven into frenzied campaigning hour after hour, mouthing the same few sentences and being shielded from any freelance questioning. At the same time, their consulting media managers are discouraging the ground game to get out to vote in favor of nonstop video/television/radio ads that are either unmemorable or irritate their tired audiences. It would not occur to these corporate-conflicted advisers to urge candidates to campaign with popular local civic groups and their leaders, providing fresh commitments and identifications for a bored media. Not when they can reap 15 percent commissions on ad buys secured weeks or months earlier.

Veteran Democratic supporters such as Joel Rogers and Nick Johnson in Iowa—a former FCC Commissioner and a savvy communicator—would suggest top Democratic politicos for us to call in the close elections. Calls were made and not returned. Some people told us Ed Rendell, former governor of Pennsylvania, could get through to anyone. The problem was that we could never get through to Rendell, who was told what we were trying to do but turned his back.

After many weeks of this incommunicado phenomenon, another potential news story emerged—about the non-communicators. They were into their own silos, cocoons, cul-de-sacs—call it what you will—but they were, of their own making, protecting themselves from any accountabilities and rationalizing failure afterward by saying their consultants told them to do this and that. A DNC staffer blurted out to me that in 2020 the DNC couldn't get through to Amy McGrath's disastrous $80 million campaign to replace Mitch McConnell.

By October 28th I was putting in calls by the hour to offices of candidates in close races and more. They included "Admiral" Mike Franken running against Senator Charles Grassley, Senators Patty Murray, Brian Schatz, Chuck Schumer (D.C.

and New York offices), Pat Leahy (longtime acquaintance), Stephen Lynch, Gary Peters, John Sarbanes, Jon Ossoff, Raphael Warnock, and Maggie Hassan. I was calling to speak with them or with any of their staff willing to convey upward the reasons for my reaching out. Several staffers called back and heard my late campaign recommendations: Get to the higher-ups with a major emphasis on raising the minimum wage to $15 an hour (go vote for a raise, you've earned it) with real lower-wage workers by your side, *slam* the GOP for blocking extension of the child tax credit, for rampant corruption (polls show this issue resonates), talk about putting Main Street over Wall Street (the class issue), do midnight campaigning at different work locations—starting with the midnight shift change at a large hospital and other attention-catching motivations pulled from WinningAmerica. net. Make news, not just rerun old ads. As Election Day nears, more and more people pay attention.

I kept trying to get some media attention about this effort, calling the veteran Greg Sargent of the *Washington Post* and Jim Fallows of the *Atlantic* ("Biden has terrible speechwriters"). Marjorie Margolies said she sent the WinningAmerica project to her sister-in-law, Hillary Clinton, but received no response.

I called Ben Winkler, a Democratic leader in Wisconsin, about the Barnes/Johnson race. No return calls. I conversed with Miles Rapoport, coauthor of *100% Democracy* (argues for voting as a legal duty) and well-connected to Democratic politicians. He threw up his hands, saying he couldn't help either. I called Senator Ed Markey's personal cell phone and learned that his "box was full."

David Kelley called, saying the Ryan campaign wasn't rebutting the GOP attack that he was a lapdog of Biden and Pelosi and that he should use our various advisories. I was told that Ryan's chief fundraiser, Alexandra Leventis, could get us to Ryan. Made the call, in vain. Pat Gaspard, head of the Center for American Progress and a seasoned politico, became excited when I recounted our activities. He had not heard of them earlier in the year (the media blackout again) and the hour was late.

At the same time, Mark was calling people he knew at the *New York Times* and other outlets. He is very persuasive on the phone, having made tens of thousands of calls during his many campaigns for electoral office and civic projects. He paralleled his calls with enticing emails tailored to the person addressed. He called those political podcast hosts who claim they are always looking for good material. Oh, sure! Most are in their own rut. They can't think outside their podcast routines. They just stereotype experienced civic advocates as gadflies having neither money nor influence—never mind their ideas or records of accomplishment.

That raises the question of organized labor. They have campaign PACs and they represent a not inconsiderable amount of labor earnings and pension funds. Also, it is not as if I've been without labor credentials. Having been a leader in the fight to establish OSHA in 1970, I worked with many labor lobbyists on Capitol Hill and around the country on worker health and safety, worker pension funds, and heralded union dissenters against their corporate-indentured leaders. I've been on picket lines pushing for higher minimum wages, environmental justice, and other issues I highlighted as a four-time candidate for president. Sure, I pushed some union leaders—to go vigorously for repeal of Taft-Hartley and to make Labor Day a real worker day—and probably irritated them in the process. I exposed how the CEO of DuPont had corralled the head of the AFL-CIO in 1980, Lane Kirkland, to dampen labor's enthusiasm for our nationwide Big Business Day highlighting corporate crime, fraud, abuse, and unremitting power over our society.

As 2022 wore on, I noticed that the AFL-CIO was unusually quiet. So, I called Damon Silvers, known as that organization's intellectual, and learned he had left daily tasks and become a "senior adviser" while writing a book and lecturing at the London School of Economics and Political Science. Asking what was up, he said that the AFL-CIO had decided to stay in the background and let the local unions pick up the cudgels because they were more trusted with the rank and file. He knew that it was a clever way for the AFL-CIO people in Washington to avoid having to handle some 35 percent of their member unions' workers who voted for Trump.

Damon liked the midnight shift campaign idea because it respected those workers who kept our country going while the rest of America slept and because it directly connected with them at their workplaces. It spreads a word-of-mouth sense of reaching out to see what was on their minds and gives the media a story not ever covered. Hospitals, nursing homes, all-night convenience and drug stores, fire and police departments, emergency and repair crews on standby, and three-shift factories are some stops. I sent him the package, which he sent directly to Liz Shuler, the president of the AFL-CIO. He couldn't understand why she would not go on my radio show/podcast to discuss labor/corporate relations. Bernie Sanders was barnstorming the country with his vintage progressive agenda and not getting much national coverage for his efforts. Damon decried this disinterest by the media. Yet the unions could have elevated his turnout and visibility. He promised to get our late-stage, feasible refinements calling for appealing to left/right voters on "broad and better" advances to Ms. Shuler.

Four days later he called to say she liked several of the suggestions enough to send them to the member unions en route to the locals. He also sent to the teachers union our argument for labeling the GOP anti-children on a broad range of opposed protections. His view was that the Democratic Party sticks too exclusively to its voter base because of corporate money overriding an all-out progressive agenda that can win votes.

The point is contrast, contrast, contrast—not the Dems' messaging strong suit. Even though they are not in contention at all in the red states, why not show some thirty serious livelihood indicators that are worse in these states under Republican Party domination than in the blue states? Start with the GOP governors (Texas, Florida, and others) who turned down federal Medicaid money leading to higher mortality and morbidity levels for children and poor parents there. There are books and articles on these red state/blue state differences that strike at the core of living in America which the Democratic Party strategies have mostly failed to pick up on and send over their mass-media buys and on the campaign trail. Contrast also requires repetition and memorable short slogans.

The *Las Vegas Sun* published an op-ed by us. We sent op-eds to other regional newspapers that were not published. Michael Moore's gloom-and-doom predictions for the Democrats got him on Ari Melber's MSNBC show, but Mark got no invitation to present what he had to say about how the Democrats can find bloom and soon.

A bright spot for the Democrats were the Culinary Workers Union in Nevada and Arizona who worked the old-fashioned way to get out their votes—person-to-person, meetings, rallies, and information. Unfortunately, their efforts—decisive in Nevada's electoral outcome—did not diffuse to other unions around the country at this crucial level of human energy and conviction. Maybe they should barnstorm their union brothers and sisters in time for the 2024 elections.

Ron Elving, having received our materials, called back to say, "You can only do what you're doing." When I mentioned how much coverage the *New York Times* had given to Tucker Carlson (eleven full pages over three daily editions), J. D. Vance (cover of *New York Times Magazine* among numerous prior articles), and Marjorie Taylor Greene (on the cover of the *Times Sunday Magazine*), compared to progressive leaders largely ignored, he said: "There is a peculiar fascination with these people" whose outrageous statements only get them more coverage in the *Times* and *Washington Post*. Then, of course, there were Trump's vulgar lying and false accusations, regularly reported in 2016,[1] that gave him towering media platforms for his gibberish, bigotry, false statements, and outright libel of his named opponents.

The poster man for an incommunicado elected official was my Senator, Richard Blumenthal (D-CT). I've known Dick since he was editor of the *Yale Law Journal*. He was Connecticut's Attorney General for many years. We've had occasional good back-and-forth discussions on substantive issues. He has visited events at our American Museum of Tort Law, where he voiced strong interest in going after corporate crime should he get to chair a Senate subcommittee. It stood to reason that he would be a gateway to Senator Gary Peters and his Democratic Senatorial Campaign Committee.

I stepped up my efforts to speak with him about six weeks before the election by contacting his Washington office and two local offices in Hartford and Bridgeport, and making personal telephone calls. I got to know a twenty-year-old intern, Graham, who didn't know me, while he answered the phones at the senator's office in the Senate Hart Building. I paralleled my calls with ones to Blumenthal's chief of staff, Joel Kelsey, and his communications director, Maria McElwain. After some days of no callback—he was running for an easy reelection in a small state—I enlisted my Congressman John Larson's office to second the motion to connect. Still nothing. A friend facetiously suggested smoke signals near his home in Greenwich.

I called Maureen Moriarty at Representative Larson's Hartford office to be more persistent. After intense effort, she reached Rick Kehoe, who for over thirty years was Dick's political adviser. Kehoe heard and understood my pitch three and a half weeks after Maureen first spoke with him. He replied that these ideas "make sense" and assured me that he would ask Dick to call me. I left him with the plea that if he couldn't achieve that result to let me know. He didn't succeed and I never heard from him again.

After the election, Senator Blumenthal was one of several senators urged to hold hearings during the interregnum to lay the groundwork for 2024—a period when they could breathe freely to focus on categories of public necessity for the people, instead of constantly worrying about how what they're doing would affect their big funders and corporate lobbyists. Back in 2020 during the two-month interregnum, filled with Trump still trying to overturn his 2020 election loss, the Democrats had the power, the nice committee hearing rooms, and the staff to conduct blockbuster hearings throwing contrasting cudgels at the GOP—the "Grand Old Plutocrats." That never happened. Not one of the suggested hearings in the House or Senate was even considered, notwithstanding our volunteering to suggest credible, articulate witnesses providing testimony and the names of reporters long awaiting such revelations and commitment.

Marjorie Margolies called to say that Valerie liked "very much" my suggestion that Biden deliver a major speech on "Our Children and the GOP." Marjorie then exclaimed: "It is so frustrating, I'm sick of them [meaning the Democratic Party operatives] always second-guessing themselves, no emphasis on an authentic economic agenda."

We started getting calls from people we had called weeks earlier, belatedly calling candidates' offices in really close contests, urging last-minute campaign events and language. Gershon Cohen, Alaska's leading public citizen, called from Haines,

Alaska, to say that Mary Peltola, a First Nation Alaskan, was poised to upset the mercurial Sarah Palin, former governor of the state and the vice-presidential nominee with John McCain in 2008. "She's running a great campaign, great mailers, campaigns with Republican Senator Lisa Murkowski in disaster areas and reassures people with her steadiness." Having campaigned for Alaska statehood in Washington during the summer of 1957, in addition to writing a long article published in the *Harvard Law Record* the previous year on the Indian Tribal Nations, I looked forward to speaking with her. She was finishing the congressional term of Republican Don Young, who had passed away earlier in 2022. No luck. I couldn't get through to her and people in Alaska, like Gershon, who tried to open the door, didn't succeed either. Obviously, she has come a long way without my advice.

Election Day saw the Democrats barely holding on to the Senate and losing the House by a difference of ten seats. Then bizarre things started emerging. The Democrats lost five seats they should have won in a state they control—New York—after overreaching in their redistricting. The State Court of Appeals ruled four to three that the Democratic redistricting was invalid and selected a Master to redraw the boundaries. He did in ways that allowed the Republicans to gain five seats on Election Day, including the seat won by the unvetted George Santos, who ran a fraudulent campaign to win in Long Island. It was one of the Democratic Party's worst miscalculations/blunders in its history. The redistricting fiasco was almost the difference in the party's loss of the U.S. House of Representatives. No one was fired. The chair of the state Democratic Party retained his position. This lack of accountability is an immolating pattern of behavior in Washington and the states.

Omnipresent around most congressional Democratic candidates were the consulting firms largely staying in the shadows from the largely disinterested media. An exception was a long treatment by *The Intercept* in April 2021 titled "The Democratic Party's Consultant Factory."[2] The context for this feature was the loss in 2020 of a thirty-four-seat cushion for the Democratic Party in the House, down to just a nine-seat majority. People of color were the majority of voters in seven of the seats the Democrats managed to lose. The loss of minority voters who had generally voted for Democratic candidates was an ominous sign. *The Intercept* warned that "the same miscalculations could cost the party its thin majority, and with it the ability for the Biden administration to legislate." Which is exactly what happened. Pelosi's Democrats lost the House in 2022 by ten seats.

As noted, during 2022, the Democrats were overtly fearful, even defeatist, consequently their campaigns remained overly cautious and unimaginative in attracting and motivating voters. Their slide to near defeat in 2020 prompted *The Intercept* to say that, "In most industries, a failure that stark would lead to an autopsy, a round of firings, and a reformulation of strategy to make sure it doesn't happen again. . . . Instead, according to a review of federal election records and interviews with senior party operatives, the calamity has led to promotions and expanded business opportunities for those at the top."

Whereupon *The Intercept* plunged into a narrative of top staffers leaving the party to start or join lucrative media firms, or spinning off new groups from established ones, taking on all kinds of corporate clients along with reaping the rewards of a party that constantly was expanding its riches to outsource its future performance to corporate-conflicted consultants. The demands for diversity among paid political consultants and campaign staff by women, African Americans, and Hispanics were mostly about carving up the piles of money, not about agendas, revised strategies, or becoming closer to working and jobless people's perceived needs. Polling was deliberately self-censoring of corporate abuses and focused on picking a very few dominant themes at a sufficiently general level, like "healthcare," to carry the campaigns and not upset "the self-dealing nature of party leadership transitions"[3] over controversies of substance.

Recognizing that the overall pipeline of consultants "had" grown significantly more diverse, *The Intercept* found that "the consulting ecosystem has absorbed these new voices with no disruption to business as usual, leaving in place a structure in which major Democratic Party firms spend part of their time working on behalf of candidates and the party, and the rest of their time working for corporate clients. Firms and operatives who reject that approach continue to be shut out, as the party's position with working-class voters of all races continues to weaken."[4] Note that this dual client structure was not necessary to keep these groups paying their bills. On the contrary, the enormous amount of cash from the political side just expanded these operators' ambitions for growth by servicing major corporations.

Jockeying for positions with intrigue and blacklists, rewarding abject loyalty over critical thinking, advancing by way of know-who and sycophancy—instead of know-how and the peoples' inter-est—were rife. The back-and-forth between the major Democratic Party committees—the Democratic National Committee (DNC), Democratic Congressional Campaign Committee (DCCC), the Democratic Senatorial Campaign Committee, the Democratic Governors Association, and the commercial consulting firms was like an incestuous parody of their declared charters.

The overlap is just normal and taken for granted by House and Senate Democrats. After all, both work overtime to raise money from these same corporate sources. *The Intercept* again: "Many of the firms who manage to get business from the party, whether white-owned, minority-owned, or a blend, may be limited by the substantial amounts of corporate work they do at the same time—work that often conflicts with Democratic voters' priorities." *The Intercept* reports, "House Majority Forward, the dark-money group aligned with House Democrats, and House Majority PAC have done work with HIT Strategies, which lists Big Pharma as a client" and also lists progressive organizations as clients.

"After working on the Obama campaign in 2008 and then becoming executive director of the Democratic National Committee, Jen O'Malley Dillon cofounded Precision Strategies, which combined political work with consulting on behalf of health insurers, Silicon Valley, Bank of America, and other major corporations. In 2020, she became Joe Biden's campaign manager after he had sewn up the nomination.[5]

"Dewey Square Group . . . does work for the party as well as major corporate clients, including fighting to roll back Ohio's renewable portfolio standards.

"SKDK . . . a firm staffed by former DCCC operatives that does millions of dollars of work for the DCCC and the party, also does corporate work for clients like Gillette and American Airlines."

While first Native Americans and their supporters were doing nonviolent civil disobedience, getting arrested in freezing weather in several states against TransCanada's Keystone XL Pipeline Project, SKDK helped develop the company's propaganda campaigns against them.

You may be wondering why we thought our Winning America campaign had a chance to ever get a foothold on this political/corporate money pot. True, we avoided any contact with this boiler room hustle. Instead, we took the high road, stating that the Democrats were in trouble and could learn from outside civic groups some things about winning votes. At the outset, we didn't quite realize how rigidly these consulting firms held the reins and controlled the doors for just talking with candidates. The dependency had devolved so far in recent decades that the "agents" played the role of the "principals."

In conversation after conversation with reporters, editors, and producers, I would urge them to investigate this coercive operating dependence. Instead, the media would focus just on the periodic reporting of money raised and, to the extent feasible, who was donating it to the candidates. Often, the main pollsters publicized by this same media were part and parcel of this political/media consulting complex.

So embedded were these polling subsidiaries that the Commission on Presidential Debates selected them to determine whether third-party candidates had the requisite 15 percent support to qualify for all-important presidential debates drawing up to one hundred million viewers. Fifteen percent was a staggering hurdle, given how little media is given to small parties and their candidates. But the commission—created in 1987 and controlled by leaders of the Republican and Democratic parties—was taking no chances. Naturally, no third-party candidate, including Ross Perot in his second run, could overcome that barrier.

Admittedly we had to be a bit naive, if only to keep going against the odds. One of the subjects of our naivete was Stan Greenberg. You'll recall that earlier we had asked him to support our project, and he declined, saying it should be exclusively on corporate power and the economic agenda. Stan had recently turned over the ownership of his giant consulting firm, GQR, to his daughter and other partners.

Here is *The Intercept*:

GMMB, a DCCC mainstay that is stocked with veterans of the organization, also does corporate work . . . Greenberg Quinlan Rosner, the DCCC's lead polling firm, also does heavy corporate work in banking, healthcare, and tech, and has represented everyone from Monsanto and Verizon to Blue Cross Blue Shield and UnitedHealthcare. In 2020, the firm listed the Business Roundtable, a collection of the nation's largest corporations, as a client . . . Stan Greenberg was the top pollster for President Bill Clinton.

Mark, who had read Stan Greenberg's book and other writings, kept trying to get him back on the phone to see if, at least, he could open some doors and suggest sources for funds. His calls were not returned. Stan must have thought we were afflicted with a severe dearth of realpolitik. Didn't we know what he had been doing getting superrich all these years after a short stint as a Yale political scientist?

Hart Research, another DCC polling company, left nothing to inference, listing major trade associations from major sectors of the economy and named corporations. One was Eli Lilly, the producer of insulin that was the subject of lawsuits against its skyrocketing price terrifying people with diabetes. From all its findings, *The Intercept* dryly concluded that "corporate conflicts might narrow the horizons of what Democrats advocate for in the economic sphere . . . that creates incentives for the party to push on the cultural front but not on economic issues, regardless of the electoral implications." Too bad the mainstream media did not pick up from *The Intercept* any interest in making this consulting world part of their election period beat.

Here is one example of monetized consultancies from Texas. In 2020, the 10th Congressional District running from Austin to Houston was 40 percent Black, Asian, and Hispanic. The Democratic candidate, Mike Siegel, secured the support of the DCCC in a drive to flip a Republican seat. Siegel wasn't satisfied that the consultants given him knew how "to run a real left campaign." He told *The Intercept*: "There's not like an alternate framework or ecosystem of pollsters, and consultants who are like: No, this is how you can win with a populist message."

As Jim Hightower would say—you can't beat Texas Republican incumbents with corporatist Democratic candidates. One way or another, the Democratic Party shows who they are beholden to on the critical issues, beyond the existing social safety net. Many millions of voters stay home because they have learned that the party doesn't deliver for them. Unless, that is, there is a pandemic catastrophe when the Democrats overrode unanimous Republican opposition in Congress to enact the laws providing temporary relief to millions of Americans and their families irrespective of their political identities. The GOP's contribution was to shrink the original legislative packages sent to Congress by President Joe Biden. This pipeline is starting to dry up because the programs were time-limited.

Shrugging off their corporate conflicts, the largest firms boast heartily on their websites. SKDK touts itself as, "There is no better place than SKDK if you are in need of strategic communications advice to manage a crisis, protect a brand, advocate an issue, or win an election . . . our experience and track record are second to none." The firm doesn't provide a scorecard of wins and losses for electing "hundreds of members of Congress, senators, mayors, governors, local elected officials and spreading winning ballot initiatives." To do so would require distinguishing between safe seats or one-party districts and its record in any fiercely contested elections or representing underdog candidates. Not to mention their taking credit for elections that were foregone conclusions. SKDK is not alone in its braggadocio. Greenberg, Quinlan, Rosner (GQR) has a similar website. They're all pumping themselves, knowingly oblivious to the hard reality that they are working with golden handcuffs and split loyalties. That is a big reason why tens of millions of Democratic voters stay home, because as they say year after year to pollsters, "They think voting doesn't matter or isn't worth their time."

The interregnum had one electoral run-off that had to be decided in Georgia in January between incumbent Democratic senator Raphael Warnock and Republican Herschel Walker. As was Warnock's first victory two years earlier, the runoff was viewed as a razor's edge contest. I tried to get our usual simple campaign forays and slogans that can be conducted immediately and inexpensively to Warnock and his campaign staff. As with Warnock's first campaign, we were told by longtime supporters and engagers with the Democratic Party that getting through to anyone on this campaign was a formidable task. They had tried and failed, no matter that they were donors, experienced professionals, or academics long engaged in electoral politics. We found them accurate. Warnock squeaked through with 51 percent of the vote, giving the Democrats and three Independents a 51 to 49 majority, with two very shaky Democrats indeed—Senators Joe Manchin (D-WV) and Kyrsten Sinema (I-AZ). This was an ominous cliffhanging win in the Senate election that had twice the number of Republicans up for election as there were Democrats. Ominous because, in 2024, the Democrats have twenty-three incumbents (including three Independents who vote with the Democrats) up for election while the Republicans have only eleven incumbents, mostly in red states. Up against these odds, the Democrats are going with the same playbook, the same ineffective Senator Gary Peters as chair of their Senate campaign committee, and the same crew running the Democratic National Committee (DNC). There are no indications of any shake-ups, changing of the guard, or anything resembling an expressed urgency or dissent that questions the continuance of the status quo mentality. What's more, the Dems have their favorite scapegoat on most state ballots—the Green Party and their fallback scapegoat—the few hard-core Progressives talking out of turn.

Accordingly, let's turn the page and indulge in some observations and recommendations for 2024—a critical year for the two-party duopoly and what remains of democracy in the United States.

CHAPTER 9

Some Obvious but Ignored Paths to Victory with Mandates

Albert Einstein broadly observed that, "No problem can be solved from the same consciousness that created it." This insight requires that the Democratic Party bring into its ranks new dynamic operatives, listen to outside advice, and hear the alarms of more realistic retired politicians for the final months of the 2024 campaign. It is probably too late to expect a changing of the guard at the top of the national and most state political committees. It is not too late to realize that entrenched complacency and conformity comprise a deadly cocktail for November 2024. It is not enough for the Democrats to win by a margin so close that one or two Blue Dog Democrats can "Manchin" the majority into paralytic pastures ripe for majority GOP congressional subversion. Well-known were Senator Manchin's one-vote grips on the Democrats that blocked major portions of Biden's pandemic-era legislation and appropriations. Less well known is how Senator Sinema blocked Biden's modest corporate tax reform package, including the removal of the notorious "carried interest" loophole for the private equity crowd.

Complacency marked the celebration post-November 2022 by the Democrats because they didn't lose the House of Representatives, as previously noted, by as much as some polls predicted. But they *did lose* the House to a GOP whose record should have subjected them to a very major defeat. The new House leader of the Democrats, Representative Hakeem Jeffries (D-NY), told the *Washington Post* in January 2024 that, "Democrats defied political gravity." Jeffries's job is to be optimistic, but projecting that trait with the words, "We were told that the red wave was coming, because of concerns related to the economy and the President's unpopularity. The exact opposite happened," becomes political puffery. No, Representative Jeffries, the "exact opposite" did *not* happen. The GOP took control of the House from Speaker Nancy Pelosi and has been torturing the Democrats every day since. The Democrats, especially in Jeffries's state of New York, handed the House and the well-being of children, low-income people, and the climate to the ravages of a cruel Republican regime, controlled by a tiny clique of mad-dog right-wingers willing to inflict the pain of a government shutdown on its own people. A culture of complacency is one of lowered expectations and heightened contempt for invigorating dissent. We do well to remember that dissent has been the motion of assertion in American history.

Conformity is another name for closing doors to anyone who thinks that the Democratic Party apparatchiks could use some policy and pragmatic advice. Listen to James Carville, described as "the blunt-talking Democratic strategist," saying to a *New York Times* reporter in mid-January 2024:

According to Democratic strategist James Carville, "The DNC, the state party chairs, the labor people, the progressive advocacy groups, they all want a seat at the table. You can have a seat at the table as long as you keep your mouth shut."[1]

In short: no debates in the Democratic primary, no public or private proposals to excite the deadened electorate and give them tangible and aspirational reasons to go and vote. Just shut up and follow the party's orders that again and again have deep-sixed the party at the state and national levels in languid contests with GOP horror shows. Go along with the Democratic Party's blunders, cowardliness, withdrawal from the country, inbred campaigns, and downright surrender of their prospects to an avaricious political/media consulting complex. A network whose main purposes are profits and incestuous backslapping each other as they slip in and out of their corporate-conflicted outfits from the ranks of the party's staff.

The party scarcely knows how to learn from its failures, hold people accountable for them, and replace them with fresh energetic talent. The headlines do not ever read "Democratic Shakeup for Coming Election." Instead, it's largely the same old recycled crowd of sinecurists who don't know how to get out of the way.

The result is what psychologist Irving Janis called "groupthink." As related in James Surowiecki's best-selling book *The Wisdom of Crowds: Why the Many Are Smarter than the Few and How Collective Wisdom Shapes Business, Economies, Societies and Nations*,[2] "groupthink" emerges when "decision makers are too much alike—in worldview and mindset."[3]

According to psychologist Irving Janis, "Homogeneous groups become cohesive more easily than diverse groups, and as they become more cohesive they also become more dependent on the group, more insulated from outside opinions, and therefore more convinced that the group's judgment on important issues must be right. These kinds of groups," Janis suggested, "share an illusion of invulnerability, a willingness to rationalize away possible counterarguments to the group's position, and a conviction that dissent is not useful."[4]

The small number of people in charge of the Democratic Party's strategic and tactical choices fit this profile of groupthink and go beyond not being receptive to dissent. They are not receptive to pragmatic ways to get more votes by more effective communication, real outreach to voters and the all-important people who usually do not vote but can be persuaded to do so with amplification of people-sensitive approaches. Moreover, outside advice can help in deflating the opposition, placing Republican candidates on the defensive, making them seem as not caring for people and being too cozy with cruel and power-hungry profiteers, who are already perceived by many desired voters as preying on them and their communities. It is important to note that asking people and local civic groups what is harming their livelihoods and what they wish for their children gets away from the usual polling questions that reflect the predetermined issues constantly repeated in the media. For example, a January 22, 2024, *Washington Post* article referenced several typically unimaginative poll questions.[5] These repeatedly polled issues become the straitjackets of campaign managers, who often boil poll themes down to a couple of issues defining the entire campaign, as with abortion and expanded costly health insurance. These are indeed strong issues for the Democrats, but they cannot carry the burden of persuasion by themselves. Especially because a narrow agenda may not motivate sizable blocks of voters who want assurances on other actual or looming conditions affecting them, their localities' special problems and needs. This is not an argument for an endless laundry list of issues that some politicos think confuses and dilutes people's attention. It is a plea for a broader number of topics that candidates can champion, depending on timing, place, and audience.

The Democratic Party leaders need to become open-minded and flexible about the ways they can reset campaign strategy and tactics. They also need to break through the clique of political/ media advisers who are often encumbered by self-interested ways and means of running campaigns. Many of those in the consulting class run losing campaigns, depart with their large retainers, and get hired again by clueless Democrats.

All these discussions of messaging must not obscure that the candidates must stand out as appealing, authentic, caring, and knowledgeable representatives of the people.

To open vistas of electoral success, candidates can start by absorbing the six and a half hours of succinct presentations by twenty-four civic leaders of proven accomplishment available on WinningAmerica.net. A summary of their presentations is also on that website under the title "Crushing the GOP—2022." Not only are their issues compelling, they motivate eligible voters to vote, and they cut through the labels given to categories of voters to attract the support of all workers, consumers, patients, elderly, young people, and parents with children. Civic advocates have to speak universally instead of with partisan language to prevail. This approach decisively succeeds if it catches two-thirds to three-fourths of the left/right voters addressed. I've listed some two dozen reforms and redirections strongly supported by this unbeatable left/right coalition, and I'll bet there are plenty more that you can add from the local to the national arenas (see the Appendix).

Here is where my earlier point comes in about contrasting a candidate's record with that of an opponent. Contrast allows you to project a positive narrative of your candidacy while degrading that of your opponent, instead of starting with the latter "slash and burn" which turns off many voters. In 2022, for WinningAmerica.net, we designed such a contrast handout which can be inexpensively printed in the millions. You can design a handout that asks voters to poll themselves on one side of the flyer and then see which candidate agrees or rejects positions on the other side. The value of this handout is that it can score with the "five-minute voter" as well as voters who take more time figuring out their decisions.

Painting the GOP as the party of *no* over the past century lets you contrast the Democratic Party of *yes*—Social Security, Medicare, unemployment compensation, right to unions, worker safety, women's and civil rights, consumer protections (including protecting children), environmental protection, auto safety, and clean water. On these and many other advances, the GOP historically has been the party of *no, no, no.*

YOUR CHOICE in 2022

COMPARE Dems & GOP

1. Raise frozen Minimum Wage
2. Strengthen gun safety laws
3. Tax wealthiest firms and the SuperRich
4. Guarantee freedom for women—Roe
5. End Citizens United and dark $$
6. Provide Medicare-for-All
7. Raise frozen Social Security benefits
8. Restore voting rights
9. Fund child care and sick leave
10. Fight climate violence with renewable energy
11. Reduce skyrocketing RX prices
12. Increase funding to prosecute corporate crooks

WHO'S ON YOUR SIDE?

	DEMS	GOP
1. Minimum Wage	YES	NO
2. Gun Safety	YES	NO
3. Tax Richest	YES	NO
4. Roe & Freedom	YES	NO
5. Dark Money & Elections	YES	NO
6. Medicare-for-All	YES	NO
7. Expand Social Security	YES	NO
8. Voting Rights	YES	NO
9. Child Care/Sick Leave	YES	NO
10. Climate/Renewables	YES	NO
11. Reduce Drug Prices	YES	NO
12. Prosecute Corporate Crooks	YES	NO

Recounting this history up to the present cuts through the camouflaged imagery the GOP place in their political ads and propaganda. People have to be reminded of past records of politicians, and recent records such as that of Donald Trump, who covers over his failures and damage to the American people every day, with little rebuttal. This makes the very useful book *Wrecking America: How Trump's Lawbreaking and Lies Betray All* by Mark Green and me into a veritable handbook for campaign managers. We even address Trump voters, within their various frameworks, in the last chapter "Whose America?"

It is a good idea when you bring together many of the changes and protections you are campaigning for to put them under a bright umbrella—call them, say, "A Compact With the American People." In the 1994 congressional campaign, when Clinton was president, the insurgent Republican Newt Gingrich (R-GA) put together his "Contract for America," with ten promises so dubious and deceptive that critics called it a "Contract *on* America." People heard his standing for something title over and over again, far more than its corporatist contents. He toppled several House Democrats and became speaker of the House.

A *Compact* can also convey the necessary sense of urgency in a more formidable style than using frightful adjectives and adverbs, and project the Democratic Party as the party of *yes* for immediate improvements in the livelihoods of millions of families. These issues embrace extending the child tax credit, paid family sick leave, and childcare paid for by reversing the Trump tax cuts for the under-taxed top 1 percent and big business. Punctuating the *Compact*'s commitments with actual

House and Senate bills and public hearing numbers show the Democratic Party and its candidates to be serious.

The more the Democratic Party focuses on "kitchen-table" improvements where people live, work, and raise their children, the more a left/right support pattern replaces the GOP's empty promises with vague or fabricated cultural values.

However, the GOP, having little real record of caring for "ordinary people," will persist in trying to divert voter attention to the culture wars. The aforementioned "Kentucky Values" contrasts a dozen values reflected and supported throughout our country. The Kentucky Values shows how the GOP's positions and voting records are directly destructive of the civic fabric of our nation. Remember, the GOP blocks raising the federal minimum wage from its present frozen $7.25 per hour—many of the congressional Republicans do not believe in any minimum wage. This poverty ideology by the Grand Old Plutocrats slams hard against Americans believing "that a hard day's work deserves a fair day's pay." This messaging allows easy focus on a key vulnerability of the Trump GOP, that is the widespread revelations in the media, the courts, and congressional hearings of historic levels of blatant corruption involving breaking laws and violating norms of decency and public trust. Nonpartisan revulsion against corruption ranks near the top of political polls all over the country and the world.

Getting more volunteers and getting the best out of them ends up being subordinated to fundraising efforts. How can we increase volunteer time commitments in addition to fundraising? Remember, under the conflicted control of political consultants, there is ample evidence that the more money that is raised the more it is wasted, in addition to enriching the paid firms marketing candidates. Paying legitimate expenses for volunteers, including applying the best-known techniques to have great numbers of lawn signs, candidate campaign buttons, and other indications of vigorous outreach, is a far better way for retaining voter attention than a rip-off ad campaign for another repetitive and forgettable thirty-second TV ad. Campaign staff and volunteers can compile the *best practices* from past and current campaigns to adopt. Candidates don't have the time to reinvent the wheel. Sometimes business marketing techniques can be useful. Netflix pays great attention to choosing the best one or two words for a penetrating description of each of their films or programs. The right words can catch people's attention for candidate proposals.

There are so many fun ways to succeed in getting people's attention so you can then motivate them to vote. Here are a few: When you hear a candidate speaking to an audience, touting themselves, ask them a question almost never asked of them by any voters. "Candidate, you can't do these things by yourself up against the Fat Cat lobbies, how do you specifically propose to empower us, the people, so that we and you can carry the day?" You can add that the great ancient Roman lawyer Marcus Cicero defined for the ages the word "freedom" as "participation in power." The discussion that follows such an opening really stirs up crowds in thoughtful, constructive ways. The jaded reporters and TV crews will take notice as well. Massively repetitive, routine, dull campaigns give candidates all kinds of ways to lose, unless, that is, they are incumbents from a safe seat. In that case, you should be looking for mandates that are perceived as benefiting people. Smug safe seat incumbents have cost the Democratic Party elections by not having dynamism in contested elections. Whatever the complexion of a district and state, it is a very good idea for candidates to figure out how to run *with* the people, *with* the civic groups instead of parading in front of populaces.

Running *with* the people quickens not just candidate causes, but sparks voter idealism and supports what we should aspire to for our country. This is far more effective than just advancing what is already on the table. A major illustration here is the public funding of political campaigns. Most candidates have accepted the current system of nonstop requests for contributions. That shouldn't stop candidates from communing with citizen organizations striving to get on the table, eliminating this gross method of donations for quid pro quo acceptance of the special interest groups' agendas or legislation. Privately, the vast majority of members of Congress hate having to hold out the "tin cup" day after day. The fact that they have the power to completely change this corrupt system should not be ignored by the usual declaration, "I'm not going to engage in a suicidal unilateral disarmament." After all, when candidates speak of the American dream, they address the alleviation of people's anxieties, dreads, and fears of everyday life but also reach for the transformative ideals people like and are ready to embrace.

At this writing, it seems likely that the GOP candidates are going to run unconditionally with their presidential nominee,

Donald Trump. This total loyalty to the bombastic, foul-talking Trump opens the opportunity to demand that GOP candidates disavow or reject any number of his blatant false statements, crazed smears, and opinions. Refusing to do so out of fear of an immediate Trumpian denunciation keeps the Republican candidates on the defense in any formal debate or interaction. This tactic will produce stories that often have legs extending beyond the first day, because they generate comments from various identity groups, which can lead to increased energetic voter turnout.

All the intricate preparations and campaigning outlined here are directed toward getting out more Democratic votes than Republican votes. Effective GOTV efforts require laborious preparation to succeed. That is why GOTV has to have its own singular initiation teams weeks before voter registration and the Election Day push to the polls. With almost half of the eligible voters not voting, the reservoir of nonvoters to turn into voters is huge and, one might add, hugely neglected. The emphasis and polling and targeting is mostly on "likely voters." GOTV efforts focused on the nonvoting pools have proven to be chronically difficult because the outreach has been chronically unimaginative and underfunded. Lower-income Americans are disproportionately nonvoters, and the Democrats can appeal to them against the GOP party of *no* on treating their dire necessities. Devoting the resources to enlist the influencers in their midst and arranging for many personal gatherings in homes, service clubs, and eateries to hear about community needs and frustrations, starting before Labor Day, gives nonvoters time to register and spread the word about the need to vote.

Much can be discovered in the campaigns within the overall campaign to convert nonvoters. Many neighborhood assistance groups, churches, soup kitchens, and assorted charities would be eager to assist in voter education that goes beyond slogans and robocalls. They are the bridge to the civic community that is more trusted by millions of citizens so long wary and weary of betrayal and broken promises.

Another discovery is that it is perfectly legal to offer any voter (regardless of party affiliation) lottery tickets or tickets to musical and sporting events as they leave the voting precinct to boost voter participation. The same goes for passing out invitations, again indiscriminately to departing voters, for a free lunch or dinner at locations such as church basements to meet other neighbors in a celebratory, festive get-together. This also can work to attract a line of food trucks prearranged to receive vouchers for prompt fulfillment. These social inducements address the immense loneliness and withdrawal from anything resembling civic participation by people who are destitute or afflicted. That is why social modes of free transportation to the polls with others from the neighborhoods are such an essential expenditure for GOTV. Exhorting, expensive TV ads are a caricature of GOTV attempts.

Information feedback from the economic underclass about how they are exploited and ignored shows that the Democrats have long since abandoned them at a wholesale level. This political redlining, as Bishop William Barber II has pointed out in vibrant speeches about this "political underclass" around our country, has cost the Democratic Party dearly.

Overall, the Democrats need a public philosophy of governing, not just a better set of strategies and agendas for winning elections. The test for the Democratic Party is what occurs *between the elections* that it wins to the people who have been left behind for so long. With the unimaginable riches accruing to the top one percent, the extension of reality is that about half of American families fall into the category of "poor" and "near poor." The ravages of that economic status go far beyond the customary statistics for these tens of millions of people, especially their children.

Therefore, personal contacts with a massive GOTV drive opens up the necessity for helping and facilitating the entry of these voters into civil society, starting with their neighborhoods. There have been enough "pilot project" successes in so many of these areas of deprivation to learn from. This is a major purpose of assembling these new voters right after they vote at gatherings where they can dine and forge bonds with one another.

Conclusion

Our democracy needs a public philosophy of what is needed to lift up the lives and livelihoods of nearly half of America's populace. It must transcend intense election goals and offer initiatives delineating the broader purpose of "politics" and "democracy" for all. Enough of candidate manipulative "metaphors" and campaigns. We are beyond the point where elections have become off-limits to "democracy" as they increasingly become instruments of plutocratic autocracy, if not worse.

The Democratic Party's regulars, distant as most are from the strains and the pains of so many, need to understand the problems of the people, so as to be part of the solution. I have compiled Five Omnicides to increase practical frames of reference and to broaden the horizons of enlightened self-interest for people and their posterity. These omnicides (See Appendix B), when their perils and proximities are integrated functionally in one's worldview, tend to have unifying impacts overriding the pettiness and short-sightedness that plague the human condition.

Election victories should be viewed as "commencements," not just celebrations, for moving forward fast toward the common good for a good life in the spirit of our Founder's phrase, "the pursuit of happiness."

The Appendixes

The following material amplifies many of the points made in this book. Additional material is available at our website, WinningAmerica.net and at Nader.org.

Appendix A

Reforms and redirections strongly supported by this unbeatable left/right coalition

1. Require that the Department of Defense (DOD) budget be audited annually, and disclose all government budgets. Secrecy destroys accountability.
2. Establish rigorous procedures to evaluate the claims of businesses looking for a government handout which would end most corporate welfare and bailouts.
3. Promote efficiency in government contracting and government spending.
4. Adjust the minimum wage to inflation.
5. Introduce specific forms of taxation reform as well as push to regain uncollected taxes.
6. Break up the "too big to fail" banks.
7. Expand contributions to charity, using them to increase jobs and drawing on available "dead money."

8. Allow taxpayers the standing to sue, especially immunized governments and corporations.

9. Further direct democracy—initiative, referendum, and recall, for starters.

10. Push community self-reliance.

11. Clear away the obstacles to a competitive electoral process.

12. Defend and extend civil liberties.

13. Enhance civic skills and experience for students.

14. End unconstitutional wars and enforce article 1, section 8, of the Declaration of War Act.

15. Revise trade agreements to protect US sovereignty, and resume full congressional deliberations, ending fast track.

16. Protect children from commercialism and its physical and mental exploitation and harm.

17. Control more of the commons that we already own.

18. End corporate personhood.

19. Get tough on corporate crime, providing penalties and enforcement budgets.

20. Ramp up investor power by strengthening investor-protection laws and by creating a penny brigade to pay for an investor watchdog agency.

21. Oppose the patenting of life-forms, including human genes.

22. End the ineffective war on drugs.

23. Push for environmentalism.

24. Reform healthcare.

25. Create convergent institutions.

---

*List is excerpted from chapter 4, page 65 of *Unstoppable*

Appendix B

Five Omnicides Facing Our Unprepared World
By Ralph Nader
January 12, 2024

The countries that straddle our tormented world are woefully unprepared to counter and prevent five omnicides already underway or looming menacingly on the horizon. This is increasingly true with the yearly passage of neglected opportunities. The gap between our mounting knowledge and its application to these global threats is widening.

1. The climate crisis, better called climate violence, producing record storms, wildfires, droughts, sea-level rises, floods, and unprecedented heat waves, is omnicidal. The year 2023 was the hottest in recorded history. Millions of lives are already being lost, with even more people suffering from climate-related illnesses and injuries. In addition, property destruction is rampant. The consequential effects of natural disasters are mounting in terms of damaged agriculture, soil erosion, habitat destruction (leading to species extinction), and the regional spread of insect-borne diseases such as malaria.

    Promised investments for mitigation and prevention made at the international "climate change" conventions have not been fulfilled. Renewable solar energy is growing, to be sure. However, the pace of proven responses required by the accelerating global warming is at abysmally low levels.

2. Viral and bacterial pandemics are looming larger by the decade. Faster transport carriers of infections often zoonotically transmitted, poor collaborations such as between China and the United States, and increasing human-driven mutations from e.g., reckless overuse of antibiotics are exacerbating these problems. The proliferation of laboratories with inadequate safeguards for their "gain of function" and viruses and bacteria breaching containment all are raising alarming scenarios by scientists from many disciplines.

    The COVID-19 pandemic has taken approximately fifteen million lives between 2020 to 2021, according to the World Health Organization. Specialists are saying it is not a question of "if" but a question of "when" future pandemics will occur.

3. The omnicidal perils of nuclear, chemical, and biological weapons are not being confronted with the requisite international arms control treaties. Indeed, the existing treaties between the United States and Russia are being rescinded or suspended, and the remaining ones are in danger of not being renewed and updated. The use of these weapons and their delivery capabilities is becoming decentralized with fast-innovating drones and smart bombs.

    Our Congress has no countervailing forces in motion, no serious hearings, no champions confronting the necessities of applying knowledge to action and compelling an empire-building White House to work to mobilize allies and non-allies alike around the world to negotiate peace treaties which are in everyone's perceived self-interest. (Remember the treaties between the former Soviet Union and the United States.)

4. "Artificial intelligence" or "AI" is viewed by leading scientists and technologists as the ultimate tool capable of advancing an out-of-control doomsday future. Machines replicating themselves and turning on their creators is no longer science fiction. A coherent warning came from computer expert Bill Joy in his seminal article published by *Wired Magazine* on April 1, 2000, titled "Why the Future Doesn't Need Us." He included in his triad of plausible horrors, AI, biotechnology, and nanotechnology and how they are interwoven with one another.

    Without any regulation to speak of, these technologies are being driven by commercial/corporate short-term profit priorities, with heavy government subsidies and contracts. The citizenry's input is not part of the equation.

    In 2014, heavyweights in science and technology, led by Stephen Hawking, released a letter to the world warning of robots that could take control of their operations and replicate their algorithms resulting in direct control of human beings, autonomous weapons, and other seizures of decisions from the human species. It was a one- or two-day story in the mass media followed by a global shrug and back to business as usual. Congress and the parliaments of other nations are unprepared and have done little to develop the enforceable legislation necessary to thwart this relentless self-inflicted momentum to omnicide.

5. Then comes the foundational omnicide stemming from a
    wave of elected dictators enabled by an excluded, deterio-
    rating civil society. Political and corporate power is increas-
    ingly concentrated in the hands of the few at the expense
    of the many. In most countries, the political economy has
    converged into an ever-maturing "corporate state" about
    which President Franklin D. Roosevelt issued a warning in
    a 1938 message to Congress:

    > The first truth is that the liberty of a democracy is not
    > safe if the people tolerate the growth of private power to
    > a point where it becomes stronger than their democratic
    > state itself. That, in its essence, is Fascism—ownership of
    > government by an individual, by a group, or by any other
    > controlling private power.

    Kleptocratic regimes come in various styles, depending
    on the nation's stage of development, and operate by steal-
    ing from the future to enrich and entrench themselves in the
    present. Both in so-called developed and developing coun-
    tries, they are displacing any semblance of modestly func-
    tioning democracies able, with the primacy of civil values
    and the rule of law, to foresee and forestall these approach-
    ing omnicides.

    Where is the hope? Where it always has been, in soci-
    eties with deliberative democratic practices and traditions
    of civic engagement that lean toward governments of, by,
    and for the people. Just 1 percent of the people resolving
    to commit and connect can start reversing these ominous
    drifts toward the cliffs.

As Thomas Jefferson said, "I know no safe depository of the ultimate powers of the society but the people themselves; and if we think them not enlightened enough to exercise their control with a wholesome discretion, the remedy is not to take it from them, but to inform their discretion by education."[1]

Appendix C

Suggestions for Successful Elections in 2020 at All Levels
By Ralph Nader
October 2020

The following are *Eleven Suggestions* for getting out more progressive voters to the polls in the approaching elections at the local, state, and national levels. For a variety of reasons and causes, tens of millions of eligible Americans do not vote. These ideas can spark interest and participation by these citizens, and regular voters, in shaping a more productive and fair democratic society. Spread the word.

The following items were assembled before COVID-19, which means that some of them need to be altered accordingly, while the majority are not significantly affected.

Corporatist right-wingers prefer to campaign on "values" and not on their voting records. They cannot answer the question—"Which side are you on?"—in ways that appeal to voting families. Right-wingers will describe deceptively a law they voted for, such as the tax cut for the rich and the corporations (2017), but for the most part, they block or oppose votes to provide necessities for the people. Right-wingers prefer campaigning about "values" and abstractions. Consequently, in 2014 when Senator Mitch McConnell was up for reelection, I drafted a list of Kentucky Values and compared them to the contrary positions and votes of McConnell. The latter were clearly contrary to broad Kentucky values. A member of Congress hand-delivered to McConnell's opponent this list of values in the context of McConnell's votes. McConnell's opponent declined to use this approach in the campaign. The *Louisville Courier-Journal*—the state's largest newspaper, thought enough of the message to print it as an op-ed by me.

Of course, every state—Texas, Georgia, Wisconsin, Minnesota, etc.—can be seen as having similar broad and appealing values. Comparing an incumbent's vague embrace of values to the incumbent's specific votes and positions is powerful and can motivate voters to look beyond campaign slogans and platitudes. It makes the "values rhetoric" clash with the reality of the incumbents' actions. No more using abstractions as camouflage for the misdeeds on the ground. It makes the politician's *record* matter.

Getting out the vote by telephone banks, postcards, or door knocking is important but has several limitations. It doesn't work very well with nonvoters or people who do not see that the election matters to them where they live, work, and raise their families. (The "pox on all your houses" people.) This memo—*pre-COVID-19*—emphasizes the importance of early person-to-person conversations and developing relationships in neighborhoods organized and staffed by full-time organizers and local "influencers." The memo suggests transportation options and then postelection celebrations to solidify voter participation and future civic and electoral action. The price tag is half of what Mr. Bloomberg spent to end up winning American Samoa in the Democratic presidential primary. Adjustments here need to be made for much greater mail voting.

The theme of *corruption* must be prominent and continually restated. No matter the polls or the country, when people are asked what they dislike the most about government and politicians, corruption is almost always near or at the top of their concerns. The Trump administration is the most deeply overt, covert, and varied *corrupt* regime in US history—think of the daily impeachable offenses such as spending unauthorized money, also a federal crime under the Anti-Deficiency Act, and defying scores of congressional subpoenas that reflect corrupt Trumpian practices. *Corruption* is a word that sticks in people's minds. Use it, repeat it, exemplify it to strike home.

Make the voting record of the incumbent—and the positions taken—specific and personal to voters. Here is one approach (call it a "Voter Self-Help Guide"—Where do you stand?). On one side, you ask the voters yes or no questions on several important issues. On the other side, you can then compare candidate answers with the positions of their opponents and yourself. Of course, there can be different designs, including ones suited to social media. But the goal should be to show that the incumbent *disagrees* with the voter and the challenger *agrees* with the voter.

The many bad votes of the adversary need to be publicized for a deep imprint. It is remarkable how little attention is given to this strategy. The aggregate votes show that the "whole is larger than the sum of its parts." On television or in social media, this aggregate list can be broken down into a serial rendition—showing a string of votes over days. This will be both dramatic and compelling and will have a deep imprint, unlike a conventional thirty-second ad.

Millions of Americans who work the midnight shift are keeping the country going while we are sleeping. These include healthcare workers, nursing-home staff, police, firefighters, convenience store clerks, fast-food restaurant employees, gas station attendants, and other all-night workers at retail stores (e.g., drugstores and grocery stores), all-night factories, security guards, etc. The candidates can issue a one-page press release describing the categories of workers and thanking them. These workers are not part of campaign events, and they know they are marginalized by candidates. Candidates can show these workers how valued they truly are. Candidates who campaign at night, starting at the midnight shift before the largest hospital in your district or state, will see the benefit of visiting workers from midnight until 3:00 a.m. or so, especially with likely news coverage and social media outreach. Candidates as "midnight campaigners" will be much appreciated, and word of mouth will spread the news of the "midnight" candidate's concern for the forgotten workers.

Winning elections without *mandates* will leave a cynical trail among voters. Empty ads violate the principle that *policy* precedes *message*. Candidates need to persuade people that they want to win with mandates from the people, that they know where they came from and won't forget the specifics on which the candidates campaigned. Campaigning on mandates will produce supportive feedback for campaigns from tens of thousands of active people. Mandates mean postelection accountability and preelection contrast with one's opponents.

Trump has shown the power of his *nicknames*. Why? Because, astonishingly, the mass media keeps repeating them over and over again (including during the 2016 campaign) without offering the target of his pejorative nicknames a chance to reply. Ordinarily, candidates do not use nicknames, and principled candidates don't want to descend to his level. But as a top Trump campaign official gleefully said on NPR—they work, why not use them? Nicknames *in return* blunt Trump's nicknames from working. Giving a bully his own medicine, including circulating millions of buttons, signs, and posters, will either help get equal time or stop the initiator from engaging in this branding tactic.

In Florida, ex-felons, owing a few hundred dollars in unpaid prison fees, court costs, etc., still may be obstructed from voting despite Florida overwhelmingly passing a constitutional amendment allowing them to vote. With the governor opposed, the courts still in process, it is worth expanding on LeBron James's $100,000 down payment to the Florida Rights Restoration Project to start paying off the debts, with more money to come from his new "More Than a Vote" organization. But will it be enough? A Michael Bloomberg level contribution is needed for the hundreds of thousands of ex-felons who know the specific amount owed. Others await notice of the amounts due. It is a mess but very worth addressing, given how close and consequential Florida elections have turned out to be.

Candidates running for Congress or for the governorship of states need better coaching for candidate debates. There are times while watching these debates when it is difficult to distinguish between the positions of Democrats and Republicans. Too many Democrats have lost when they should have easily won given the voting record and/or public stands by the Republicans. The Democrats too often come across as tentative, cautious, defensive, and seemingly unwilling to let the audience really know the difference between them and their opponents (answering the perennial question "Whose Side Are You On?"). Why? Because they often don't really know who they are—and because they are coached by dim or conflicted consultants, Democratic candidates also don't seem to know how to reply and gain the momentum by ending a response and answer that opens new attack themes. The questions asked by debate moderators and reporters are part of the problem. More attention needs to be paid to training candidates to propose consequential questions during debates. There are reasons why the Democrats have lost four of the last five House elections to the worst, most vicious, anti-worker/consumer, corporate cronyism party in GOP history.

Debate content, timing, and techniques need to be the subject of national training sessions. The ads that will follow can present powerful themes and be worth their price because they will be more memorable for word-of-mouth communications.

In 2018 the Democrats could have won four more Senate seats had Democratic candidates not tried to sound like Republicans—and talked about what families and young voters really need and want from the most powerful (under the Constitution) branch of government (e.g., making livelihood protections that elaborate the disgraceful status quo).

Candidates need to develop *powerful uniform themes,* grouped as a highly visible "commitment to voters," that attract more left/right support from people who have household and neighborhood conditions on their mind, *writ small* and *writ large* (living wage to healthcare costs and access to job-intensive infrastructure projects in their community—to cite three of many). Focus on what the perceived necessities and injustices are by families, regardless of the political labels they place on themselves.[2]

There are many issues bringing left/right voters together just waiting for elaboration and authentic candidate stands. Put simply, a left/right approach nationalizes the election and recognizes that conservatives, liberals, progressives all get ripped off by companies, all are exposed to toxic pollution, crumbling public services, the many controls of big companies, health and safety hazards, and most have a surplus of *anxiety, dread, and fear* about the future. The Democratic Party can take command of agendas and reforms that Republicans will not support and cannot be blurred, or credibly denied and are on most people's minds.

One such long overdue non-blurrable issue is raising the federal minimum wage from its long-frozen level of $7.25 per hour to $15 an hour. The party needs to make its existing support more vocal, visible, and repeated in many human-interest contexts. The party should accelerate its implementation and not wait for five years as did the House-passed bill. Over twenty-five million workers will benefit in intangible ways. The message must be authentic, vivid, front and center, and not just seen as the political rhetoric from past years.

An authentic and well-publicized *contract with America* needs to be drafted and widely disseminated by all Democratic candidates after Labor Day. Veteran politicians have told me people do not know what the Democratic Party stands for—its agenda is too piecemeal. Look at their weak slogans. Even with the Republicans blocking the next massive relief bill, already passed by the Democrats last May, the contrasting message of what the Democrats stand for is not getting through to the majority of the voters. If the message, in its granularity, were getting through, the polls would be plummeting for the GOP, not merely sliding.[3]

Appendix D

Unmasking Phony Values Campaigns by the Corporatists
By Ralph Nader
October 17, 2018

Corporatist candidates like to talk up *values* without getting specific and without drawing attention to how their voting records put the interests of big financial backers against the interest of most voters. This election season is no exception, from Florida to Texas to California to Ohio to Wisconsin. In 2004, I wrote the following article for the Louisville *Courier-Journal* comparing Kentucky values to the starkly opposing record and behavior of Senator Mitch McConnell.

All current candidates for elective office who stand for "we the people" and believe that big corporations should be our servants, not our masters, may find this list of values applicable in their states. Corporatist opponents' voting records, positions, and their campaign contributors' interests can be clearly compared with civic values and any other values voters and candidates wish to highlight. This kind of comparison can only help to turn out larger numbers of voters who want to elect candidates who will champion consumer, worker, children, and small taxpayer causes.

From my travels throughout Kentucky, starting with the late 1960s campaign for coal miners' health and safety laws, I've observed that Kentuckians would like their politicians to be driven by Kentucky values. This election season, voters must be wondering: How has Sen. Mitch McConnell lived up to key Bluegrass State commitments?

1. Rewarding hard work

Kentuckians don't want handouts—they believe in working for a living. That's why they believe in a fair day's wage for a fair day's work.

Mitch McConnell is worth more than $27 million, but has blocked efforts to prevent the minimum wage from seriously eroding due to inflation. He would rather allow McDonald's and Walmart have taxpayers, through the earned income tax credit, pay for their workers' public assistance than raise their minimum wages to meet workers' basic needs.

2. Honoring your elders

Many Kentuckians follow the Fifth Commandment: Honor thy father and thy mother. They believe our elders, after a lifetime of work, deserve a decent living standard.

Mitch McConnell dishonors our fathers and mothers when he says that the government should cut funding for Social Security and Medicare, programs that give Kentucky elders, who paid into these safety nets, much-deserved security in their golden years.

3. Practicality

Kentuckians want politicians to have the same practical problem-solving spirit that they and their neighbors exhibit in daily life.

Mitch McConnell has called himself a "Proud Guardian of Gridlock" in Washington and, as the *Washington Post* wrote, has "raised the art of obstructionism to new levels."

4. Respecting women

Kentucky women have made sure that respect and equality for women is a pillar of Kentucky culture.

Mitch McConnell has shown where he stands on disrespecting women: He has voted against helping mothers take leave for sick children, domestic violence victims seeking justice, and working women seeking fair pay.

5. Being forthright

Kentuckians don't like politicians talking behind their back—saying one thing to them in public and another in closed rooms full of fat cats.

Mitch McConnell does just that, meeting privately with the multi-billionaire Koch brothers and promising even more Senate opposition to raising the minimum wage, extending unemployment benefits, and helping students pay for college.

6. Responsibility

Kentuckians believe people should be held responsible for how they treat others. They believe corporations should be held responsible for the harm they cause to their workers.

Mitch McConnell has helped roll back safety measures that hold corporations responsible for worker safety. At the urging of business groups, he helped pass a resolution declaring that

Clinton administration safety rules protecting against repetitive-stress injuries "shall have no force or effect." The United Mine Workers of America's legislative director Bill Banig said McConnell has "not done anything to help us with mine safety."

7. Love thy neighbor

Kentuckians don't want their neighbors in hard times dying because they're struggling to make ends meet. That's why they don't want their neighbors subjected to "pay or die" healthcare, whether it is because of the staggering prices of drugs, operations, emergency treatments, or health insurance.

Mitch McConnell stands opposed to the most efficient healthcare system, single payer, or full Medicare for all: everybody in, nobody out, with free choice of doctor and hospital. He even campaigned vigorously against Kynect, which has helped hundreds of thousands of Kentuckians sign up for healthcare.

8. No one being above the law

Kentuckians do not believe anyone should be above the law. They want Wall Street crooks who crashed our economy and were bailed out by taxpayers to be prosecuted and put in jail.

Mitch McConnell is an avid Wall Street protector in Congress while he takes campaign cash from Wall Street bosses who he works to keep above the law. He has pledged to "go after" Dodd-Frank financial protections and has been a vocal opponent to the law-enforcing Consumer Financial Protection Bureau. According to the Center for Responsive Politics, Wall

Street was the No. 1 contributor to McConnell's campaign committee from 2009–14.

9. Defending the Constitution

Kentuckians defend the Constitution and especially believe in its first phrase: We the People. They believe that corporations are supposed to be our servants, not our masters.

Mitch McConnell has said that the "worst day" of his political life was when Congress passed the bipartisan McCain-Feingold campaign finance reforms aimed at limiting corporate influence on governance. He proudly told a group of billionaires that the *Citizens United* decision allowing floods of corporate money into elections was a victory for "open discourse."

10. Patriotism

Kentuckians love the commonwealth and the nation. They honor our soldiers and the fallen for their loyalty to America.

Mitch McConnell has allied with disloyal, unpatriotic corporations who are abandoning America. He voted against laws that would help stop outsourcing and voted for tax breaks that perversely reward corporations for shipping American jobs overseas.

McConnell also voted in 2003 to defeat an amendment to provide $1 billion in lifesaving body armor for the National Guard in Iraq and later in 2005 voted against an amendment to provide $213 million for more protective Humvees from roadside bombs in Iraq.

As Kentuckians head to the polls this November, I hope they keep these facts in mind about how McConnell has opposed these long-standing Kentucky values.[4]

Appendix E

An Invitation to a Conversation
January 2018

Investment in a recovering democracy produces the greatest all-around returns for our country. Investment in a tightening plutocracy disintegrates our society and its prospects. What follows is a proposal for an enlightened citizenry funded by the enlightened affluent starting now. Compare the proposed investments with what are the benefits of having a Congress that is accountable to voters and that respects the just rule of law starting in January 2019.

Objective: Organize a Civic Initiative to get out the votes of *ten million Americans* who otherwise would not have voted in selected states and congressional districts, laying the basis from April to November 2018.

It is likely, based on the 2014 turnout, that over two-thirds of the voting-age voters will stay home for the midterm congressional elections of November 2018. That numbers about 150 million people! If a *different Congress* is not elected, all the present "clear and present dangers" will receive two additional years of accelerating implementation with all their serious direct and indirect harms to our county at all levels among the populace and to our country's posterity.

Traditional partisan political efforts to bring out the vote from this vast pool of about 150 million nonvoters—phone banks, advertisements, mailings, and other unilateral exhortations—have not been very successful. We have ample warning that 2018 could give us the same-old, same-old practices and the same fate of past years. There has been no shake-up of the political bureaucracies, political consultants, and their traditional single-issue allies for more vigorous, more creative, and more intensive get-out-the-vote efforts. Another disastrous specter of déja vu is clearly ahead of us. We need a fresh, new entry for bringing out a significant and decisive number of new voters in strategically selected congressional districts.

What is proposed here is a *civically driven* labor-intensive, educational, neighborhood effort over about seven months to bring out adequately informed, motivated voters who, registered or not currently registered, have usually stayed home. This civic drive would be enhanced by often discussed, fair and prudent redirections, reforms, and realistic visions for the good society enabling better livelihoods and the good life for millions of deprived people and families.

There would be lively discussions, more formal teach-ins, get-togethers for neighborhood feedback, and daily contacts by locally respected "influentials" in various residential venues. The necessities, wants, and values of the voters would be related to Congress to which so much of the sovereign powers of citizens have been delegated under our Constitution. This mutual learning/educational process will use the most effective person-to-person and modern media techniques of achieving regular preelection attendance, increasingly motivated as their perceived empowerment increases.

This week after week of *personal* attention is designed to bring out new voters to the polls en masse. Citizens will have been properly registered, and voters will be trained to overcome other, in time, Election Day hurdles to voting. Organizers will carefully plan for Election Day so that voters' voices are heard at the ballot box.

Past low voter turnout by citizens living within communities in need of a sensitive, responsive Congress will receive foremost attention.

Too many members of Congress focus on indicators such as GDP, the stock market, corporate profits, and the increases in wealth (the greatest percentage of wealth gains going to the top one percent). Unfortunately, too few members of Congress truly focus on the daily life and livelihoods of the majority of Americans and the impoverishment, debt, anxiety, dread, and the fear people have for their family's future. Let's face it, half of the people are poor, given what economists think is required for a family of four to have the basic necessities. Collectively, many people have given up on "politics," which they view as a dirty word, which of course, assures that we get dirty politics created by such mass withdrawal from the electoral political process writ large, before and beyond Election Day.

Why would ten million nonvoters become voters in 2024? Because for seven months they will be respected—and located, informed, and connected to their friends, neighbors, relatives, and recognized "influentials" in their communities. Because they will be discovering themselves as sensitive, reflective citizens—much as the poor farmers and their travelling lecturers did in East Texas around 1887 to start the greatest political reform movement in US history around fundamental issues of power, economics, and accountability spearheaded by their own candidates (see *The Populist Moment* by the late Lawrence Goodwyn, Professor of History at Duke University). With seven months of interactions and elevated aspirations, the usual stereotypes of get-out-the-vote campaigns are replaced with lengthy educational and motivational sequences for a better life.

It comes down to advancing prospects for a better life and livelihoods in safe, "neighborly" neighborhoods with the essentials of living wages, universal health insurance, decent shelter, safer consumer goods, especially food and drugs (environmental protections, air, water, soil, and climate), properly maintained public facilities, and effective community services. Responsive governments and political reforms also will be necessary to sustain these advantages.[5]

Notes

Chapter 1: "What's Past Is Prologue . . ."

1   Norah O'Donnell, "Are Members of Congress Becoming Telemarketers?," *60 Minutes*, April 24, 2016, https://www.cbsnews.com/news/60-minutes-are-members-of-congress-becoming-telemarketers/.

2   Timothy H. Edgar, ACLU Legislative Counsel to Interested Persons, memorandum, September 13, 2002, "War Powers and the President's Authority to Launch Military Operations Against Iraq," ACLU, https://www.aclu.org/documents/interested-persons-memo-war-powers-and-presidents-authority-launch-military-operations-against.

3   Norman Solomon, Karen Bernal, Pia Gallegos, and Sam McCann, "Autopsy: The Democratic Party in Crisis," https://democraticautopsy.org/democratic-party-in-crisis/.

4   Glenn Kessler, Salvador Rizzo, and Meg Kelly, "Trump's False or Misleading Claims Total 30,573 over 4 Years," *Washington Post,* January 24, 2021, https://www.washingtonpost.com/politics/2021/01/24/trumps-false-or-misleading-claims-total-30573-over-four-years.

5   Glenn Thrush and Coral Davenport, "Donald Trump Budget Slashes Funds for E.P.A. and State Department," *New York Times,* March 3, 2017, https://www.nytimes.com/2017/03/15/us/politics/budget-epa-state-department-cuts.html.

6   Sharon Lerner, "How Trump Gutted OSHA and Workplace Safety Rules," *The Intercept,* October 20, 2020, https://theintercept.com/2020/10/20/trump-osha-workplace-safety-covid/.

7   "FTC Budget Would Shrink under Trump Plan," Bloomberg, May 23, 2017, https://news.bloomberglaw.com/esg/ftc-budget-would-shrink-under-trump-plan.

8   "Trump Administration Cuts NHTSA Vehicle Safety Budget by 40 Percent," Safe Braking, November 15, 2019, https://safebraking.com/trump-administration-cuts-nhtsa-vehicle-safety-budget-by-40-percent/.

9   Liz Alesse, "Did Trump Try to Cut the CDC's Budget as Democrats Claim?," ABC News, February 28, 2020, https://abcnews.go.com/Politics/trump-cut-cdcs-budget-democrats-claim-analysis/story?id=69233170.

10 Rebecca Cokley and Valerie Novack, "The Trump Administration's Deregulation of Nursing Homes Leaves Seniors and Disabled at Higher Risk for COVID-19," Center for American Progress, April 21, 2020, https://www.americanprogress.org/article/trump-administrations-deregulation-nursing-homes-leaves-seniors-disabled-higher-risk-covid-19/.

11 Scott Cohn, "The American Greed Report: Food Safety Measures Face Cuts in Trump Budget," CNBC, July 6, 2017, https://www.cnbc.com/2017/06/30/american-greed-report-food-safety-measures-face-cuts-in-trump-budget.html.
12 Charles Piller, "Undermining CDC," *Science*, October 14, 2020, https://www.science.org/content/article/inside-story-how-trumps-covid-19-coordinator-undermined-cdc.
13 Senate Budget Committee, Trump Budget Public Health Fact Sheet, February 12, 2020, https://www.budget.senate.gov/imo/media/doc/SBC%20Trump%20Budget%20Public%20Health%20Fact%20Sheet%202–12-20%20FINAL.pdf.
14 Juana Summers, "Timeline: How Trump Has Downplayed the Coronavirus Pandemic," NPR, October 2, 2020, https://www.npr.org/sections/latest-updates-trump-covid-19-results/2020/10/02/919432383/how-trump-has-downplayed-the-coronavirus-pandemic.

Chapter 2: Floundering Democratics
1 "The Do Nothing Congress: A Record of Extremism and Partisanship," https://nader.org/wp-content/uploads/2014/02/GOP-Outrageous-Votes-10-2012v3.pdf.

Chapter 3: Early Warnings
1 Ralph Nader, "Reflections of a Trump Voter Who Still Loves President Trump," *Boston Globe*, June 23, 2017, https://www.bostonglobe.com/opinion/2017/06/22/reflections-trump-voter-who-still-loves-president-trump/uH1dbdJGEqjgc1nCusXdfI/story.html?event=event12.

Chapter 4: Winning or Losing America
1 David George Boyce, "Review of *Wars of Empire*," *The Journal of Military History* 70, no. 3 (2006): 850–51, https://doi.org/10.1353/jmh.2006.0153.
2 Ralph Nader, "Speaker Nancy Pelosi Writes to Me!," Common Dreams, August, 1, 2020, https://www.commondreams.org/views/2020/08/01/speaker-nancy-pelosi-writes-me.
3 Links to columns, the Ralph Nader Radio Hour, letters, and tweets can be found at: https://nader.org/.
4 Nadja Popovich, Livia Albeck-Ripka, and Kendra Pierre-Louis, "The Trump Administration Rolled Back More Than 100 Environmental Rules. Here's the Full List," *New York Times*, January 20, 2021, https://www.nytimes.com/interactive/2020/climate/trump-environment-rollbacks-list.html.
5 Chuck Marr, Samantha Jacoby, and George Fenton, "The 2017 Trump Tax Law Was Skewed to the Rich, Expensive, and Failed to Deliver on Its Promises." Center on Budget and Policy Priorities, March 5, 2024, https://www.cbpp.org/research/federal-tax/the-2017-trump-tax-law-was-skewed-to-the-rich-expensive-and-failed-to-deliver.

Chapter 5: Ideas and Action for Change

1 The presentations from the Breaking Through Power conference can be found at: https://www.breakingthroughpower.org/.

Chapter 6: Building on the Foundation

1 Office of Technology Assessment Archive, https://ota.fas.org/otareports/.
2 A 12 Point Plan To Rescue America: What Americans Must Do To Save This Country, https://rescueamerica.com/12-point-plan/.
3 Doug G. Ware, "'This Was Not a Surprise': Pentagon Again Fails Annual Audit of $3.8 Trillion in Military Assets," *Stars and Stripes*, November 16, 2023, https://www.stripes.com/theaters/us/2023–11-15/pentagon-failed-audit -shutdown-funding-12064619.html.

Chapter 7: Lights, Camera, Action—or Inaction

1 "Political Issues that Matter," http://votenader.org/issues/.
2 Mark Green and Ralph Nader, *Wrecking America: How Trump's Lawbreaking and Lies Betray All* (New York: Skyhorse Publishing, 2020), 85.
3 Ibid., 261.
4 Mark Green and Ralph Nader, *Crushing the GOP, 2022* (Washington, DC: Essential Books, 2022), Robert Kuttner, 7–9.
5 Ibid., David Cay Johnston, 9–11.
6 Books by Thom Hartmann available only online can be found at: https: //www.thomhartmann.com/thom/books.
7 Green and Nader, *Crushing the GOP, 2022*, Thom Hartmann, 11–14.
8 Ibid., Dr. Steffie Woolhandler, 15–17.
9 Ibid., Dr. Irwin Redlener, 17–19.
10 Ibid., Richard Aborn, 21–23.
11 Ibid., Russell Mokhiber, 23–25.
12 Ibid., Notes, Richard Aborn, 25–26.
13 Ibid., William Hartung, 27–28.
14 Ibid., Ret. Col. Lawrence Wilkerson, 29–30.
15 Ibid., Marielena Hincapié, 30–33.
16 Ibid., Robert Fellmeth, 33–32.
17 Ibid., Jamie Raskin and Mark Green, 35–37.
18 Ibid., Notes, Mark Green, 37–40.
19 Ibid., Mark Green, 41–44.
20 Jim Hightower's columns are available at: https://jimhightower.substack .com/.
21 Green and Nader, *Crushing the GOP, 2022*, Jim Hightower, 45–47.
22 Ibid., Anat Shenker-Osorio, 47–49.
23 Ibid., Bill Hillsman, 49–52.
24 Ibid., Notes, Mark Green, 52–53.
25 Ibid., Mark Green and Heather McGhee, 55–57.
26 Ibid., Robert Weissman, 57–59.
27 Ibid., Ruth Ben-Ghiat, 59–61.
28 Ibid., Ruth Ben-Ghiat and Mark Green, 61.

29 Ibid., Notes, Mark Green, 61–66.

30 Ibid., Annie Leonard, 67–68.

31 Ibid., Notes, Mark Green, 69.

32 Ibid., Mark Green and Joe Madison, 70–71.

33 Ibid., Ralph Nader, 73–79.

34 For additional information, see: https://winningamerica.net/.

Chapter 8: Before the Fall

1 Kyle Cheney, Isaac Arnsdorf, Daniel Lippman, Daniel Strauss, and Brent Griffiths, "Donald Trump's Week of Misrepresentations, Exaggerations and Half-Truths," Politico, September 25, 2016, updated September 25, 2016, https://www.politico.com/magazine/story/2016/09/2016-donald-trump-fact-check-week-214287; Alan Yuhas, "How Does Donald Trump Lie? A Fact Checker's Final Guide," *The Guardian*, https://www.theguardian.com/us-news/2016/nov/07/how-does-donald-trump-lie-fact-checker.

2 Ryan Grim and Rachel M. Cohen, "The Democratic Party's Consultant Factory: An intercept investigation finds that a revolving door of friends and colleagues at the top echelons of the DCCC reinforces its corporate sensibility," *The Intercept*, April 6, 2021, https://theintercept.com/2021/04/06/democratic-party-dccc-political-consultant-factory/.

3 Ibid.

4 Ibid.

5 Ibid.

Chapter 9: Some Obvious but Ignored Paths to Victory with Mandates

1 Michael D. Shear and Katie Rogers, "Democrats Fret That Biden's Power Players Are Not at His Campaign Base," *New York Times*, January 14, 2024, https://www.nytimes.com/2024/01/14/us/politics/biden-democrats-campaign-base-delaware.html.

2 James Surowiecki, *The Wisdom of Crowds: Why the Many Are Smarter Than the Few and How Collective Wisdom Shapes Business, Economies, Societies and Nations* (New York: Doubleday & Co., 2004).

3 Ibid., 36.

4 The Wisdom of Crowds, chapter 2, part IV, http://wisdomofcrowds.blogspot.com/2010/01/chapter-two-part-iv.html.

5 Dan Balz, Scott Clement, and Emily Guskin, "Trump Leads by Wide Margin in N.H. Primary, Post-Monmouth Poll Finds," *Washington Post*, January 22, 2024, https://www.washingtonpost.com/politics/2024/01/22/trump-leads-new-hampshire-post-monmouth-poll/.

Appendixes

1 Ralph Nader, "Five Omnicides Facing Our Unprepared World," Nader.org, January 12, 2024, https://nader.org/2024/01/12/five-omnicides-facing-our-unprepared-world/.

2 See this excerpt from my book *Unstoppable*: https://nader.org/2014/04/27/unstoppable-25-proposals/.

3   Ralph Nader, "Suggestions for Successful Elections in 2020 at All Levels,"
    Medium, October 9, 2020, https://rnader.medium.com/suggestions-for
    -successful-elections-in-2020-at-all-levels-782c5e236c21.
4   Ralph Nader, "Unmasking Phony Values Campaigns by the Corporatists,"
    Nader.org, October 17, 2018, https://nader.org/2018/10/17/unmasking
    -phony-values-campaigns-by-the-corporatists/.
5   Ralph Nader, "An Invitation to a Conversation," Winning America, January
    2018, https://winningamerica.net/an-invitation-to-a-conversation/.

Index